Cause-Marketing for Nonprofits

PARTNER FOR PURPOSE,
PASSION, AND PROFITS

DAW

WILEY

John Wiley & Sons, Inc.

To my mother, Grace Baird Daw—
Economist, educator, author, and
inspiration to her five children

For general information on our other products and services or for technical support, please contact our Customer Care Department within the United States at 800-762-2974, outside the United States at (317) 572-3993 or fax (317) 572-4002.

Wiley also publishes its books in a variety of electronic formats. Some content that appears in print may not be available in electronic books.

For more information about Wiley products, visit our web site at www.wiley.com.

Library of Congress Cataloging-in-Publication Data
Daw, Jocelyne.
    Cause marketing for nonprofits: partner for purpose, passion, and profits / Jocelyne Daw.
       p.   cm. — (The AFP Fund development series)
    Includes index.
    ISBN-13: 978-0-471-71750-8 (cloth)
    ISBN-10: 0-471-71750-9 (cloth)
    1. Social marketing. I. Title. II. Series.
HF5414.D39 2006
    361.7'630688—dc22   2005031933

Printed in the United States of America

10 9 8 7 6 5 4 3 2 1

Contents

Foreword

We adore worthy causes—so much so, in fact, that the planet now boasts more than 1.5 million nonprofit organizations. These nonprofits bravely battle everything from cancer to child abuse, from poverty to pollution. But given their proliferation, more and more of them risk becoming as forgettable as they are noble. Not counting the Red Cross, most donors can't name the world's top 10 nonprofits, much less the 10 most effective.

Indeed, nonprofits have a problem: cause inflation, meaning their numbers are growing so fast that most have trouble standing out. What can we do? Invent better, livelier, more focused, and creative strategies to capture the public's imagination and make sure that every nonprofit gets the support it deserves. That is what the brand strategy and communications firm I founded, Cone Inc., does and has been doing for 25 years. And it is also the topic of this excellent book by my friend Jocelyne Daw.

Suppose your organization is just one of many focusing on a particular sliver of the charitable pie. How do you go about spotlighting yours to make it the number one charity that comes to a donor's mind? How will you compete to turn your nonprofit into a synonym for that particular cause? The message that we believe needs to be heard and understood by not-for-profits is this: Being a nonprofit doesn't mean being noncompetitive.

It's a common temptation among nonprofits to think that having a different tax status means they are different in every way. They don't foster long-term, vibrant relationships with donors; they make inspiring presentations. They don't cater to segmented markets; they appeal broadly to the public. They don't conduct customer-satisfaction research; they collect data on awareness.

Of course, anyone who emulates a business or joins forces with a company risks being accused of "selling out." But far from selling out, acquiring for-profit-like marketing know-how and strategies for interacting with sponsors, donors, and volunteers is essential to getting your voice heard in the cacophony.

We at Cone Inc. have been listening to and studying that noise and have spotted numerous trends. Here are a few.

Number one, relationship management utilizing tailored communications and specialized experiences. Effective nonprofit communications today means much more than simply telling the public about your cause. Monologues are out, dialogues are in. You must engage your target audiences in two-way conversations that work to build long-lasting, multidimensional relationships. And you can do that by first developing a strategic focus that best fits your mission, and then directing a well-honed but simple and consistent message toward those whom you've previously determined will be most receptive. To make sure your message continues to resonate with your chosen audience, frequently ask them what they think. Actively solicit feedback and allow your supporters to help you fine-tune your unique proposition to keep it relevant.

In promoting interaction with your partners, donors, and volunteers, remind them regularly of the value of giving and the good their efforts and dollars are accomplishing. Take your cue from Save the Children and report back at least once a year, more often if possible. To put it in business terms, manage your customer relationships and make use of the multiple means of communication available to you.

Another emerging trend involves passion marketing, in which you touch upon people's emotions and turn targeted individuals into evangelists for your cause. Personalized communications and messages that link local donors to the bigger picture aren't just emotionally satisfying; they also encourage a long-lasting commitment to your cause. Demographic profiles have long been used to identify cause-receptive markets, but tapping into people's personalities, psyches, and interests will increase your chances of success. For proof, look no further than the Susan G. Komen Breast Cancer Foundation. It has been particularly successful at getting people to sing, bowl, cook, walk, and run "For the Cure."

A third trend is reciprocity, in which the giving goes both ways. No matter how you attract your donors and volunteers, make sure that they receive something from you in return. That something may be access to support services and timely Internet content, the ability to expand one's sphere of influence, or thank-yous in the form of invitations to free events. The point is to engage with your supporters, interacting with them for reasons other than appeals for donations. By engaging people in a pleasant chain of experiences that remind them of you and your cause, you will foster loyalty and encourage their inclination to act, recommend, remember, and give.

Which nonprofits will show the questing spirit needed to embrace these trends and innovate for growth and future gains? Those that find the courage to accept risk, foster agility, and be, above all, market-driven will win the public's continued attention and support. The payoff isn't just greater sophistication, efficiency, or even improved fund-raising success and service delivery—though all those are included. The ultimate reward is the confidence and energy your success will instill throughout your entire organization.

A case in point (and a case I'm flattered to find included in this book) is the American Heart Association (AHA). When we began working with the AHA, many of its executives and volunteers deeply valued their heritage and unmatched credibility in science, but could see that the science in and of itself would not guarantee public support in the future. They had to make their brand more relevant to both current and new constituents. One audience the association wanted to target and grow was women. So, we set out to create a powerful emotional bond with this audience, and that meant enlivening the AHA's "white lab-coat" image by adding some sassy red to it. We worked together to create Go Red for Women, a national campaign designed to increase awareness, change behavior, and raise funds for the battle against heart disease, the number one killer of women.

The AHA launched the campaign by releasing new scientific guidelines concerning women and heart disease and concurrently debuting its distinctive red-dress icon. Also, we designated February 4, 2004, as the first National Wear Red Day for Women. With that, a loud rallying cry was sounded by our "partners," many of whom were television news anchors across the country decked out in red, as well as hundreds of newspapers and magazines. Even towns and cities across America festooned themselves in crimson to promote the campaign, celebrating "Seattle Goes Red," "Atlanta Goes Red," "Boston Goes Red," and so on, all of which made for an unusually rapid infiltration into the popular culture.

To date, Go Red for Women has been a stunning success, generating more than 2.3 billion media impressions to increase awareness of heart disease in women, $45 million in new contributions, including lead cause support from Pfizer and Macy's, and the participation of some 8,000 corporations in the 2005 Wear Red Day. And, now, as a testament to the power of the message, the World Heart Federation is taking Go Red for Women around the world.

But I didn't know how well we had succeeded until one day when I was driving on Route 128 outside Boston. I was on a conference call—with AHA executives, as it happened—when a flash of red caught my eye, or make that a flash of Go Red! There, spinning on the massive tumbler of a cement truck, was the Go Red for Women red-dress icon. Via this wholly unlikely medium, hundreds of drivers were getting our message: Wear red to show your support for the fight against heart disease in women.

How I loved that cement truck. After just 15 months, we had triumphed with a vibrant campaign to seize the public's imagination, garner donor support, and energize the American Heart Association, its associates, and millions of volunteers.

But sophisticated, innovative marketing is only part of the story. In this book, Jocelyne issues a call for nonprofit organizations to reach out to corporations in ways that truly make sense for both parties. Her advice is timely and wise. For example, Cone research shows that the public welcomes partnering between nonprofits and for-profits. Eighty-two percent of Americans say they have a more positive image of a business when it joins hands with a nonprofit, and 76 percent have a more positive image of the nonprofit when it partners with a company. If those statistical haloes don't convince you, here's a clincher: Seventy percent say they are more likely to donate to a charity once they know it has a corporate partner.

Over the years we have developed and played matchmaker for cause-branding efforts, and, through this, we have seen nonprofits and for-profits move closer together. We know first-hand what can be achieved when extraordinary organizations partner with one another. The results have been remarkable. Think Yoplait, the Susan B. Komen Foundation and the battle against breast cancer; ConAgra Foods, America's Second Harvest, and fighting to end child hunger; or J.C. Penney, the YMCA, and Boys & Girls Clubs of America, creating safe after-school programs. All were relationships that we were fortunate enough to help along, and the results have been gratifying in every case.

Want those kinds of results for your own nonprofit? Read on. The journey will be rewarding in unimagined ways.

Carol Cone
Chairman and Founder,
Cone, Inc.
Boston, Massachusetts
November 14, 2005

Acknowledgments

This book is part of the Association of Fundraising Professionals (AFP) and John Wiley & Sons Inc. series on fund development for the nonprofit sector. The concept for the book started with the kernel of an idea—to write on cause marketing for the nonprofit sector, a new and emerging field of corporate–nonprofit collaborations. This was an area not only of personal interest but also one where I had learned from the ground up as a nonprofit cause-marketing pioneer and professional of over 15 years.

But my personal interest and experience could never have been enough to write a book of the scope that I hoped would be a significant contribution to the nonprofit sector. It was only possible with the major input, sharing, and advice I received from professionals working in the for-profit and nonprofit sector—on both sides of the border. Spirit of generosity is the only way I can describe the kindness and enthusiasm of people who helped make this book possible. This spirit reflects the business mind and passionate heart of those working in this evolving discipline and their commitment to the field, the advancement of the nonprofit community and the good of society.

My first thanks and acknowledgment go to Carol Cone, Chairman and Founder of Cone Inc., and her team, particularly Kristian Darigan, Cone Vice President. Carol Cone and Cone Inc. are internationally recognized for their work in Cause Branding®, strategic cause marketing, and corporate social responsibility. Cone is both a pioneer and leader in building collaborations between the private and nonprofit sector and a knowledge leader with their 10 plus years of Cone research reports. The research series tracks trends and attitudes, and the findings and longitudinal analysis have made them the preeminent leader on corporate cause information for the media, corporations, and nonprofit sector.

Right from the beginning Carol was enthusiastic and supportive of the book project. Carol kindly agreed to write the foreword, generously shared all of the Cone/Roper and Cone research reports, and provided in-depth information on their recent work with the American Heart Association's "Go Red for

Women" cause initiative. The book considers their work, and Part I on the cause-marketing movement builds on the long-term research undertaken by Cone Inc. I feel privileged to have had Carol's involvement and support from the Cone Inc. team.

David Hesskiel of the Cause Marketing Forum (CMF) was a great source of information, knowledge, and encouragement. He met with me early on in the project and provided me with a strong list of contacts to interview. His innovative Cause Marketing Forum, Web site (www.causemarketingforum.com), teleclasses, and national conference were a great resource, and as a result of the Forum he has created a strong community of practice network for those working in the cause-marketing field. Through the cause-marketing forum I connected with Mollye Rhea, a regular presenter for the CMF and President of For Momentum. Mollye hosted me when I was in Atlanta, connected me with some leaders in the field, and challenged me to write "the resource book." I am grateful for her support and her friendship.

Jerry Welsh, President, Welsh Marketing, former Vice President of American Express and originator of the cause-related marketing concept, was generous with his time and insights on the history, goals, and focus for cause-related marketing. My friend David Barnes, Vice President, Public Affairs, American Express Canada, was enthusiastic and supportive right from the start of the project. He provided his own insights and knowledge and helped connect me with the New York office of American Express.

My husband, Bob Page, a member of the World Business Council on Sustainable Development (WBCSD) as TransAlta Corporation's representative, invited me to attend a number of their meetings (Boston, Geneva, Montreux, Stockholm, Paris), where I heard many speakers, including WBCSD President, Björn Stigson, discuss the role of business in the community and the organization's mission "to provide business leadership as a catalyst for change toward sustainable development, and to promote the role of eco-efficiency, innovation and corporate social responsibility."[1]

The case studies in Part II, "Best Practices Cause Initiatives," and Part IV, "Making it Happen," could not have been possible without the generosity with which cause marketers shared their cause-marketing initiatives The in-depth case studies in Part IV, "Making It Happen," involved extensive interview time and approvals, and I would like to express a special thanks for their time and commitment to Kyle Zimmer, Executive Director and Co-Founder of First Book for sharing First Books' innovative cause-marketing focus and specifically their "Dr. Seuss Cat in the Hat Challenge" cause-marketing promotion; Kathy Rogers, VP, Cause Initiatives and Integrated Marketing, American Heart Association; and Kristian Darigan, VP Cone Inc., for their contribution on the AHA's innovative "Go Red for Women" cause initiative; Gregory Boroff, Vice President, External Affairs and Matthew Goldstein, former Director Business Partnerships receive my thanks and gratitude for sharing the Food Bank for New York City's story on developing a cause-marketing orientation and emphasis and specifically their Bank-to-Bank cause-marketing program; and Karina Chow, Division Manager, Community Fundraising and Karen Bronstein, formerly of the Vancouver District chapter, now with Hospice Calgary, shared their cause-marketing experiences using the "Daffodil Campaign" with the local districts of Vancouver and Vancouver Island of the British Columbia and Yukon Chapter of the Canadian Cancer Society.

The overall book was made possible by the input of many fellow cause-marketing professionals who generously shared their experience, expertise, and advice, all of which are a vital part of this book. I hope that the final product is a reflection of that generosity of spirit and that the result created is a contribution to this growing discipline. I express a sincere thank-you to the following people, who kindly participated in interviews and provided information.

Alison DeSilva, Vice President, Cone Inc.

Anne-Marie Grey, Chief, International and Corporate Alliances, UNICEF

Barbara Tombros, Director, Alliance Development, Novartis Pharmaceuticals Corporation

Bob Page, Vice President, Sustainable Development, TransAlta Corporation

Carol Cone, Chairman and Founder, Cone Inc.

Carrie Suhr, Vice President, Corporate Development, KaBOOM!

Chris Pinney, Former Director, IMAGINE program, Canadian Centre for Philanthropy, now Program Director, Boston College

Cindy Schneible, VP, Cause-Related Marketing and Sponsorship, Susan G. Komen Breast Cancer Foundation

Clam Lorenz, Director, Communications, MissionFish

Cornelia Higginson, Vice President, Philanthropic Programs, American Express Company

Cynthia Currence, National Vice President, Strategic Corporate Marketing Alliances, American Cancer Society

D'Arcy Levesque, Vice President, Public and Government Affairs, Enbridge Inc.

David Barnes, Vice President, Public Affairs, American Express Canada

David Hesskiel, President, Cause Marketing Forum

Doug Davidge, Senior Advisor, Partnerships, Public Works and Government Services, Canada

Drew Robertson, Area Marketing, Atlantic Canada, Investors Group

Elizabeth Hackbarth, Corporate Relations Director, National Kidney Foundation

Gigi Politoski, Vice President, Programs, National Kidney Foundation

Gregory Boroff, Vice President for External Relations, Food Bank for New York City

Harry Abel, Vice President, Strategic Alliances, National Mental Health Association

Howard Byck, Chief Marketing Officer, Director of Corporate Development, Share Our Strength

Jamie Niessen, Director, Marketing and Communications, Burnet, Duckworth and Palmer LLC

Jim McCoy, Event Coordinator, Children's Hunger Alliance

John Good, Executive Director, Canadian Parks Council

John Mikkelsen, Assistant Vice President, Corporate Partnerships, TELUS

Josh Knights, Director, Development, Nature Conservancy

Judy Tenzer, Vice President, Public Affairs and Communications, American Express

Julie Dawson, Manager, Partnerships, Evergreen Public School District

Karina Chow, Division Manager, Community Fundraising, British Columbia and Yukon Division, Canadian Cancer Society

Karen Bronstein, Director Marketing and Development, Hospice Calgary

Kathy Collins, Vice President, Marketing, Lee Jeans

Kathy Rogers, Vice President, Cause Initiatives and Integrated Marketing, American Heart Association

Kelly McMackin, Vice President, Cause Marketing and Media Partnerships, Kinterra

Ken Hubert, Sales and Marketing Director, McKinley Masters

Kevin Martinez, Director, Community Affairs, Home Depot

Kristian Darigan, Vice President, Cone Inc.

Kurt Aschermann, Chief Marketing Officer and Head, Corporate Opportunities Group, Boys and Girls Clubs of America

Kyle Zimmer, President and Cofounder, First Book

Laurelea Conrad, Formerly, Senior Manager, National Corporate Alliances, Heart and Stroke Foundation

Laurie Leier, Manager Fund Development, EPCOR Centre for the Performing Arts

Mark Hierlihy, National Director of Development, Canadian Breast Cancer Foundation

Martha Parker, former Executive Director, Volunteer Calgary

Mary Norman, Group Vice President, Strategic Marketing Alliances, Arthritis Foundation

Mary Beth Salerno, President, American Express Foundation, American Express Company

Matthew Goldstein, Former Director, Business Partnerships, Food Bank, New York City

Michael Robinson, President and CEO, Glenbow Museum

Miriam Lennett, Director, Corporate Marketing, National Trust for Historic Preservation

Molly Rhea, President, For Momentum

Nancy Muller, Vice President, Public Affairs, American Express Company

Pam Brandt, Brandt Communications

Richard Irish, Vice President, Public Affairs and Area Marketing, Investors Group

Richard Maoire, Former Manager, Corporate Relations, Reading Is Fundamental

Ron Defeo, Community Affairs Dept., Home Depot

Stephanie Robertson, Simpact: Social Impact Strategies

Sue Tomney, Vice President, Corporate Social Responsibility and Donor Awareness, Imagine Canada

Vicki Gordon, Senior Vice President, Corporate Affairs, Intercontinental Hotels Group

Jerry Welsh, President, Welsh Marketing

A FEW PERSONAL THANKS . . .

A special mention must go to my former colleagues at Parks Canada and the board members of the Canadian Parks Partnership from 1988 to 1997. This includes, but is no means limited to: Luc Gendron, Lilian Tankard, Erica Alexander, Sylvia Worrall, Cathy Cuthiell, and Ken Norman of the Canadian Parks Partnership; Gary Lindfield, John Good, Tanya Middlebro', Ian Rutherford,

Christina Cameron, Mike Porter, and Tom Lee of Parks Canada. John Ewart of Howell, Fleming in Peterborough, Ontario, provided pro bono legal advice during my involvement with the program. A special mention to my key collaborator in Parks Canada, Doug Davidge, and the ying to my yang; his innovative thinking, willingness to partner, and pure energy and enthusiasm was critical to both the development of the strategy and the ongoing implementation of the cause-marketing program. Without his input, guidance, wonderful second sober thoughts, and collaboration, the program could not have achieved the level it did.

Sincere thanks also go to my colleagues and friends at Glenbow Museum. My team in the Enterprise Unit pitched in, covered some of my workload (Tas Rahim, Brent Buechler, and Marilyn Field) when I was writing, and cheered me on. My boss, Glenbow Museum President and CEO Mike Robinson, generously supported this work and provided lots of encouragement and critical questioning of the cause-marketing concepts and principles.

I would like to thank my editor, Susan McDermott, for her encouragement and faith that I could produce a book worthy of the AFP/Wiley series. This book would not have been possible without the financial support of the following: Ministry of Community Development, Province of Alberta for their research grant, administered through Museums Alberta; Association of Fundraising Professionals, Calgary Chapter, who enthusiastically provided a grant for the Cause Marketing Forum conference attendance and travel; and finally to the Joy Harvie McLaren Staff Scholarship at Glenbow Museum for a grant to support administrative assistance for permissions and final work. Thanks also must go to Amber Loewen, who provided administration support for the permissions and formatting of the final product.

IT COULDN'T HAVE HAPPENED . . .

Without the love and encouragement of my family, my mother Grace Daw, children Kate and Doug Page, friend, Amber Loewen, and especially my husband, Bob Page, who somehow always believed I could do it. He encouraged me every step of the way; listened to, challenged, and discussed my ideas; read my initial work; provided feedback; and supported me right to the end. I couldn't have done it without him.

Jocelyne Daw
March, 2006
Calgary, Alberta, Canada

ENDNOTE

1. http://www.wbcsd.ch.

Introduction

My Journey: Partner for Purpose, Passion, and Profits

Innovation and change start with an idea, the imagination to see the potential, the courage to try it, and the patience to see it through. Cause marketing is one such idea: a new way of business, nonprofit causes, and community and company stakeholders aligning to work in a mutually beneficial relationship. This is a relationship that finds the intersection between societal needs, corporate marketing goals, and individual interests, that consciously marries the credibility and assets of nonprofit organizations and the public's desire to support them to marketing goals that achieve business and societal benefit and satisfy stakeholder needs.

Cause marketing is a collaboration between corporations and nonprofit causes that ultimately engages company stakeholders from employees to suppliers, to retailers, eventually reaching consumers. It brings together business and nonprofit causes' assets in a value exchange: to market and position products, brands, and companies, which creates shareholder value; to achieve a nonprofit's mission, which creates social value; and to communicate the values of all involved.

This is a book about a growing model for business and nonprofit involvement—a new way of working together for mutual benefit: partnering for purpose, passion, and profits. It's about strategic mutually beneficial alliances that can be formed and synergies built. It's about enterprising nonprofits who use their brand and assets to achieve mission and generate revenue; socially responsible corporations who see the business benefit of supporting a cause with the power of their brand, marketing, and people to achieve profitability; and socially engaged publics who contribute back to society and reward community-oriented companies through their loyalty and consumer dollars.

The new model can provide not only concrete benefits but also a complex mix of challenges and risks. For nonprofits it opens up the possibility of productive and broader support as cause-marketing relationships brings value beyond just dollars. They further validate nonprofit activities, help achieve mission, create brand awareness, disseminate information, change behavior and attitudes, bring valuable corporate expertise, and help leverage additional resources.

Corporations recognize that more active cause-marketing relationships give the company a competitive advantage by creating tangible value and increasing their profitability by helping them attract employees; selling products; managing their reputations; increasing their bottom line; appealing to employees, customers, and stakeholders; and securing the license they need to operate in many markets.

But both sides have to think carefully before taking this route. Nonprofits must recognize the potential challenge of commercial pressures and staying true to their mission. Relationships can be time consuming and require internal structures to support, and direct financial benefits are often small, with less than 10% of overall private giving coming from the corporate sector and even less from cause-marketing relationships. To be successful, nonprofits must know their mission and goals and what they can legitimately offer in cause-marketing partnership arrangement.

Corporations face nonprofit capacity questions, cultural differences, and alignment fit with their nonprofit partners. Top-down commitment to the relationship and overall corporate social responsibility is a must if cause marketing is to work. However, well-executed programs can provide significant benefits, risks can be managed, and steps taken to accomplish purpose and ensure gains are greater than costs.

The goal of this book is to help nonprofits recognize the opportunities provided by cause-marketing relationships, while minimizing potential challenges. *Cause Marketing for Nonprofits: Partner for Purpose, Passion, and Profits* seeks to help build productive relationships. First, the book looks at cause marketing in a broad social context to see how it has developed and evolved and the benefits and challenges this new way of thinking and acting can bring. Second, it works to provide those interested with an emphasis on the nonprofit sector, with a thorough understanding of this program delivery, marketing, and fundraising approach and the practical tools needed to successfully develop strategic cause programs that maximize the benefits for all. Last, the book aims to inspire critical and creative thinking and to encourage continued growth of corporate–cause-marketing collaborations.

My Cause-Marketing Journey

This book builds on my own personal cause-marketing journey and experience; draws on discussions and learning from cause marketers in the nonprofit and for-profit worlds; and uses literature and research that has been written on this topic since the early days.

I first came upon the concepts of cause-related marketing in 1988 when I attended a one-day Canadian Center for Philanthropy–sponsored seminar presented by Richard Steckel. At the time, I was the newly appointed founding Executive Director of the Canadian Parks Partnership, and we were looking for a way to implement our mission, raise revenues, and build our profile. Dr. Steckel, a pioneer in the use of strategic alliances between for-profits and nonprofits as head of the Denver Children's Museum, discussed his experience and introduced the early cause-related marketing concepts from his book, *Filthy Rich and Other Nonprofit Fantasies.* The session was magical: here was an innovative and unique way to partner business and nonprofit organizations for mutual benefit and to use social enterprise to support nonprofit causes. Richard's enthusiasm, encouragement, and information became an inspiration for my thinking and for building a cause-marketing program for the Canadian Parks Partnership.

The Canadian Parks Partnership (CPP) is a national umbrella organization providing support to the network of "friends" groups working in national parks and historic sites from coast to coast. The cooperating association "friends" group was a program established in the early 1980s to engage Canadians in supporting the education, protection, and preservation mandate of individual national parks and historic sites. Parks Canada is the government agency responsible for managing Canada's system of national parks, national historic sites, and heritage canals.

In 1988, as a newly established national organization, our board of directors needed to develop a strategy to achieve financial self-sufficiency while simultaneously fulfilling our mandate to support and enhance Canada's national parks and national historic sites through citizen involvement. At the time we had limited human and financial resources and a low profile, and our mission, although strong, was not well known. Our strengths lay in our relationship with Parks Canada and our network of 36 groups representing over 10,000 Canadians working directly in national parks and national historic sites to support heritage and environmental education, protection, and promotion.

At the same time that I attended Richard Steckel's session, Doug Davidge joined the Cooperating Association program in Parks Canada's headquarters in the newly created position of Product Development Officer. Doug had led an innovative product-licensing program in the Atlantic Canada office of Parks Canada. He saw the potential to expand this work and to collaborate with the Canadian Parks Partnership to build a national program.

With Richard Steckel's teaching, Doug's experience, Parks Canada's commitment to our organization, and the need for the Canadian Parks Partnership to achieve its mission, raise revenue, and build both organizations' profiles, the idea to develop a joint purpose-built cause-related marketing strategy emerged.

My Journey Begins: Supporting Canada's National Parks and Historic Sites

With the support and involvement of our government partner, Parks Canada, and with consulting input from the Business Development Bank (formerly Federal Business Development Bank), we put together a joint cause-marketing strategy. The plan involved using the strength, assets, and brands of both organizations to partner with businesses to involve Canadians in supporting national parks and historic sites while simultaneously raising revenue and the profile of our organizations. "The big, simple idea" was to "do only what others could not do for us"[1] by using the assets and brand of Parks Canada and the Canadian Parks Partnership to partner with corporations combining our strengths with theirs for mutual benefit to achieve purpose, inspire passion, and generate profits.

Our strategy, developed in 1989, determined three mechanisms to achieve these goals "through a joint marketplace fundraising concept: i) product line strategy; ii) national 'branded' products through licensing, endorsement, partnership/joint ventures, premium marketing, services; iii) and public membership. The CPP's commingling and merging concept is to piggyback onto existing and new products and services in cooperation with the business community and the public, merging the Partnership's unique raison d'être, its partnership base, pristine reputation and its fundraising needs with the everyday flow of *commercial trade*."[2]

This was a completely new way of thinking and doing for both organizations, especially a federal government agency. Creating an innovative joint marketing and fundraising program to develop three-way commercial arrangements among the not-for-profit, public, and private sectors was unique for its time. More often than not, it was win-win-win, and we did a lot of things right. Because this was totally new territory, we had to do what Doug Davidge called "balancing innovation with good governance." Although many people were nervously supportive, there were many who were looking for us to make mistakes, especially in the area of risk management. So we carefully crossed the *T*'s and dotted the *I*'s and put in place five basic elements to manage the program and potential risks.

1. A comprehensive master licensing agreement signed and approved by the board of the Canadian Parks Partnership and senior management of Parks Canada

2. Carefully outlined approval processes to ensure good-fit partners that brought the right attributes and had excellent ethical and environmental records

3. Detailed signed agreements with every partner that clearly outlined expected deliverables and roles and responsibilities

4. Tools for managing partnership activities, including timetables, strategic road maps, joint meetings for sharing information, and regular review of the strategic plan and direction with the CPP board and Parks Canada

5. Constant communication that was open, honest, and sincere and a relationship that was built on mutual trust and respect[3]

In 1990, the program was launched. The willingness to try something new and the faith that was put in the staff of both organizations was visionary, daring, and demonstrated a true spirit of partnership.

Implementation and Input

As the strategy was being developed and implemented, we gained valuable information and support from other nonprofit organizations on both sides of the border. The World Wide Fund for Nature, Canada (formerly World Wildlife Fund) provided important advice and shared information on researching possible partners, making the pitch, negotiations, and legal agreements. Their international headquarters had launched a cause-marketing strategy several years earlier, and the Canadian arm was well underway with its own program.

In 1993, we traveled to Washington, D.C. to meet with the National Park Foundation (NFP) and the National Parks Conservation Association (NPCA). Both had cause programs, and they kindly shared much information and learning and even suggested some of their own partners as ones that could be possibly shared through Canadian offices. Our relationship with Eureka Vacuum (Frigidaire) was launched thanks to the National Park Foundation (NPF) support and introduction. In turn, we introduced the NPF to one of our cause partners, Hi-Tec Sports (hiking boot and outdoor clothing manufacturer).

Interest in the innovative partnership was high and through speeches, conferences, and meetings we shared much of our strategy, learning, and processes with corporations, other nonprofits, and government organizations. The relationship and partnership risk structure was also emulated, and parts of it were used by other federal government departments, including the Royal Canadian Mounted Police, Fisheries and Oceans Canada, Health Canada, and the Prime Ministers' Awards. The cause-marketing strategy was shared with other nonprofit organizations, including Volunteer Calgary, Alberta Association of Fundraising Professionals and students at the Arctic Institute of North America.

Results of the Cause-Marketing Program

From 1990 to 1997 more then 25 corporate cause-marketing relationships were developed. We undertook everything from short-term cause promotions to longer-term licensed product, product purchase, and promotional programs to cause-branded relationships for ongoing programs and events. Every product, promotion, and program featured key messages about parks and historic sites and gave Canadians an opportunity to extend their support, become involved, and learn more about our national system.

A Movement Was Begun

The dollar raised provided a valuable contribution for the work of the Canadian Parks Partnership and its local cooperating associations in support of heritage and environmental education, research, and protection in national parks and historic sites. But more significantly, a movement was begun—a movement that for the first time ever reached out and involved Canadians, especially those who lived beyond the park gate in major urban cities, directly in supporting our system of national parks and historic sites. We moved them from being merely consumers of national parks and historic sites to engaged citizens dedicated to supporting these national treasures—a key mission of our organization.

The cause program reached Canadians in untraditional ways through products and promotions in untraditional places—retail outlets, on the back of cereal boxes, on products, and through millions of impressions. It raised both our organizations' profiles, enabled us to get out key messages, and allowed us to uniquely work with companies to infuse passion in their employees, suppliers, retailers, and individual consumers.

The program expanded beyond products and promotions and moved into deeper cause-branding relationships for our national event, "Take a Hike," and national education initiative, "kids@parks." Both of these signature programs were made possible with the marketing and financial support of our corporate partners and allowed us to engage Canadians beyond purchases to link them directly with the work of our organizations.

By partnering with companies and finding the intersection of where our interests and goals met theirs and that of their stakeholders, we uniquely built a program that was win-win-win. With a very low financial investment, but lots of hard work and enthusiasm, we extended our reach and achieved objectives that never could have happened without this corporate support. Like many organizations that have successfully used cause marketing, it helped us get to our end result faster and more efficiently than any other strategy could have done. The program enabled us to reach a wide range of Canadians, connect with their values, and engage them in a growing movement to support our national parks and sites.

Cause-Marketing Highlights

These concrete examples demonstrate the vision and the substance of this evolving field.

- *Post Cereal Fruit and Fiber, Support Canada's National Parks promotion:* Our first initiative was in 1991 when we undertook a short-term cause promotion "Supporting Canada's National Parks." Fruit and Fiber was a Post cereal marketed to people looking for a healthy lifestyle and an interest in the great outdoors. There was a natural link between the product line and our goal of reaching Canadians with an interest in national parks. The program included multiple elements: information about national parks and the importance of completing the system, an opportunity for cereal purchasers to write for information or to make a donation, a contest to win five trips to national parks in various regions of the country, and a donation from Post to support the cause.

  Results: For a three-month period from January 1991 to March 1991, the promotion was featured on the back of over 2 million cereal boxes, directly reaching more Canadians than any Parks brochure could ever have during the same time frame or longer. One of the winners was so taken with his experience that when he married two months later, he and his bride asked all their guests to make contributions to the Canadian Parks Partnership to support national parks and historic sites in lieu of a wedding gift—promotion combined with passion.

  Key Learning: Cause marketing could be so much more than just immediate corporate support: the product promotion was a great way to build an individual giving program, and the passion that came from these relationships could be infused to build stronger support. A second learning: although a good way to start the program and learn, a one-off promotional cause program had short-term impact and was time consuming. A goal became to build longer-term, deeper relationships.

- *Hallmark Canada, National Product Line:* The card company developed a product line featuring images from national parks and historic sites including cards, note paper, journals, and travel diaries. Developed in the early 1990s when environmentally appropriate products were being demanded by consumers, Hallmark was interested in partnering with an organization with an environmental mandate.

  Results: The products, all developed using recycled paper, were sold in Hallmark's 3,300 stores and outlets nationwide and through the network of Parks stores reaching thousands of Canadians with messages featured on the back of every card and product.

  Key Learning: Small beginnings, done right, can turn into bigger things. Our relationship continued to grow and, over the five years it lasted, extended into signature cause event partnership and an employee involvement program that raised revenue and the profile of the organizations and helped us reach Canadians beyond the park gates. It also introduced us to the value of engaging corporate partner employees and the value and passion they could bring to the cause.

- **Kodak Canada:** For a three-year period, from 1992 to 1995, a donation was made for every single-use camera and film canister that was returned for recycling. Although 97% of the single-use product could be recycled, Kodak was under scrutiny for creating what was perceived as a throwaway product.

  Results: By partnering with our organizations, purchasers of the single-use cameras were rewarded for returning their cameras to be recycled, thereby triggering a donation to support Canada's national parks and historic sites. All the advertising on the program featured information on national parks and how to become an individual supporter.

  Key Learning: Success breeds success. The recycling promotion became the foundation of a larger program that included philanthropic support as well as support for the national event "Take a Hike."

- **Hi-Tec Canada:** This multilayered program was one of the most extensive of all the cause collaborations. As a hiking boot company, Hi-Tec had a keen interest in being aligned with organizations that supported and managed national parks, a key place for their consumers to use their products. Developed in 1993 with input from Canadian Parks Partnership and Parks Canada, Hi-Tec created a special "Parks" boot and a full line of clothing ("everything but underpants" was what we used to say) that carried the logo of the Canadian Parks Partnership.

  Results: A wide-ranging advertising campaign featured national TV advertising, a special 1-800 telephone number on information about Hi-Tec products and national parks, and point-of-purchase displays and swing tags on all products that focused on providing park information and encouraging individual donations. All hiking boot boxes included a brochure, donation card, and return envelope to encourage individual support. Early in our four-year relationship, we jointly developed a strategic road map for our collaborative alliance that established goals and objectives for each partner and outlined a long-term strategy for the relationship. Revenue generated from the program went toward supporting educational and environmental programs in national parks across Canada.

  Key Learning: Even the strongest relationships don't last forever. What had been planned as a long-term relationship was terminated shortly after the then-president and CEO of Hi-Tec Canada was promoted to head up Hi-Tec worldwide. One of my most challenging cause-marketing experiences was overseeing the dissolution of what had been a rich and highly innovative partnership: making sure our organization received what had been promised, while leaving on positive terms.

- *Marci Lipman:* As a small independent retailer based in Toronto with a clothing line distributed throughout Canada, Marci was personally committed to supporting national parks.

    Results: A portion of the proceeds from a number of T-shirts to support our cause. Included on each product was a hangtag that both provided information on Canada's national system of parks and historic sites and encouraged individual involvement and support.

    Key Learning: Cause programs could be developed with any size business if the alignment is right and the benefits mutually advantageous.

- *Eureka Vacuum* donated a portion of the proceeds from every World Vac vacuum cleaner sold. Eureka, a product line of Frigidaire, wanted to be positioned as supporting a high-profile environmental cause. Information on the program and our organizations was featured on the vacuum packaging and in all their associated advertising. The program ran over a seven-year period and provided an unusual vehicle to create awareness and support for Parks' mission and mandate.

    Key Learning: Partnering with not obviously aligned companies helped to reach a new audience and present the organization in a different light.

- *Subaru* became the title sponsor of our signature national cause event, "Take a Hike," launched in 1995 to celebrate and engage Canadians in supporting parks and historic sites. Subaru's customer base was defined as environmentally conscious and outdoor oriented. As we were told, "go to any park and look at the parking lot—it will be filled with Subarus." For Subaru the fit was strategic and targeted to reaching their core users and protecting what was critical to them; for CPP, the support enabled a major national event that helped our local network of "friends" group raise profile and revenue for their local activities and programs. Subaru was actively involved in the event helping with a major advertising campaign and organizing a "Take a Hike" employee event.

    Key Learning: Deeper programs that were turnkey could extend corporate involvement and involve employees more directly. The event also introduced a new level of complexity in our cause relationships: coordinating nationally, while executing at the local level. Early buy-in at the local level, providing tangible local value, and developing national template material that could incorporate local messaging and supporters was critical.

My Journey Continues

Although I left Canadian Parks Partnership in 1997, cause marketing has continued to be an important mission-based marketing and fundraising tool for me. I have actively used it to advance community needs and programs in support of the environment, heritage, health care, and arts and culture. Most recently, as Vice President, Enterprises at Glenbow Museum, cause marketing has become a mainstay of the fund development and marketing programs. As one of the most enterprising major museums in Canada, in 1999 Glenbow implemented a long-term strategy aimed at moving from what was a "largely curator-driven, collection-based museum with passive public programming" to an "audience-driven, educationally active museum relevant to the community." Our immediate focus was to change exhibitions regularly, create signature turnkey cobranded exhibition opportunities for potential corporate partners, develop multiaged, engaging programs, rebrand to have stronger public appeal and with an emphasis on families, and actively market and focus on being publicly driven and customer service oriented. We repositioned ourselves as a continuous learning institution dedicated to telling the story of our area and the world beyond. This new approach has enabled an active cause-marketing program to support this work.

Like cause marketing's evolution, our programs reflect the latest approach: less focused on product sales and short-term relationships to being longer term and program-oriented, and cause branding and corporate social responsibility focused. A small sampling follows.

- *Enbridge Inc.* is a leader in energy transportation and distribution in North America and internationally. Operating in Canada and the United States, they manage the world's longest crude oil and liquids pipeline system. One of our city's most innovative cause marketers and branders, Enbridge is known for its commitment to the arts and environmental sustainability. Most recently, they worked with our institution to be the cobranded supporter of a special exhibition on water and sustainability, "Our River: Journey of the Bow" and an accompanying publication.

  When we first talked to them about the exhibition, they had just completed market research on public understanding of their community involvement. Believing in the importance of measuring the company's progress to gauge the impact of their community relationships, the research demonstrated that although the community admired the company, there was a lack of appreciation for their environmental work.

  The company had also just adopted a new corporate social responsibility policy (CSR) with a renewed commitment to environment, health, and safety and to a broad concept of CSR that included sustaining communities and sustaining the environment where they operated. The exhibit and book were a perfect alignment to reinforce this commitment. Enbridge was featured as the title supporter of the exhibition in the museum's advertising and promotion. On their side, they extended messaging through a series of their own ads featuring our president and their commitment to environmental sustainability (see Exhibit I.1). Using their support as a signature

EXHIBIT 1.1   SIGNATURE CAUSE—ENBRIDGE

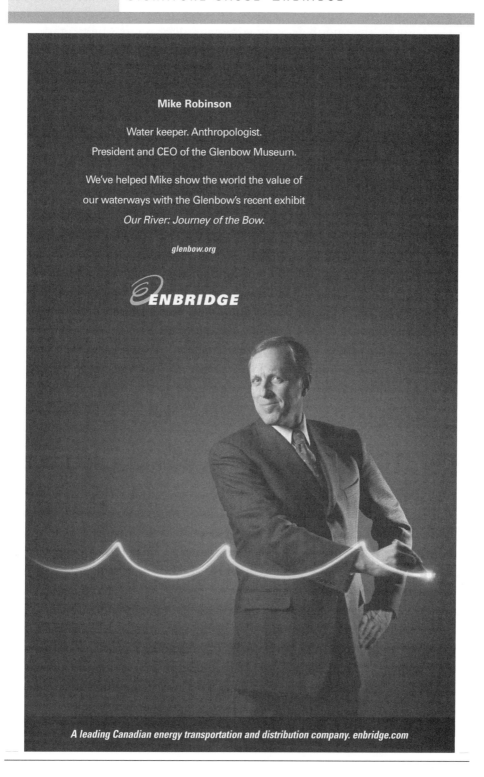

cause program for the year, they featured the exhibition and the museum as a tie-in with their annual general meeting.

Through this and their other corporate social-responsibility work, Enbridge was recognized in 2005 by the Davos World Economic Forum as one of the Global 100, a new global business ranking identifying the top 100 companies that are leading the way to a more sustainable world.[4]

- *American Express* continues its leadership in the cause-marketing field through support of Glenbow Museum international exhibitions. In addition to traditional corporate philanthropic support through their Foundation, American Express public relations and marketing arm uses their involvement to provide special benefits to employees and cardholders and to connect to merchants by encouraging use of the card in restaurants near the museum during the run of the exhibition. Their advertising campaign that accompanies this commitment extends our message and marketing reach.

- *Key Porter Books* is a leading Canadian publisher. Glenbow Museum licenses intellectual content and material developed by our curatorial team in the form of books to Key Porter. Key Porter edits, designs, prints, and markets the books through their channels, and the museum earns a royalty for every book sold. Additionally, books are distributed beyond the museum providing us with a vehicle to achieve our mission of sharing the history and art of Western Canada.

CENTRAL THEMES

Our changing society calls for new ways of thinking and doing. Societal issues are too great to be dealt with by using only the old ways; life is too complex to go it alone. As society has changed, so have relationships between business and the nonprofit sector. Cause marketing's development and growth is a reflection of this change.

Cause marketing is a corporate-nonprofit partnership that aligns the power of a company's brand, marketing and people with a cause's brand and assets to create shareholder and social value and to publicly communicate values. It is a mutually beneficial relationship where the sum of the two parts can be greater than the individual ones alone; where self-interest can be combined with altruism, marketing with philanthropy, awareness with fundraising, mission achievement with business objectives, cash support with in-kind leveraged contributions—all in an effort to achieve mutual benefit. Above all, cause marketing is where purpose, passion, and profits meet in a productive, strategically aligned partnership. All

EXHIBIT I.2   CENTRAL CAUSE MARKETING THEMES

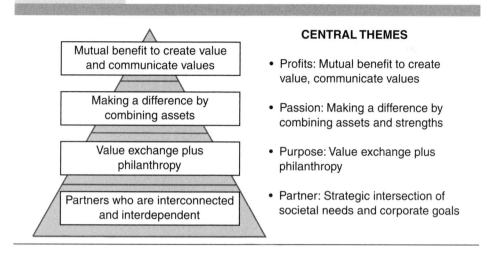

CENTRAL THEMES

- Profits: Mutual benefit to create value, communicate values

- Passion: Making a difference by combining assets and strengths

- Purpose: Value exchange plus philanthropy

- Partner: Strategic intersection of societal needs and corporate goals

successful cause-marketing programs have four common elements; describing, understanding, and using them forms the foundation of this book (see Exhibit I.2).

 ## Partner: Strategic, Mutually Beneficial Collaboration

First, cause marketing brings together business and nonprofit organizations in strategic, collaborative partnerships that are interconnected and interdependent. It is the intersection where societal needs and corporate goals meet and can come together for mutual benefit. The partners must be aligned with one another's mission and goals. The relationship must be based on mutual respect, open communications, and trust and be transparent, authentic, and honest if it is to be successful. A good collaborative alignment will see each partner actively seeking to advance each other's agenda and sharing responsibilities, contributions, and risks.

 ## Purpose: Value Exchange Plus Philanthropy

Second, cause-marketing relationships are uniquely different from traditional corporate philanthropy or sponsorship. Corporate community investment programs are charitable, usually focused on strategic areas of support and with only a modest expectation of recognition or reputation enhancement. Sponsorship is focused on the need to achieve specific marketing goals and is driven by impressions and tied to product sales, not by a commitment to the cause.

Cause marketing initiatives is the third way. It is a combination of philanthropy, support for a cause and its purpose, and marketing, the tangible business benefits from a charity alignment and the assets they bring to a relationship.

EXHIBIT I.3   INTERSECTION OF INTERESTS

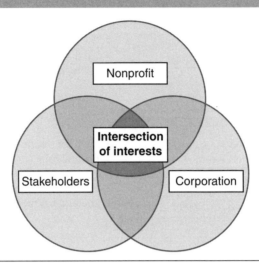

Cause marketing is the new marketing and corporate citizenship tool focused on driving corporate profitability through cause relationships.

To be successful, nonprofits must think like businesses and understand their needs and objectives. They must recognize the valuable assets they can bring, including their brand, reputation, community linkages, and networks and programs. Equally, they must see and understand the important assets and contribution beyond finances that corporations can make to support their cause and efforts. Cause marketing is the new fundraising and marketing tool that helps raise revenue and awareness and achieve important mission goals.

Passion: Making a Difference by Combining Strengths and Assets

Third, cause marketing is about passion, bringing companies together with nonprofits who share a commitment to achieving societal good and benefits and making a difference. Cause marketing creates synergies by building on strengths and assets of each partner, making the sum of the two parts greater than each individual part. Ultimately, a third element critical in all cause-marketing relationships is the end target, stakeholders, including employees, community leaders, government officials, suppliers, retailers, and consumers (see Exhibit I.3). Employees are increasingly becoming the reason why companies undertake cause-marketing programs. People want to work hard, get promoted, and be fairly compensated. But they also want to work for a company that makes a difference and that is doing great things in their community.

EXHIBIT I.4   COMMITMENT AND PARTICIPATION

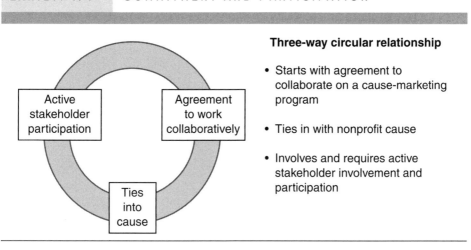

Three-way circular relationship

- Starts with agreement to collaborate on a cause-marketing program

- Ties in with nonprofit cause

- Involves and requires active stakeholder involvement and participation

Individuals in the community are looking for ways to give back, to be engaged in community support, and to do it in a way that is convenient and can publicly demonstrate their values and support. Their passionate commitment and active participation ensures cause-marketing programs will work and continue to grow (see Exhibit I.4).

Profits: Mutual Benefit to Create Value, Communicate Values

Finally, cause marketing is a new discipline in the corporate citizenship palette, one that includes use of a company's brand, marketing, and people to create mutual benefit, shareholder, and social value and reflect the values of those involved. Each element builds on the others, with the ultimate results being value creation and value reflection for the corporation, nonprofit organization, and in the end stakeholders engaged in supporting and participating in cause-marketing programs. In the current business environment, it is important to be publicly demonstrating support for wider social issues as part of corporate citizenship.

MAKING IT HAPPEN

The potential for nonprofits in this area is just beginning to be tapped. The growth in cause marketing, as tracked by a number of organizations such as IEG (International Event Group), Cause Marketing Forum, Cone Inc., and Britain's Business in the Community: Cause Related Business Campaign initiative, is clear. This discipline within overall corporate giving has seen solid growth in the 2000s, especially after September 11, 2001 and the post-Enron, Tyco, WorldCom era.

The public has demanded greater corporate accountability and commitment to the community. Companies in turn have recognized the competitive advantage that can be achieved by presenting a human face, including being a compelling place to work, welcomed in a community, and increasing sales profitability.

As leading companies demonstrate the benefits, more will follow in their wake. Nonprofits who proactively build their capacity in this area stand to gain and enhance their ability to achieve their mission, engage a wide range of people in supporting their mission, build brand and message awareness, raise revenue for their work, and provide societal benefit.

Corporate–nonprofit cause-marketing alliances possess tremendous potential to meet both business and mission goals—at a national level, in a regional area, and in local communities. However, the changing environment surrounding collaborative alliances also presents new challenges for these relationships. Cause marketing when properly developed can be a powerful symbiotic tool, but only if the circumstances are right and the sense of common purpose is clear. By knowing the foundations and focus of a program, nonprofits can determine if they have the interest and capacity to move forward.

Part I: The Cause-Marketing Movement

The first part of the book looks at the cause-marketing movement. The first chapter discusses cause marketing as the new way corporations are engaging with nonprofit organizations in the community. Viewed as the "third way," it is a middle ground between philanthropic support and commercial sponsorship programs. The second and third chapters build on the pioneering research and analytical work of Cone Inc., an internationally recognized consultancy in the field of strategic cause branding and strategic cause-marketing programs for over 20 years. Cone Inc. produced 11 seminal research reports from 1993 to 2005 that have provided analysis and insights on cause collaborations between the corporate and nonprofit sectors. The second chapter defines the cause-marketing process as integrating value and values and looks at the trends that have driven its growth in the corporate world, nonprofit sector, and community at large. The third chapter looks at how cause marketing has evolved over its 25 plus-year history.

Part II: Cause-Marketing Initiatives: The Seven *P*'s: Best Practices, Case Studies

The next section looks at the seven *P*'s of cause marketing relationships, from products type relationships (product purchases, purchases plus, and licensed products) to promotional issues and messaging to the deeper forms of cobranded promotional events and programs and public social cause marketing programming relationships established to impact and change behavior. Here specific best practices cause-marketing arrangements are presented along with key elements of each, benefits, challenges, and learning from those working in the field. Many nonprofits and for-profit companies shared their cause-marketing initiatives, and these examples represent best in class cases.

Part III: Getting It Right: Framework for Success

The third part of the book outlines the framework for success, "Getting It Right." Building a cause-marketing program doesn't require grandiose plans or a big bureaucratic structure to make them work, and small beginnings can turn into significant programs. But getting a cause-marketing relationship right takes thought and a strategic approach.

Presented in three chapters are the seven components of a cause-marketing framework, the how-tos: to organize internally, selectively build, and maintain cause-marketing relationships and programs; to maximize benefits and leverage opportunities to integrate cause marketing into overall fundraising and communications; and to incorporate many of the principles and collaborative techniques into the way both partners think and do business.

The seven *C*'s: cause readiness, collaborative fit, combining assets, creating value, executing the program, communicating values, and achieving corporate and community goals are the foundation of any successful cause-marketing program. Cause collaborations can be designed, structured, nurtured, and maintained in a manner that enables both partners to contribute to solving pressing social problems and to fulfilling important strategic objectives for companies and nonprofits. Knowing and understanding these seven steps will help guide nonprofit organizations through their thinking and planning.

Part IV: Making It Happen: Best Practices Case Studies

The final part of the book takes the seven steps from the "Getting It Right" cause-marketing framework and uses four case studies to demonstrate how to turn principles into reality. Four nonprofit organizations are featured. The first two are national nonprofits: American Heart Association, a health charity with over 1,000 chapters and a 50-year history, and First Book, a national nonprofit formed in the early 1990s that focuses on literacy, education, and underprivileged children. The second two charities are local ones: Food Bank of New York City, a social service agency, and the Vancouver and Vancouver Island District Chapters of the British Columbia and Yukon Division of the Canadian Cancer Society, a community-based organization aimed at the eradication of cancer and enhancement of the quality of life for people living with the condition.

To end the book, I have dedicated a chapter to cataloging the cause principles and cautions. This chapter enumerates the Seven Golden Rules and then looks at the Seven Deadly Sins of cause marketers, as outlined by pioneers and leaders in the field. Finally, the concluding chapter looks at cause marketing as a new discipline and growing form of corporate–nonprofit engagement and challenges both the corporate and nonprofit sectors to build for the future.

Reflections on My Journey

Through the research and writing of this book I have explored and learned of the depth, breadth, and creativity of cause-marketing programs and how my experiences are similar to other pioneers and leaders trying to chart their course in this new and growing field. I have interviewed for-profit and nonprofit professionals collaborating in every cause area from the arts, environment, and social services to health care and contributing at the national, regional, and local levels.

Done with care and thought, cause marketing can be a powerful tool for nonprofit organizations in achieving in their mission, building their brand, generating revenue, increasing awareness, engaging individuals, changing behavior and attitudes, and making a difference in their community. It can help companies increase their bottom line, attract employees and create pride, appeal to customers and stakeholders, and secure the license they need to operate in many markets. When they combine they can be a powerful force for community good. I hope this book will give you the insights and tools needed to successfully partner for purpose, passion, and profits.

ENDNOTES

1. The Canadian Parks Partnership, "*Strategic Marketing Plan: Fundraising Products and Services*," October 1989.
2. Ibid.
3. Doug Davidge, May 10, 2005.
4. Enbridge was one of six Canadian companies recognized as a leading company in sustainability by the Davos World Economic Forum, February 2005.

PART I

The Cause-Marketing Movement

CHAPTER 1

The New Corporate–Nonprofit Engagement

Corporations have long been involved in supporting community, but when the first cause-marketing programs were successfully implemented, it signaled a dramatic shift in nonprofit–for-profit relationships: one that recognized corporate community support could be positioned at the intersection of business objectives and societal needs.

Cause marketing was initiated over 25 years ago. At the time many nonprofit professionals viewed it as a fledgling idea, one that should not be considered part of any serious fund development or nonprofit program. As well-constructed programs reaped benefits for companies and nonprofits alike, the number of programs continued to grow. Now more than two decades later, cause marketing has evolved and developed into a firmly established practice, a new way for corporations and nonprofits to achieve significant bottom-line results and community impact.

CAUSE MARKETING: A TURNING POINT IN CORPORATE–NONPROFIT RELATIONSHIPS

Cause marketing was officially launched by American Express in the early 1980s. Between 1981 and 1984, American Express used this approach to support more than 45 local causes. Jerry Welsh, a senior vice president of American Express at the time and the architect of the cause-related marketing concept, believed that by giving people a local cause to rally around, it would encourage card members to use their American Express for local purchases.[1] "We were giving money away, but we're doing it in a way that builds business and helps the cause." he explained. The cause promotions were successful and as then-Chairman of American Express Travel Related Services, Louis Gerstner Jr., said, "We now know we can do well by doing good."[2]

The early success of their local San Francisco cause-marketing initiatives led the company to coin and trademark the term "cause-related marketing" in 1983. That same year American Express pioneered the concept at a national level when it launched a three-month marketing campaign around the Statue of Liberty Restoration project. The objective: to increase card use and new card applications and at the same time raise money, awareness, and support for the nonprofit Restoration Fund. American Express donated one cent for every card transaction and one dollar for every new card application. The company also made donations based on purchases of their travelers' checks and travel packages, excluding airfares, sold through its vacation stores.

American Express supported the promotion with a $4 million advertising campaign to reach existing customers and encourage new ones. The results were impressive. In just three months, the Restoration Fund raised over $1.7 million, and American Express card use rose 27%, while new card applications increased by 45% compared to the previous year.

When its first national cause-related marketing (CRM) program was initiated, then–Chairman and CEO James D. Robinson III sensed the company was introducing an innovation that could support a nonprofit organization while simultaneously increasing use of their card and differentiating the company. What he didn't realize was that this early cause-related marketing program would be a turning point—one that demonstrated that mutually beneficial relationships could be built; nonprofit organizations had valuable assets and brands that, when combined with a corporate partner's brand, marketing, and people, would appeal to the public and create shareholder and social value and publicly communicate the value of those involved. Cause marketing was to take corporate–nonprofit relationships to a new plateau.

Growing in Number, Range, and Sophistication

Over the past two decades, cause marketing has manifested itself in various ways and from its early beginning has grown in numbers, range, and depth. Today, cause marketing can include product sales, promotions, and program-driven collaborations between companies and nonprofit causes. The relationships include everything from one-off cause sale promotional activities to broader, longer term marketing relationships to what industry expert Carol Cone today calls Cause Branding: companies that make long-term commitments to causes that eventually become part of their corporate identity, culture, and corporate social responsibility palette.

Whatever the type or level, cause marketing can be seen everywhere. Check out at the drugstore and support the local food bank by adding a donation to your bill. Go to your local hair salon and a portion of the proceeds from the day's sale goes to support the woman's shelter in your town. Pick up a recent issue of a prominent women's magazine, and readers will find ads encouraging them to "Go casual for a cause." For almost 10 years, Lee Jeans has supported Lee National Denim Day, the world's largest single-day fundraiser for breast cancer research, by encouraging women to wear jeans to work for a $5 donation. Since 1996, Lee National Denim Day has raised more than $40 million to benefit the Susan G. Komen Breast Cancer Foundation. At the grocery store, your purchase of a box of Cheerios during their three-month "Spoonful of Stories" promotion supports the national charity, First Book, with the goal of "encouraging kids to read" and supporting literacy. In Canada, support breast cancer research by signing up for the Canadian Breast Cancer Foundation CIBC Run for the Cure at the local bank branch.

Although many programs are straightforward, American Express, a leader in cause marketing, is an example of growth in sophistication and complexity of many of today's cause-marketing initiatives. Beginning in 2003, AMEX Blue Card teamed up with VH1's Save the Music Foundation to support school music programs while connecting with younger consumers. Through a series of year-round events, programs, and exclusive offers, American Express Blue Card members had unique music experiences that lent support to the Foundation.

The Blue for Music program and the Save the Music Foundation launched a year-long fundraising Blue for Save the Music at the Grammy Awards with a Grammy Viewing Benefit Event. Tickets for the benefit were available first to Blue customers. Proceeds from the evening went to the program. Following the launch ceremony, musical instruments and memorabilia used by awards show performers were auctioned via an Internet auction.

The goal of the partnership was to bring greater attention to the lifelong benefits of music education and to help restore music education in America's public schools. Blue from American Express pledged to raise at least $1 million during 2003 toward restoring public school music education programs. In addition to financial support American Express contributed significant visibility via promotions, special events, and advertising. Boyd Tinsley, along with artists Sheryl Crow, Mary J. Blige, The Counting Crows, and Wyclef Jean, appeared in nationwide Blue for Save the Music PSA-style television ads that reveal how music has influenced their lives.

The multilayered program involved as part of the larger Blue for Save the Music Initiative an "Amplify Tomorrow" tour. This saw Infinity Broadcasting, one of the world's largest radio broadcasting companies, and Blue from American Express conducting fundraising events in New York, Los Angeles, Chicago, Boston, and San Francisco through the summer of 2003. Many events were hosted at concert venues by station DJs and featured music performances by some of the industry's hottest talent. Infinity Stations provided a series of on-air promotions and specialty programs. Onsite at the events, concert attendees were encouraged to visit the "Amplify Tomorrow" school bus and to purchase raffle tickets for musical instruments and memorabilia signed by famous artists. In addition, funds were raised through special ticket packages for concerts and exclusive showcases.[3]

The Nonprofit Response

In some nonprofit circles, the early cause-marketing programs were viewed with apprehension. Would cause-marketing programs satisfy individuals' charitable commitments and result in a decline of individual support? Would programs commercialize nonprofit organizations and take them away from their mission focus and scare off loyal donors? Would it result in corporations cutting back on their traditional philanthropic charitable giving?

Charitable donation concerns proved unfounded; despite a few bumps commercialism has not overtaken nonprofit–corporation relationships, and what was viewed with skepticism is being recognized as a way to build new corporate and individual revenue sources, extend message reach, and achieve important mission, project, and behavioral outcomes. Equally important, nonprofit organizations have begun to realize they too have valuable assets, including their own brand that could appeal to potential corporate supporters and be leveraged for significant additional support.

Harry Abel, a nonprofit pioneer in cause marketing, was hired from a marketing position at Coca-Cola to start a corporate relations department at the Arthritis Foundation. Joining the organization in the late 1980s, he took the advice of a corporate colleague and aimed to "think like a for-profit." "I was advised to think linkages and to look at opportunities that could work for both our organization and a corporate partner."[4] It was a new way of thinking for nonprofit organizations, and Harry oversaw the launch of a number of cause-marketing programs including the first corporate–nonprofit commendation program. The Arthritis Foundation's "Ease of Use" is a seal of approval for particular product attributes of benefit to arthritis sufferers that companies could apply and receive approval, for a fee, to use the logo on their product. He initiated a number of cause-marketing initiatives for the organization. He states, "Have senior leadership buy-in, chose your partners carefully, do risk assessment, and have carefully considered processes and procedures in place."[5]

Many national nonprofit organizations were leaders in creating cause-marketing relationships. Companies were looking for national causes with local implementations possibilities. Today, nonprofits at every level—local, regional, and national—are entering the field and developing purpose-built cause-marketing initiatives, hiring dedicated staff, and putting a major push on using cause marketing to leverage corporate resources.

The Food Bank of New York City is a great example of a nonprofit that has recognized the potential to generate additional corporate support, extend awareness and reach, and advance the mission. The 23-year nonprofit organization established an external outreach unit in 2001–2002 with a focus on building longer, deeper corporate cause-marketing partnerships. The program has helped to generate new funds, expand the amount of food collected, and extend awareness for the organization. Although corporate philanthropic financial support is still larger, cause-marketing relationships are growing in importance and provide significant awareness value as well as financial support.[6]

AN ESSENTIAL NEW LINK FOR CORPORATE–NONPROFIT ENGAGEMENT

Since the first cause-marketing programs were launched, the face of corporate community support has transformed and expanded. Corporations are moving beyond traditional philanthropic giving where they were anonymous, benign donors to an active and engaged approach that looks to create marketing and business benefits for the company and broader financial and resource benefits for the community.

With the ever-present emphasis on shareholder value, community involvement and corporate social responsibility are often being tied to business and marketing objectives, to ensure corporate profitability, manage costs, and creatively extend limited corporate resources in a competitive environment. As well, it isn't enough for companies to do good; they want to be seen doing good and to obtain business and marketing benefits beyond just a halo effect.

As cause marketing becomes more prominent and the benefits proven, corporations are taking this new approach that combines corporate self-interest with altruism. According to experts in the nonprofit field, more and more traditional corporate philanthropic support is being replaced or augmented by cause-marketing arrangements and business-driven objectives. As a result, these more active cause-marketing relationships, although a component of corporate giving and social responsibility, are emerging as the new way many corporations are contributing to the community.

Marketing professors Philip Kotler and Nancy Lee's 2005 book, *Corporate Social Responsibility: Doing the Most Good for Your Company and Your Cause*,[7] looks at the role of corporations in contributing to social causes and initiatives. Of the six areas they describe, cause-marketing elements are squarely attached to three: *corporate cause promotions, cause-related marketing*, and *corporate social marketing*. Cause marketing is indirectly linked to two other areas: *community volunteering* (frequently a component of cause-marketing programs) and *socially responsible business practices*. The latter includes "investments to support causes," an example of which is Starbucks working with Conservation International to support farmers to minimize impact on their local environment. Starbucks' advertising of their involvement falls into the cause-marketing realm. Only corporate philanthropy described in the book lacks a connection to cause marketing. Clearly, cause marketing is an important tool in the corporate social responsibility palette.

The Committee to Encourage Corporate Philanthropy (CECP) is a national organization whose membership represents companies that account for 45% of all reported corporate giving. Their tracking reflects this shift to cause-marketing-oriented giving. In 2004, "traditional" charitable giving by CECP members represented just under 49% of all corporate giving. Strategic giving, much of which is cause-marketing driven where a company's community support closely aligns with commercial and strategic business needs, represented 36%, and strictly commercial relationships was 15%. Together strategic and commercial relationships represented the highest percentage of corporate giving. The Committee analyzed where corporate community support emanated, finding that 36% came from corporate community affairs, 27% from corporate foundations, and the rest, 37%, coming from corporate operations, including marketing budgets.[8]

The overall trend line is now well established. According to nonprofit and industry experts backed up by available statistics, more and more philanthropy involves input from the marketing team, and if a nonprofit can't offer concrete ways for businesses to connect with tangible benefits including cause supporters or target audience, funding is less likely. The formerly quiet philanthropy providing support to a variety of deserving comers is being replaced by an emphasis on bottom-line, market logic for a growing portion of corporate support. Cause marketing is becoming the new corporate marketing and citizenship tool.

Supporting a specific cause and being public about this support gives companies identifiable personalities, demonstrates what they stand for, and helps them connect with customers, suppliers, investors, employees, and the community. Today consumers, employees, and other company stakeholders are thinking with their hearts, not just their heads, when they consider whom to work for or do business with.

The New Third Way: Cause Marketing—Part Marketing, Part Philanthropy

For nonprofit organizations, cause-marketing relationships are uniquely different from traditional corporate philanthropic gifts or sponsorship. Building the case for support and making the "ask" is the focus of philanthropic corporate giving. Philanthropic support is often centered on specific areas such as education, health care, or arts and culture and strategic in its approach—giving in specific geographic regions or to matters that are of interest to the company or their employees. Contributions are provided to support good causes without the expectation of profile beyond customary recognition in annual reports or on the Web site. Sponsorship, the most commercial form of corporate community involvement, focuses on a value exchange, the measurable value a business can get from sponsoring a specific event or activity. Sponsorship is guided by the hope and goal of so many impressions and specifically tying it to product sales spike, tank, or level set.

Cause marketing, the new third way, is the intersection of the two (see Exhibit 1.1). In cause marketing the emphasis is on an exchange of value, how a nonprofit relationship and nonprofit assets can help a company achieve marketing and business goals with a direct link to providing a philanthropic component that advances the organization's mission: self-interest combined with altruism; marketing combined with corporate social responsibility. Occasionally, cause marketing is called different names—from philanthropic marketing to values-led marketing to gift-based marketing to corporate citizenship. But whatever it may be called,

EXHIBIT 1.1   THE NEW THIRD WAY

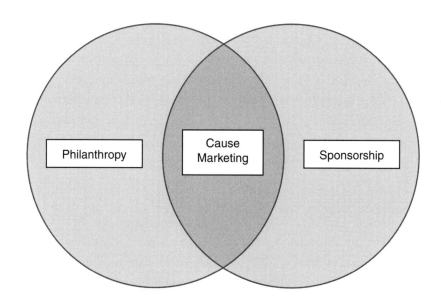

what is happening is clear. Corporate support is being tied to company marketing and business objectives geared to affecting the bottom line.

Cause marketing is a combination of philanthropic benefits, support for a cause, and tangible business benefits focused on driving profitability. Sometimes the benefits are overtly commercial, designed to increase sales and market share; other times they are more subtlety focused on positioning and building the reputation of a product, brand, or company. Either way, the goal is clear. Companies are seeking to strategically align their support of a cause with critical business objectives to achieve mutual benefits of creating social and shareholder value; connecting with key stakeholders, including employees and consumers; and publicly communicating values and contribution to community.

Often confusion exists between sponsorship and cause marketing. Kevin Martinez, Director of Community Affairs at The Home Depot, a leader in cause marketing, is an advocate of the difference. He asserts,

> Cause marketing is not about sponsorship. It is about a partnership that advances and forwards a community based organization, and marketing that allows us to enhance our core profitability, service, and product. Cause-marketing relationships allows us to mentor, advance the mission or vision of our partner nonprofit organization. The relationship is always with a community-based institution in the 501 C3 area.
>
> Our cause-marketing partnerships include as part of our responsibility to also get that mission statement out there. So when we do sell a product through cause marketing or align a service through cause marketing the question is do the consumers also understand the mission of the nonprofit that we are advancing. If they don't we have failed. That's a critical thing. In most companies, the marketing department drives sponsorship while community affairs drive partnership. When we do cause marketing, both come together and both are measuring different things. You have to have great corporate culture that affords you to have both those conversations.[9]

Kathy Rogers, Vice President, Cause Initiatives and Integrated Marketing at the American Heart Association, also believes there is an important difference between cause marketing and sponsorship.

> Our first national sponsorship program was the American Heart Walk. The corporate support was very much around the event and the benefits and value we could provide, not around supporting the cause. These early corporate sponsorship relationships were very important in helping us to learn how to work with companies. However, they were not tied to cause, the mission of the cause or to helping us to promote the cause and achieve our mission. Cause marketing and cause branding programs give us a higher level messaging and provide business benefits, but are very much tied to helping our cause promote and achieve its mission."[10]

ACHIEVE MISSION, GENERATE REVENUE, AND OTHER BENEFITS

Cause-marketing benefits go well beyond a traditional donation. Take the example of IKEA contributing to the UNICEF's Right to Play program. They could make a direct cash donation that is a direct contribution to the program. Rather, by selling a specially designed Brum Bear with a portion of the proceeds going to the program, their public values are communicated; IKEA's message about the program is more broadly disseminated, and revenue is contributed to the program; individual consumers purchasing the bear feel they have made a contribution; and IKEA's staff has a sense of pride in (and knowledge of) their company's community commitment.

Cause marketing allows a corporation to put its brand, marketing might, and people behind a nonprofit cause that can provide significantly more benefits than a straight philanthropic gift. In fact, these other mission-based benefits can be more important than the financial contribution. First and foremost, every cause-marketing initiative must be done because it advances a nonprofit mission.

Mission-Related Benefits:

- *Access to a Wider Audience:* Cause marketing offers the potential to gain marketing exposure. At no direct cost to the nonprofit, they can reach the public in nontraditional places (i.e., shopping centers, car dealerships) and ways (ads, marketing collateral pieces such as in-store promotions, hangtags on products, events) through programs that can raise awareness of both their organization and the cause. Cause marketing offers visibility, public awareness of issues, and an innovative way to reach a broad base of consumers with important educational and action-oriented messages. Cause marketing enables nonprofits to reach audiences they would normally never reach.

  For example, the Susan G. Komen Foundation, leaders in cause marketing, have developed a relationship with Ford Credit, a subsidiary of Ford Motor Company, and NASCAR Race Events that has helped them reach a whole new audience with educational information that encourages them to think about breast health and action through early detection. "Race Fans for the Cure" also provides a way for fans to support the Komen Foundation. For a $1 donation at the booths, fans will personalize a pink paper ribbon for inclusion on a banner that is displayed at Ford Credit's end-of-year check presentation to the Komen Foundation. Ford Credit helps make fan support go even further by matching dollar-for-dollar every donation made.

- *Promote Mission-Based Messaging and Action:* Nonprofit organizations can take full advantage of cause programs to engage potential supporters and to move them from awareness of an issue to action. American Express's cause program, "Blue for Save the Music" in support of music education in schools, is a good example of how this can be achieved. In advertising and promotional material developed for the program, specific information is provided on how to save music education programs in local communities. As well, people are encouraged to write their congressional representative (names and addresses supplied) to advocate for music education.

Cause programs can encourage and modify behavior through broad awareness and action-oriented programs. Their effectiveness can be greater than any traditional brochure or education program undertaken by a nonprofit organization. As one cause marketer stated, "When we're on the back of a cereal box which is read on average 8 times by multiple viewers and it has a shelf life of 3 weeks the potential to impact behavior is huge. What brochure gets read that many times—ever?"

Financial Contribution:

- *Direct Revenue:* Cause marketing provides new sources of revenue beyond the traditional community investment pool. Marketing and other corporate budgets are accessible for nonprofit support. As well because cause marketing is a value exchange, not just a direct donation, dollars generated are not necessarily tied to a specific program or activity. They can be applied to the overall work of the organization and help pay critical operational costs.

- *Additional Financial Support:* Active cause-marketing relationships can result in significant additional financial support for the cause. For example, some cause-marketing programs will trigger additional financial support. Walgreen's cause-marketing program, *Hope Blooms with You*, gives individual consumers a chance to make a donation directly at the checkout to support breast cancer programs of the American Cancer Society. The cause relationship between Canadian Imperial Bank of Commerce and the Canadian Breast Cancer Foundation sees the bank selling pink jelly beans, circle-of-strength necklaces, and pink bracelets at the teller's desk and online, all in support of the cause.

- *Employee Volunteers:* Encouraging employee volunteers can be drivers in cause-marketing programs, and nonprofits can benefit enormously from this support. Cause partners can be critical sources of human muscle and brain power for cause programs like events or programs. London Children's Museum's cobranded program, "3M Science in Your World Gallery," would not have been possible without the financial commitment of 3M. But equally significant was the contribution of the company's science staff in developing messaging, experiments, and activities that made the gallery come alive.

- *Extend Existing Fundraising Programs:* Cause-marketing programs can and should extend nonprofit organizations' traditional fundraising tools. They will never replace traditional philanthropic approaches, but used strategically cause marketing can be a tool to enhance nonprofit fundraising initiatives. Cause-marketing activities can help nonprofit organizations link with their corporate partner's employees, for both individual donations or through an employee contribution foundation. They can also enhance the credibility of nonprofits with other funders who see that organization as passing a corporate acceptability test. As an added bonus, partnering with one corporation can create a multiplier effect; one collaboration leads to another. Cause marketing should also strengthen links with existing individual donors and introduce new donors to the cause. Innovative tools can help build lists of people interested in the nonprofit's work through information or contests. They can also provide nonprofits with immediate financial contributions and in-kind support as well as the potential to build future revenue opportunities.

- *In-Kind Support:* In addition to a financial contribution, many organizations also receive valuable in-kind support such as goods or services that add to an organization's bottom line. In-kind corporation contributions can include involving product donations and additional marketing support. These can be central benefits for nonprofit organizations involved in cause-marketing programs.

VALUE OF CAUSE MARKETING

Cause-marketing support has grown enormously in the last two decades as companies, nonprofits, and constituents from employees and suppliers to retailers and consumers continue to react positively to the outcomes and benefits of joint business collaboration. The result: companies continue to find more money and resources in their budgets. The numbers tell the real story.

Putting a true cash dollar value on cause marketing is a challenge. However, the International Events Group (IEG) began estimating spending in 1990. IEG, established to make sponsorship the fourth arm of marketing, alongside advertising, promotion, and public relations, provides services, research, and advocacy for the profession. They estimate spending only "on payments by corporations to nonprofit sponsors in unrestricted fees in exchange for a marketing affiliation or relationship." As they themselves note, many cause-marketing initiatives combine contributions from philanthropic, advertising, and other company budgets."[11] However, by looking at the IEG numbers, it is clear to see the growth in cause marketing.

In 1990 IEG estimated that $125 million was being spent. In 1998, it had jumped 400% to $545 million, and by 2003 cause-marketing spending had almost doubled to $922 million. This rapid growth continues, and in 2004 cause-marketing spending grew by 7.5% to just under $1 billion; by 2005 it rose to $1.08 billion, a 9% growth.[12]

In addition, IEG projects the value of additional in-kind marketing benefits, including advertising and media exposure, which extends messaging and builds brand awareness for the nonprofit recipients, to be approximately three times the amount of the cause-marketing fees themselves.[13] Add in the value of cause relationships helping achieve mission, gaining corporate expertise, and assistance, and the contributions to nonprofit organizations increase significantly. As outlined earlier, not only do companies make contributions to support their chosen cause, but the programs also themselves frequently trigger additional donations and support from employees, consumers, and other company constituents.

Philanthropic Giving versus Cause-Marketing Support

Historically, funding from corporations has been a relatively small portion of the support base of nonprofit organizations. In 2003, Giving USA estimated that individuals, estates, foundations, and corporations gave $240.72 billion to charitable causes. Of that, corporate support represented about 5.6%, at $13.46 billion (cash and in-kind). In Canada corporation contributions represent a higher percentage of overall support. Relatively new to the philanthropic marketplace,

WOMEN'S HEALTH ISSUES: BREAST CANCER

Avon's Breast Cancer Crusade and Worldwide Fund for Women's Health raised and contributed $300 million in its first 11 years since it committed itself to raising breast cancer awareness in 1993. Avon's program is particularly focused on medically underserved women and to encouraging early detection of the disease through self-examination. Avon's sales representatives regularly distribute educational materials on breast cancer awareness including information about making additional donations. As well, their support of the annual fundraising walk, Avon Walk for Cancer, drew over 600,000 participants in 2004. Revenue is generated by financially contributing to the walk and by pledges collected by walk participants themselves. In addition, the value of the promotion and awareness created through the program has made a major promotional contribution to the profile of the issue of breast cancer—one that is difficult to value financially.

UNICEF

Although there are a few nonprofit organizations that generate the majority of their support from cause-marketing relationships, organizations like UNICEF are more typical of the financial benefit of cause marketing. In 2004, they generated $65 million in corporate gifts. And although the majority of that support comes from philanthropic gifts, the fastest growing area is from cause-marketing programs.[14]

Canadians' charitable contributions in 2003 were estimated to be at $9.105 billion. Individual giving accounts for the highest percentage of contributions at 72% of total Canadian giving. Corporations follow in second place at 16%, and foundations provide 12% of all recorded giving.[15]

Comparing this traditional philanthropic support with cause marketing is difficult, if not impossible; a quick calculation demonstrates how cause marketing has become a growth area for nonprofit support. In 1990, traditional philanthropic corporate giving in the United States was pegged at about $7 billion (cash and in-kind).[16] By contrast, cause marketing's value, cash and in-kind, was approximately $500 million ($125 million plus approximately $375 million in-kind), representing about 14% of corporate philanthropic support.

In 2003, corporate giving (cash and in-kind) was about $13.46 billion. When compared with recorded cause-marketing dollar contributions (approximately $1 billion direct and $3 billion in-kind) at the same time, these more active and engaged corporate–nonprofit relationships had grown to represent about 29% percent of overall corporate giving, up from 14% in 1990, a dramatic rise, demonstrating its rapid growth and increasing importance.

Another way to look at it is strictly from a growth perspective. Cause marketing grew from $125 million in 1990 to just under $1 billion by 2003, a 900% increase. During the same time frame, corporate giving rose 200%—from approximately $7 billion in 1990 to just under $14 billion in 2003. Either way, cause marketing is here to stay and grow.

CAUSE-RELATED MARKETING INTERNATIONALLY

Cause marketing is not restricted to North America. It is now a global phenomenon. Campaigns are prominent throughout Britain, Europe, and Australia. Jerry Welsh, the originator of the concept of cause-related marketing, has established programs in China.[17]

The UK in particular has put muscle behind a national campaign to encourage cause-marketing programs. In 1995, the UK national organization Business in the Community launched an initiative to develop a center of knowledge, information, and best practices to promote cause-related marketing (now called Cause Related Business Campaign) as a means of making a positive impact on key social issues.

In the UK, Business in the Community's Cause-Related Marketing Tracker 2003 presented the amount raised for charities and good causes. Pegged at £58.2 million or over $90 million U.S. contributed through cause-related marketing programs, this is an increase of over 15% from 2002. Of this, £24 million or $37.2 million U.S. dollars were funds leveraged through staff, customer, and supplier fundraising.[18] This amount focuses on the dollars raised in 2003 and does not include the other benefits associated with cause marketing. During this year 67 businesses and 64 charitable causes collaborated and undertook 82 cause-related marketing programs.

European Experience

Europe, a latecomer to the field, is starting to recognize the value cause marketing can provide businesses, nonprofits, and the community. In 2000, CSR Europe released it first report on cause-related marketing (CRM), looking at this growing trend in Europe. CSR Europe, the organization dedicated to encouraging corporate social responsibility, looked at how CRM is proving itself as being the "first step towards profitably combining social and commercial marketing goals."[19] The report highlighted the changing consumer attitude and expectation of social and environmental need, coupled with the desire to see companies do more to address these issues. Although used by a relatively small

TESCO, COMPUTERS FOR SCHOOLS

Several major initiatives were launched, one of the best known being Tesco Computers for Schools. Started in 1992 as a one-off promotion, the program has developed into a long-term strategic initiative for the grocery chain. Tesco provides its customers a voucher for every £10 spent in-store. Shoppers donate their vouchers to the school of their choice, which exchanges them for brand-new computer equipment. Parents have collaborated to increase the number of vouchers collected for their school. Tesco continues to run the highly successful cause program. One of the interesting facets of the program is the way support is provided to the community directly from shopper to school of choice. No one nonprofit cause partner is involved.

ALLIANCE CARTON NATURE AND UNICEF (FRANCE)

The Program:

Alliance Carton Nature and UNICEF in France launched a joint initiative to recycle beverage cartons, which would then be turned into wrapping paper and sold in supermarkets to support UNICEF projects. Since the program was launched in 1996, every year approximately 300,000 children ages 9 to 11 are invited to participate in the project. The children bring empty beverage cartons to school, which are then sent to a recycling factory. The cartons are turned into wrapping paper. Through a contest organized in the schools, a child's drawing is selected to decorate the wrapping paper. Each Christmas the paper is sold through retailers in France. The projects from the sales are contributed to a different UNICEF initiative each year.

Program Goals:

Entitled "Brikkado" the project was initiated to improve the environment while helping children in developing countries. Alliance Carton Nature, the French arm of the Alliance for Beverage Cartons and the Environment, aimed to develop policy makers' and public authorities' awareness of the effectiveness of recycling beverage cartons. They also wanted to present beverage cartons as being ecologically friendly and to communicate complex environment issues to the public and businesses through the help of educational institutions.

UNICEF's main objective was to reach families and the general public through children about their organization. As well, they wanted to develop a product that would complement, not compete with, their UNICEF Christmas card program.

Results:

The project continues today, and the profits from the program contribute to different major UNICEF projects each year through a direct donation from Alliance Carton Nature. Since its inception well over 800,000 euros were donated through the Brikkado wrapping paper program.

The program has received significant publicity and several major awards. In 2004, for the second year in a row, the UNICEF Christmas Wrapping Paper was designated as an environmentally sustainable product by the French Ministère de l'Environnement et du Développement.

Employees, clients, suppliers, retailers, and schools are regularly updated on the program. Since its inception, millions of children have participated in the recycling program. The project has become a model for cause-marketing collaborations. UNICEF and Alliance Carton Nature brought together two different cultures, an entrepreneurial and nonprofit ethos to make the project work.

number of companies to date, CRM programs were touted as a way, if part of a broader CSR program, to "make good, profit making, business sense."[20]

Conclusions

When cause marketing was launched over 25 years ago, it was viewed as a fledgling idea. Today, cause marketing is a global phenomenon that has developed into the new way for businesses and nonprofit causes to collaborate to achieve mutual benefits. Cause-marketing partners a nonprofit cause's brand and assets with the power of a corporation's brand, marketing, and people to achieve social and shareholder value while communicating values.

Cause marketing has come a long way from its early days, has become increasingly sophisticated, and now includes everything from one-off cause sale promotional activities to broader, longer term marketing relationships to companies that make long-term commitments to causes that eventually become part of their corporate identity, culture, and corporate social responsibility palette. Today, cause marketing can include product sales, promotions, and program-driven collaborations between companies and nonprofit causes.

Nonprofit organizations have responded by proactively seeking cause partnerships and recognizing the value of these corporate marketing relationships and the benefits beyond traditional philanthropic contributions. Done right, cause marketing can help achieve mission, generate additional revenue, extend reach, get out important messages, change behaviors, and enhance awareness of a nonprofit and the cause.

Cause marketing is augmenting traditional corporate philanthropic support and becoming the new way corporations and nonprofits organizations are working together. Different from philanthropy or sponsorship, cause marketing combines the two—the community benefit associated with philanthropy and the business value tied to sponsorship—self-interest combined with altruism.

Cause marketing's time has come, and companies continue to find more money and resources in their budgets for cause marketing. This segment of corporate giving and corporate social responsibility is a growing phenomenon and an important new marketing and corporate citizenship tool to create profitability and a new fundraising and marketing tool for nonprofits to generate revenue and achieve critical mission goals.

Endnotes

1. Interview with Jerry Welsh, April 6, 2005.
2. Sue Adkins, *Cause Related Marketing, Who Cares Wins* (Boston: Butterworth-Heinemann, 1999), pp. 14, 15.
3. www.home3americanexpress.com/corp/latestnews/blue-music.asp, April 17, 2004.
4. Interview, Harry Abel, January 27, 2005.

5. Ibid.
6. Interview, Matthew Goldstein, Director, Business Partnerships, Food Bank of New York City, May 23, 2005.
7. P. Kotler and N. Lee, *Corporate Social Responsibility: Doing the Most Good for Your Company and Your Cause* (New York: John Wiley & Sons, 2004), pp. 23, 24.
8. www.corphilantrophy.org.
9. Interview, Kevin Martinez, March 25, 2005.
10. Interview, Kathy Rogers, January 24, 2005.
11. Information from the 1999 Attorney General's Report, "What's in a Nonprofit Name? Public Trust, Profit and the Potential for Public Deception," www.oag.state.ny.us/press/reports/nonprofit/full_text.
12. IEG Sponsorship Report, 2004, projected a 7.5% growth from the previous year. Their recording of cause-marketing programs shows its growth from 1990 at $125 million to over $1 billion projected in 2005. Cause marketing is now the third largest sponsorship category recorded by the International Event Group.
13. Information from the 1999 Attorney General's Report, "What's in a Nonprofit Name? Public Trust, Profit and the Potential for Public Deception," www.oag.state.ny.us/press/reports/nonprofit/full_text.
14. Interview, Anne Marie Grey, Chief, International and Corporate Alliances, UNICEF, April 5, 2005.
15. "Philanthropic Trends," Spring 2005, KCI, Ketchum Canada.
16. AAFRC Trust for Philanthropy/Giving, USA 2003.
17. Interview, Jerry Welsh, April 6, 2005.
18. www.bitc.org.uk/programmes/programme-directory/cause_related_business/index.html
19. "Cause Related Marketing: CSR, Europe, 2000", Foreword.
20. Ibid. Section 1, Introduction.

CHAPTER 2

Integrating Value and Values

The American Marketing Association defines marketing as "an organizational function and a set of processes for creating, communicating, and delivering value to customers and for managing customer relationships in ways that benefit the organization and its stakeholders.[1] Cause marketing is a process that integrates value with values, connecting marketing objectives with societal needs. It creates shareholder and social value through mutually beneficial collaborative partnerships, connects with key constituents, and publicly communicates values of citizenship.

As corporations and nonprofit organizations adapt to this new approach to marketing and corporate community support, they have had to confront the blurring and blending of lines and ambiguity around the language used to describe these relationships. Although cause marketing is a well-known term, a number of names are used to describe this growing way business and nonprofit causes are aligning in mutually beneficial relationships. Philanthropic marketing, affiliate marketing, values-led marketing, cause-related marketing, passion branding, cause branding, and cause overlay are all commonly cited terms. But whatever it may be called, what is happening is clear. Corporate community support is being tied to company marketing and business objectives geared to affecting the bottom line.

CAUSE MARKETING DEFINED

Cause marketing has four key elements that define it and set it apart from traditional marketing and from other corporate–nonprofit relationships:

1. Creates shareholder and social value
2. Is a collaborative, mutually beneficial business–nonprofit partnership
3. Connects and engages constituents including employees and consumers
4. Communicates values of citizenship

Creating Value Through Mutually Beneficial Collaborations

Cause marketing's first and second distinguishing characteristics are that it is a mutually beneficial collaborative relationship that strategically aligns a company and a nonprofit cause to create shareholder, consumer, and social value. From the business perspective, shareholder value is achieved by using the relationship to drive marketing objectives that can include all aspects of corporate and brand development, advertising, public relations, sales promotion, reputation management, loyalty, and relationship marketing. Cause-marketing relationships usually are jointly developed with community relations or the foundation and the

FORD AND THE SUSAN G. KOMEN BREAST CANCER FOUNDATION

Ford Motor Company's cause program with the Susan G. Komen Breast Cancer Foundation's Race for the Cure successfully positioned Ford among a key target market: women. For Ford, this market has frequently felt disassociated with what is viewed as a more male-oriented industry.[2] This multilevel cause relationship includes product sales, such as a specially designed Lily Pultizer scarf and a song by Melissa Etheridge, both available at fordcares.com.

STARBUCKS AND FAIR TRADE– CERTIFIED COFFEE

Listening to the growing requests from their customers to purchase fair trade coffee, Starbucks makes their commitment a major part of the corporate social responsibility program and includes it as part of their marketing program. Since 2000, Starbucks has regularly bought and brewed fair trade–certified coffee and paid premium prices to ensure that farmers make a profit. Shade-grown coffee is critical to stopping the clearing of tropical rain forests. Fair trade coffee allows Starbucks to support both development issues and the environment while satisfying customer concerns—a clear example of having their cake and eating it, too!

In 2003, Starbucks provided $1 million for financing through the Calvert Foundation, giving 10,000 fair trade coffee farmers access to affordable credit. In addition, Starbucks provided another 42.5 million to Conservation International's Verde Ventures, making similar financial help available to additional farmers in Central and South America. Through the Calvert Foundation and Conservation International, they provide financial support to farmers to improve the quality of life for the farming families and their communities.[3] Starbucks publicly communicates their commitment through on-site brochures on this work available at Starbucks outlets.

company's marketing team. It can also involve human resources, employee organizations, and senior executive leadership.

Every company that gets involved in cause-marketing collaborations has goals and objectives it wants to achieve. Sometimes the program is overtly commercial and involves direct product sales that can increase a company's sales transactions, improve profit levels, or expand market share. Other times, the program is more indirect, with a focus on market positioning, building reputation or stakeholder relationships, and differentiating or branding the company tied to a cause issue.

As was previously outlined for nonprofit organizations, cause marketing is a fundraising and marketing tool that achieves social value well beyond just financial support. Specifically, cause marketing helps an organization achieve mission and program goals, expand financial support and revenue generation, increase organizational and cause brand awareness, get out key messages, and access corporate expertise and resources.

Business and nonprofit cause collaboration brings together and combines assets to create mutually beneficial value. Business brings the power of their brand, marketing expertise, connection with employees, consumers, stakeholders, and

UNICEF and Starwood Hotels Check Out for Children

Elegantly simple, but highly effective Check Out for Children is a flagship global cause-marketing collaboration between UNICEF and participating Starwood Hotels and Resorts throughout Europe, Africa, the Middle East, Latin America, and Asia Pacific. The partnership came about when Starwood Vice President and General Counsel for Europe, Africa, and the Middle East, Robert Scott, was in Ethiopia in 1995 finalizing the opening of the Sheraton Addis Ababa. Struck by the imbalance of wealth between the rich world and the poor, he determined to bring about change. As a result, one of the world's most successful cause-marketing partnerships was born.

The logistics of the program makes the process of donating incredibly simple. Upon check-in, hotel guests are invited to add one dollar (or local currency equivalent) to their bill, as a donation to UNICEF. All funds raised contribute to UNICEF immunization programs.

The program creates a win for all partners. For UNICEF, Check Out for Children™ reaches countless guests, informing them of their advocacy and commitment to children. The program had raised over US$10 million by 2004 and helped directly reach a broad audience with key UNICEF messages. For the hotels, the program offers a major public relations benefit. But most importantly, the program actively engages their staff in supporting a worldwide cause with the end result of an increasingly motivated and loyal staff. For guests at the hotel, it is a simple way to make a difference.

financial support. Nonprofit causes contribute their name, reputation, link with donors, volunteers and community leaders, and programs tied to addressing the cause issue. Credibility and the public's desire to support them is another strong asset that nonprofits bring to a relationship. An opportunity for employee engagement, volunteering, and creating pride is a new emphasis for many of today's cause-marketing initiatives. Together, the merged assets from the two partners combine to create mutually beneficial value that is greater than the sum of the individual parts.

Connecting: Employees, Stakeholders, and Consumers

The third critical characteristic is the focus on building a relationship and making a connection with constituents that involves their active participation and engagement. This can include everything from purchasing a product, to participating in a promotion, or volunteering in an event or program.

Depending on marketing goals and objectives, constituents include a range of people but almost always start at the center and move outward (see Exhibit 2.1) from employees and investors, to community influencers, NGOs, and govern-

---

EXHIBIT 2.1   MOVEMENT OF CONSTITUENTS

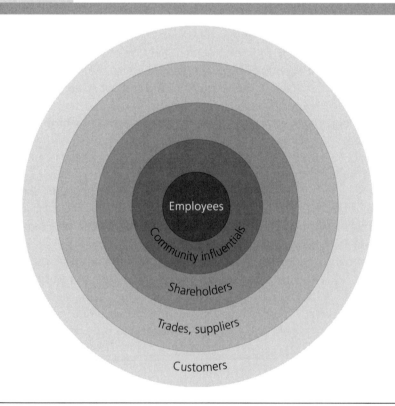

ment officials to retailers, suppliers, and trades, eventually reaching individual consumers.

Building brand identity and demonstrating their value is a major marketing goal for most companies involved in cause programs. Brands are built from the inside out, and a cause-marketing program integrates the concern and commitment for the cause into the business culture. Cause-marketing programs align with the interests of employees and constituents and engage them in making a difference. Because cause-marketing programs are so visible, they enable employees, constituents, and individual consumers to openly demonstrate their own citizenship values and commitment to supporting community initiatives and needs.

Increased employee pride, morale, and loyalty; better relations with key community influencers; and higher trade and consumer sales are all ways that cause initiatives can benefit corporations and their cause partners.[4]

ConAgra Foods and Feeding Children Better

ConAgra Foods has embraced the cause of combating child hunger with their Feeding Children Better initiative. They have underwritten over 100 afterschool cafes now serving about one million hot meals each year. Because ConAgra is not a consumer brand itself, the company's driving business goal was to strengthen ties with its employees, retailers, and food-service customers.

Food Bank for the NYC Bank-to-Bank Cause-Marketing Initiative

Launched in 2004, Bank-to-Bank is a month-long, citywide food drive that runs through November. The cause-marketing relationship sees the Food Bank of New York City partner with local banks to reach a wider range of donors. The partnership enables New Yorkers to make a different kind of deposit at their local bank branch—a deposit of canned food items for the city's hungry. The food drive is the city's largest, with a goal of raising one million pounds of food, enough to provide an additional 700,000 meals to those in need. Partner banks included Washington Mutual, Credit Suisse First Boston, Deutsche Bank, HVB Group, and Lehman Brothers. Media partners include *amNewYork, Forbes, New York Moves, Time Out New York*, WB11, and 1010 WINS. Additional partners are Bloomberg LP and UPS.

Nonprofits can also use cause-marketing programs to connect with a new group of potential supporters as well as their established donor group. This can help generate additional financial support and build further connections that enable them to expand their fundraising capacity, get out key messages, and achieve key mission goals.

Communicating Values: Corporate Citizenship Tool

The final characteristic of cause marketing is that it puts a public face on a company's community commitment and brings its values to life. Unlike traditional philanthropic gifts, cause marketing focuses on publicly communicating the support using marketing tools. Cause marketing visibly demonstrates in the marketplace through advertising, corporate, and product promotional material what a company stands for, how it contributes, and how it is making a difference at a societal level. As Carol Cone states, "Cause marketing puts a human face on a corporation and shows they are about more than just making profits, producing products or delivering services."[5]

Cause marketing is a merging of self-interest and altruism, marketing, and philanthropy. On one hand, it is a commercial activity where key marketing objectives must be met; on the other, an overarching goal is improving community and addressing societal issues. The support provided through cause programs allows nonprofit causes to channel resources to people in need, to enhance the environment, or to tackle social problems. There is a definite philanthropic element and objective inherent in any cause program. In fact, cause marketing can only exist where the social and cultural context encourages community support and action.

With This in Mind . . . A New Definition

Cause marketing is a mutually beneficial collaboration that aligns the power of a company's brand, marketing, and people to a charitable cause's brand and assets to create shareholder and social value, connect with constituents, and publicly communicate values.

CAUSE MARKETING IS MARKETING, SO A FEW VITAL FACTS

Although cause marketing combines marketing with philanthropy, it is still marketing. As cause-related marketing originator Jerry Welsh is fond of saying, "We named it cause marketing very carefully. If it were philanthropy, we would have called it marketing-related philanthropy."[6] So as Jerry states, it is important to remember a few critical fundamentals that drive corporate marketing.[7]

Focus is on the cause, not the charity:

Cause marketing is just that, an emphasis on a cause, not a specific charity. The cause is the overarching driver and the nonprofit organization the vehicle for support.[8] As nonprofit professionals know, a host of charities can play critical roles and thrive under an overarching cause. Hunger is one such example. Charities can be found working on all levels, from local (Food Bank of New York City) to national (Second Harvest) to international (Feed the Children). Donations can be made to support to everything from soup kitchens to breakfast in the classroom programs to food in Africa.

Corporate cause marketers will chose a cause that aligns with their company, brand, or product and is logical to their constituents, including employees. For example, Avon's market and staff are women, so it makes sense that their alignment is with an issue relevant to women—breast cancer.

Perhaps national in scope, but always local in impact and implementation:

Like politics, all marketing is local and cause marketing is no exception. Although national nonprofit organizations may be the focus of support, critical to virtually all cause-marketing initiatives is local impact and local implementation. "Cause marketing was started to focus in on local areas," states Jerry Welsh. "For example if you live in Dallas, the Dallas ballet or museum is more compelling to you than would be a generic ad for an American Express card."[9]

"Check Out for Children," although supporting an international charitable organization, UNICEF, is implemented in individual Starwood hotels in cities around the world. Ford's involvement with the Susan G. Komen Foundation "Run for the Cure" supports events in local communities. ConAgra Food's Feeding Children Better initiative supports over 100 local afterschool cafes. Product sales and promotions are implemented in local retail outlets, events held in local communities, and programs activated by local citizens.

Compelling and positive presentation, even of difficult issues:

Because cause marketing is very much a public activity and is meant to sell products or position the company, product, or brand, the cause issue must be presented in a compelling, uplifting way. Marketing can't be about negative consequences like breast cancer deaths, starving children, or desperate poverty. Cause marketing is about finding an answer, making a positive difference, taking charge of a community issue.

Susan G. Komen Foundation has been a leader in taking a challenging subject, women and breast cancer, and positioning it with a positive slant. The focus isn't about the negative effects of breast cancer; their message is about getting involved in finding the cure. "Cook for the cure; run for the cure; charge for the cure" all conjure up a positive message of action.

Cause-Marketing Initiatives: Usually time limited, promotion driven

Cause-marketing initiatives are usually time limited and promotionally driven. The relationship may be longer than the specific promotional period. For example, Yoplait and Susan G. Komen Foundation have had a relationship focused on the annual promotion "Save Lids to Save Lives" since 1997. The cause marketing initiative itself is for a three-month period annually. But this isn't always the case. As the field evolves, so does the approach taken.

Cause Marketing and Corporate Citizenship: Deeper relationships that are strongly marketing based:

Today's cause-marketing initiatives are the new marketing and corporate citizenship tool that is part of a company's long-term and public support of a cause that eventually becomes part of its brand equity, corporate social responsibility, and organizational identity. Avon and breast cancer, Target and schools are prominent examples. Both have cause-marketing components to their programs, but they have made such a long-term commitment they have built a reputation around their particular community support.[10]

TRENDS DRIVING CAUSE MARKETING

What are the trends driving the growth of this integration of value and values? In many ways, cause marketing's time has clearly come. While corporations and nonprofits reap the benefits and individuals continue to support these initiatives, it is here to stay and grow.

CORPORATE DRIVERS

Leading companies have long understood the importance of publicly communicating their values. John Bell, founder of Esprit clothing company, said in a 1993 interview with *The Age*, "Today a company must stand for more than just making a profit. There are two great benefits to doing that, the best people will want to work for you and the consumers will want to support you. In business today, service is not an issue; it's something you have to have. The market dictates price and styling. The only issue left is what you stand for."

Today, more and more companies are realizing they can no longer afford to be anonymous benefactors or disengaged citizens. Over the past 10-plus years, Cone research reports have tracked this trend and the changing attitudes toward cause marketing and its impact on corporations and the way they contribute to the community. Using the Cone research reports, Carol Cone and her staff have identified key motivators that are driving these changes in the corporate sector: employees, communities, and consumers are all demanding that companies play an active role in building community and demonstrate what they stand for. It is no longer good enough to be good citizens; companies need to be seen to be doing good.[11] Finally, shareholders are demanding value be created and values adhered to; cause-marketing initiatives provide a clear return on both of these requirements.

Employee Motivator

Attracting, Retaining, and Creating Pride

In global marketing, employees are a critical competitive advantage. Attracting, motivating, and retaining them are increasingly a driver in cause-marketing programs. Improved loyalty and morale, greater job satisfaction, and higher retention translate into better overall financial performance. A study undertaken by Watson Wyatt showed that companies with excellent recruiting and retention provided an 8% higher return to shareholders.[12]

The 2000 Cone study on cause marketing and strategic philanthropy indicated that using cause-marketing programs to enhance employee loyalty was one of the most important long-term objectives of a program.[13] By 2002, the Cone survey found that employees whose companies support social issues were:

- 40% more likely to say they are proud of their company's values
- Nearly 25% more likely to be loyal to their employers than those whose companies do not have such programs[14]

The 2004 Cone Corporate Citizenship Study showed a company's commitment to a social issue was important when Americans decided where to work:[15]

2004	2002	Oct. 2001	March 2001
81%	77%	76%	48%

A 2005 Canadian study, conducted by Globescan for Hewlett Packard (Canada) Co., suggests that 91% of Canadians prefer to work for a company that is socially and environmentally responsible.[16]

Cause-marketing programs are becoming an integral part of a company's culture and a major reason they are undertaken. To further reveal the importance companies are placing on employee engagement and pride, Jeffrey R. Immelt, chairman and chief executive officer of General Electric, told 200 corporate officers that it would take four things to keep the company on top. Little did they realize what would top his list. The last three things were predictable: execution, growth, and great people. What trumped those to be ranked first? Virtue.

To be a great company today you also have to be good company. "The reason people come to work for GE is that they want to be about something that is bigger than themselves. People want to work hard, they want to get promoted, they want stock options. But they also want to work for a company that makes a difference, a company that's doing great things in the world."[17] While John Bell of Esprit might have understood this critical factor in 1993, as Carol Cone stated when she presented the GE quote, "When GE's top executive believes supporting community is a have to do, it's no longer just a nice to do."[18]

Building Brand

Employees also help build a company's brands and reflect its values and attributes. Brands are built from the inside out, and when companies launch cause-marketing programs, their employees are central to their success. They need to understand and be actively engaged if a company is to receive maximum benefit from its cause-marketing endeavors.

Enhancing Skill, Providing Volunteer Opportunities

Cause-marketing relationships can connect employees with volunteer opportunities. More and more companies are recognizing the benefits of employee voluntarism in team building and skill development. Nonprofits at the international, national, and local levels are experiencing the same demand: to make cause-marketing programs accessible to employees that allow them to build pride, engage in volunteer opportunities, enhance skills, and develop team spirit. Sometimes this can be a great benefit and other times a challenge to provide the right volunteer opportunities that work for both partners.

Community Scrutiny

Post–Enron, September 11

Corporate scandals have created a new "post–Enron, WorldCom, Arthur Andersen, and Tyco" world where corporate governance is taking hold. Not only is there an expectation that corporations have to be governed appropriately; they must also give back to the community and publicly show they stand for more than just profits. Topping it off, post–September 11 communities are being forced to evaluate their relationships with the companies they do business with and for whom they work. As identified in the Cone research reports, the question repeatedly raised by consumers, employees, suppliers, and stakeholders is, "What do you stand for?"[19]

In Cone's 2004 study, 90% of respondents said they would consider switching to another company's products and services, speaking out against the company (81%), and selling investments (80%) if the company was behaving illegally or unethically.

Done right, cause marketing can build a positive emotional connection to external constituents from suppliers to community and government officials to consumers. In an era of increasing public scrutiny, communities are a force that is key in a corporation's success.

World Wide Web

Cone research has also identified the rise of the Internet and blogs as a way that provides access to all sorts of information and makes a company's activities very transparent. It allows individuals to praise or attack a company with a simple keystroke. Connecting today with consumers is no longer about advertising and having a one-way conversation; it's about a two-way dialogue that can establish trust and build an understanding of a company's community involvement. A recent example? Lance Armstrong Foundation is now encouraging cancer survivors to "Share your story at Livestrong.org."[20]

License to Operate

With the decline in government intervention, the license to operate in the community no longer comes from government alone but from constituents, employees, and the community in general. Companies have to manage in a new way and take a more proactive role in community engagement to get buy-in from a wide range of community interests. For over 15 years organizations like the World Business Council on Sustainable Development have advocated the need for companies to understand the changed landscape. Self-regulation is a focus for business, and the council encourages companies to be proactive and public to gain support.[21]

Unlike traditional corporate philanthropy, cause marketing provides an innovative and highly visible way to demonstrate support of a cause and community. Support for companies involved in cause marketing has grown since its inception. In the 2004 survey, Cone found

- 92% of Americans have a more positive image of companies and products that support causes, significantly higher than figures preceding September 2001 (81% in March 2001, 83% in 1999, 85% in 1993).
- 85% say a company's commitment to a social cause influences the decision of which companies could do business in a local community[22]

Socially Consciousness Consumers

The Cone Reports have also focused on consumer opinions toward cause marketing and the marketplace and have identified key trends as a result of their work.

Reward or Punish

Today consumers are thinking with their hearts, not just their heads, when they shop. Supporting a cause gives companies identifiable personalities, demonstrates what they stand for, and helps them connect with customers, suppliers, investors, employees, and the community. Especially since September 11, consumers are shopping with a cause in mind. Cone Inc.'s 2002 survey points out that if price and product are equal, consumers are willing to switch their purchases to products that support a cause.

- Before September 11, 54% felt this way; after September 11 an overwhelming 81% agreed.[23]
- By 2002, 84% and then in 2004 an all-time high of 86% of Americans said they were likely to switch brands when price and quality are equal to help support a cause.[24]

A similar Canadian study completed by Globescan in 2005 found 92% of Canadians surveyed are more likely to purchase products or services from companies that are socially and environmentally responsible.[25]

Time Challenged

Cone research looks how at cause marketing is also an effective way for time-crunched consumers to give back to their community through purchases and on-going loyalty. Cause-marketing programs provide a convenient way to donate.

- Cause-related shopping is the second and third means of providing charitable gifts for those who planned to give a charitable donation over the holiday season.
- Consumers and constituents appreciate that they can easily support charitable causes through cause-based programs.[26]

The British Business in the Community 21st Century Giving research showed a similar trend:

- 83% of those who participated in a cause initiative said it enabled them to support a charity more than they would otherwise have done.[27]

A very practical Canadian example highlights the interest of consumers in contributing to charitable causes through consumer purchases and loyalty programs and the corporate response. TELUS Corporation is one of Canada's leading providers of data, Internet Protocol (IP), and voice and wireless communication services and provides a full range of communications products and services. The company recently offered their premium wireless customers the opportunity to accept a gift of high-quality chocolates or a free music download.

"Our national loyalty program called Perks goes out to our high value wireless customers. We did a little test about a year ago and offered these customers two premium options as a high value customer. The value of the individual offers exceeded $25 and we gave them a choice of taking the gift or donating the money to one of three charities. Guess which one really succeeded? We were amazed that in no time at all the generosity of our customers exceeded a charitable donation of over $400,000. That's when it really dawned on us the interest in this type of cause marketing and it was our Chief Marketing Officer that got engaged," relates John Mikkelson, Assistant Vice President, Corporate Partnerships. That experience led the firm, which is dedicated to being Canada's premier corporate citizen, to launch similar initiatives with partners such as their recent investment in five Science Centers across Canada.[28]

Women and Teens

The term *consumer democracy*, described by Marc Gobé in his recent book, *Citizen Brand*, is emerging, where shopping is often values-driven behavior, especially for women and teens, which companies ignore at their peril. Women place a high value on relationships and community. Shopping is an extension of who they are and the principles they hold. They want to know what a company stands for and how it is relevant to them. Today's teens and twenty-somethings grew up viewing community service as part of their high school programs, and many colleges had it as an admissions requirement. More than 60% of teens surveyed by Alloy, a youth marketing firm, said they were more likely to buy brands that supported charitable causes. And kids have a big influence on parents' shopping decisions, including big-ticket items like cars.[29]

Women have long been a powerful but little recognized economic force. In the United States they influence 80% of products sold,[30] and not only do they have more buying power, but women are also willing to look beyond price and product to see the values the company promotes. The 2003 Cone Holiday Trend Tracker found the following.

- 77% of women are likely to consider a company's reputation for supporting causes when purchasing gifts compared to 64% of men.

- Nearly two-thirds of female shoppers (65%) say they plan to purchase a product in which a percentage of the price is donated to a cause compared to 54% of male consumers.

- Women are also more likely to buy holiday gifts from retailers that support social issues (60% versus 49%).[31]

Shareholder Value

Corporate Social Responsibility and Reputation Management

A corporation is a for-profit company and as such a major responsibility is returning an investment to shareholders. More and more companies are viewing the way they engage with the communities as important to responsible business practices. In return, responsible business practices means companies are able to hire great people and have strong reputations in the community and with their customers. Cause marketing, with the right partners and community program, can expand a company's marketing, enhance its brand, and extend the company's reputation in the marketplace. All are critical elements in ensuring value to the company and by extension its shareholders.

NONPROFIT DRIVERS

It is not surprising that the launch of cause marketing in the early 1980s coincided with the Reagan and Thatcher years when it became clear the social safety net, once considered sacrosanct, would not be spared even for those in the greatest need. Dramatic and sweeping reductions of government services abruptly ended the era of big government. And in the wake of tax cuts and ballooning deficits devastating cuts came to nonprofit organizational funding.

What was considered only a short-term phenomenon as government dealt with an immediate funding crisis has evolved into a long-term and systemic change to society. The decline of government involvement in key societal areas has continued unabated, and a steady stream of new organizations continues to spring up to address increasing collective challenges and needs. The result? A profound change to the structure of society, the way nonprofit organizations operate and fund themselves, greater accountability and transparency for the nonprofit sector and new expectations of collaboration among the three sectors for societal good: all factors driving nonprofit organizations' interest in building cause-marketing collaborations.

Resource Needs

Increased Competition

Over the past 25 years society has witnessed an explosion in the growth and number of nonprofit community organizations in North America and beyond. There are now nearly 800,000 nonprofit organizations in the United States, double the number that existed in 1990.[32] The nonprofit sector now represents almost 10% of the American workforce. In Canada, the January 2005 issue of *Forefront*, Imagine Canada's national publication, recorded 161,000 nonprofits and charities, representing 13% of the total workforce.[33] This has created a surge in funding needs for community organizations. Competition is fierce, and demand is outstripping supply. Creativity and new ideas are needed to stand out, get their message heard, and sustain and build the organization.

Need for New Revenue and Additional Resources

Corporate fund-raisers in the nonprofit sector recognize the benefits to incorporating cause marketing into their overall corporate fundraising strategy mix. In Britain, where cause marketing has been actively promoted by the organization Business in the Community, recent research reveals its importance for the charitable sector.

- 96% of respondents said cause-related marketing was important to their fundraising objectives, up from 80% in 2002. Nearly 22% said it was vital.
- 81% believed that the importance of cause-related marketing for achieving their fundraising objectives has increased over the last 2 to 3 years.
- 93% believed that cause-related marketing will increase in importance in achieving their fundraising objectives over the next 2 to 3 years. This is compared to 84% in 2002.[34]

In North America, the *PRWeek*/PainePR Survey on Maximizing Cause-Related Relationships reveals optimism for 2005 is very high among nonprofit executives across the board. Nonprofit/cause-marketing forecast predicts the level of corporate investment will increase over the next 12 months, on average, by 17%.[35]

Nonprofits at all levels are seeing the growth in relationships that are mutually beneficial and publicly presented. Leading nonprofits are actively building program platforms that can position them as cause brands.

Achieving Mission

Collaboration, the New Reality

Today's public challenges are important to all—be it government, nonprofit, or business—but too big for one sector to solve on its own. Everything from protecting the environment, alleviating poverty, and reducing crime to improving education is relevant to the three sectors. Reaching out and jointly responding can result in a significant infusion of new energy, resources, and thinking on how to counter societal challenges.

And corporate–nonprofit partnerships are viewed positively. In the 2004 Cone Corporate Citizenship Study, 89% of Americans believe corporations and nonprofits should work together to raise money and awareness for a cause.[36]

Cause marketing allows the private sector to provide more than just financial support; it helps a nonprofit achieve its mission. By creating awareness, providing corporate expertise and employee volunteers, and leveraging financial contributions, cause marketing contributes so much more to nonprofit organizations than traditional philanthropic gifts. The new corporate–nonprofit cause-marketing collaborations are greater than the sum of the individual parts.

Community Expectation

Accountability, Relevance

The growth in the number of nonprofits and increased competition has also created a need for nonprofits to be accountable and relevant to the community. In a dynamic environment where transparency, accountability, and impact are expected, nonprofits are using cause-marketing collaborations to unleash the power

KaBOOM! "A Playground within Walking Distance of Every Child in America"

KaBOOM has used cause marketing as their main fund development strategy by building a model that allows efficient and easy access for corporations to put their marketing power behind the cause, engage their employees, help sell their products, and create an integrated investment in a cause.

"It's helped us to get further, faster to our end goal," states Carrie Suhr, VP, Corporate Partnerships at KaBOOM. "In our first decade, 90% of our revenue has been generated through corporate partnerships and it has helped us achieve our mission faster and more efficiently."[37]

of strategic communications to share information about their organization and relevance to the community. Cause-marketing relationships lend credibility to a nonprofit and enable messaging to reach a broader market.

In 2004, the first Cone research on the impact of corporate–nonprofit cause relationships showed that community members are more likely to feel positively about a nonprofit organization and support the cause. Specifically,

- 76% believe that partnerships result in a more positive image of the nonprofit.
- 79% are more likely to buy a product that supports the nonprofit.
- 76% are more likely to tell a friend about the nonprofit.
- 70% are more likely to donate money to the nonprofit.[38]

As a result, leading nonprofits are building platforms that can create a focus for a cause-marketing relationship, making them more appealing to potential corporate partners and eventually individual donors. They are becoming more sophisticated about building their own brand to become a charity of choice.[39]

CONCLUSION

Cause-marketing language can be confusing, and many different terms are used to describe this new corporate-nonprofit relationship. Whatever the term, cause marketing has four key distinguishing features:

- A mutually beneficial **collaboration** between a company and a nonprofit cause that uses and combines each other's assets to **create shareholder and social value**
- A way to build a relationship and personal **connection with constituents**, from employees to suppliers, to influentials to consumers, that involves their active participation and engagement in the cause program
- A merger of self-interest and altruism to support community and citizenship that publicly **communicates the values** of all participants

Defined cause marketing is a mutually beneficial collaboration that aligns the power of a company's brand, marketing, and people to a charitable cause's brand and assets to create shareholder and social value, connect with constituents, and publicly communicate values.

Cause marketing is marketing, and it is important for nonprofits to understand how this impacts cause initiatives. The focus is on the cause, not the charity; its emphasis is on local impact and implementation. Because of the public nature of cause marketing, presentation of the cause stresses making a difference and taking action, and presents the issues in a compelling, uplifting way. Although cause marketing can be long term, the activity tends to be short term.

What are the trends that have driven this integration of value and values? Trends, as outlined by Cone Inc, and supported by their research, that have encouraged cause marketing for corporations include:

Employees: helps attract, retain, and create employee pride.

Community: corporate scandals and 9-11 have people asking what companies stand for; puts a human face on a company; license to operate; World Wide Web, which has created the need for a two-way dialogue.

Consumers: appeals to socially conscious consumers, time-crunched consumers, women, and teens as an efficient way to give; way to reward companies for their community values; and to communicate their own values.

Shareholders: a corporation is a for-profit company and has a responsibility to return an investment to shareholders. Cause marketing can enhance a company's ability to achieve profit.

Nonprofit cause marketing collaborations are driven by:

Resource Need: the growing number of nonprofit organizations has required nonprofits to look for new sources of revenue and resources to achieve their mission goals.

Mission Need: collaboration has become a critical tool in achieving mission.

Community Scrutiny: with the growing demand for accountability, transparency, and relevance, nonprofits are using cause marketing as way to extend their communications and marketing and to present to the community the programs and mission.

ENDNOTES

1. www.marketingpower.com/content4620.php
2. *Cause Marketing: BSR Issue Briefs*, published by Business for Social Responsibility at www.bsr.org/bsrresources/whitepaperdetails.cfm, copyright, 2001–2002.
3. Corporate Social Responsibility Annual Report, 2003 (www.starbucks.com/csr).
4. Although this is commonly accepted, Carol Cone first identified the role of employees in building brand and their importance in the *1999 Cone/Roper Cause Related Trends Report*.
5. Carol Cone, March 16, 2005.
6. Interview, Jerry Welsh, April 6 2005.
7. Ibid.
8. Carol Cone, Mark Feldman, and Alison DaSilva, "Cause and Effects," *Harvard Business Review,* July 2003, 3.
9. Interview, Jerry Welsh, April 6, 2005.
10. "Cause branding" was trademarked by Cone Inc. in 1999 Cone/Roper Cause Related Trends Report.
11. Cone/Roper reports from 1993–2004 track the trends and attitudes to corporate involvement in the community.
12. M. Gobé, *Citizen Brand* (New York: Allworth Press, 2002).

13. 2000 Cone Roper Executive Study.
14. Ibid.
15. 2004, 2002, 2001 (March, October) *Cone Roper Corporate Citizenship Studies*.
16. "Responsible Firms Earn Goodwill," *Calgary Herald*, April 25, 2005.
17. Marc Gunter, "Money and Morals at GE," *Fortune*, November 1, 2004.
18. Carol Cone, March 16, 2005.
19. *Cone/Roper Cause Related Trends Report*, 1999.
20. From *Vanity Fair* advertisement, August 2005.
21. Stephan Schmidheiny and World Business Council on Sustainable Development, *Changing Course: A Global Business Perspective on Development and the Environment*, Chapter 12, "Managing Business Partnership" (Cambridge, MA: MIT Press, 1992).
22. *Cone/Roper Cause Related Trends Report*, 1999.
23. *2001 Cone/Roper Corporate Citizenship Study*, 2001 annual study commission by Boston-based Cone, first phase conducted March 1–24, 2001, second phase conducted October 26–28, 2001.
24. *2002 Cone Corporate Citizenship Study, The Role of Cause Branding*, 2002 annual study commissioned by Boston-based Cone, conducted July 26–29, 2002.
25. "Responsible Firms Earn Goodwill," *Calgary Herald*, April 25, 2005.
26. *Americans Shop with a Cause in Mind This Holiday Season*, 2003 Cone Holiday Trend Tracker, an annual study commissioned by Boston-based Cone, conducted November 7–10, 2003.
27. *Cause Related Marketing—21st Century Giving Study*, June 2002.
28. Interview, John Mikkelson, Telus, August 10, 2005.
29. Lauren Gard, "We're Good Guys, Buy from Us," *Business Week*, November 22, 2004, 72, 73.
30. Karen Epper Hoffman, "Internet as Gender-Equalizer?" *Internet World*, 9 November 1998.
31. Cone Holiday Tracker, 2003.
32. Internal Revenue Services Report as presented in AFP article, Jan. 24, 2005, "*Fundraising Competition Increases as U.S. Charities Number 800,000.*"
33. *Forefront* (Vol. 1, Issue 1) front cover.
34. "*Cause Related Marketing–Reaping the Benefits (2004),* Business in the Community, www.bitc.org.uk/resources/research_publications/brand_benefit.html.
35. The *PRWeek*/PainePR Survey "Cause-Marketing Forecast Is Bright: Nonprofits Predict 17 Percent Increase for Coming Year," October 25, 2004. This survey was conducted for *PRWeek* by Impulse Research Group, a full-service public opinion and marketing research firm and was sponsored by PainePR. Interviews were conducted among 106 nonprofit executives from September 1 to October 8, 2004.
36. 2004 Cone Corporate Citizenship Study, press release, May 25, 2005.
37. Interview, Carrie Suhr, February 2, 2005.
38. 2004 Cone Corporate Citizenship Study, press release, May 25, 2005.
39. 2004 Cone Corporate Citizenship Study.

CHAPTER 3

Evolution of Cause Marketing

Cause marketing has come a long way since 1981. The Cone Reports track its development and define its evolution: from an initial one-off tactic meant to drive immediate sales to a more strategic approach geared to building customer loyalty and reputation, to deeper and longer term social commitments that brand a business and its identity with a cause, to the sophistication of many of today's leading programs that are the public face of a company's corporate social responsibility.[1]

With the wide acceptance and even embracing of cause marketing in North America and Britain by businesses, nonprofits, and community and corporate stakeholders, it is clearly here to stay. How and why it has flourished and grown parallels the underlying societal trends and demonstrates the changing relationship of corporations and nonprofit organizations. Corporate involvement in the community has been a long-established practice that has evolved significantly since cause marketing first established a presence. Relationships have advanced and altered as the demands have grown and society has changed.

EVOLUTION OF CAUSE MARKETING

Cause marketing has evolved over the past 25 years and is identified by Cone Inc. through four definable phases and approaches.[2] Each is an evolution from the earlier, but change and development is not linear. In the maturing of any trend there is overlap, not always a clearly delineated time frame, and aspects of each phase in the others.

Companies and causes just entering the cause-marketing arena often start in the early phase that focuses on more short-term product sales approaches. Leading companies and nonprofit organizations developed more sophisticated strategic corporate citizenship programs right from the beginning. Consideration of each stage, its characteristics, benefits, and challenges, demonstrates the growth and the phases of cause marketing.

- **Sales phase:** Early start-up phase, one-off promotion tactic usually tied to product focused on driving sales. First launched in the 1980s, this approach continues to be taken, especially by those just entering the cause-marketing field or looking for a short-term impact. Associated with the term *cause-related marketing*.

- **Customer loyalty phase:** The early to mid-1990s saw a growing focus on programs that were more strategic, longer term, and aimed at building customer loyalty and making broader contributions to causes. The relationship was deeper with more impact for both partners.

- **Branding phase:** Mature phase, longer, deeper connections, "Cause Branding"[3] coined by Cone Inc. in 1999 and described as a strategic, approach that integrated social issues into an organization's brand and corporate identity. This stage grew in prevalence from the mid-1990s to late 2001. The branding phase saw a shift in emphasis from product sales, where a consumer's purchase was the end result, to a cultural emphasis, publicly supporting a cause to build a company's brand and identity.

- **Social responsibility phase:** Leading companies are now using cause marketing as a tool to put a public face on their corporate social responsibility and to communicate the values of their company to key stakeholders. Since Sept. 11 and greater public scrutiny and distrust due to corporate ethics (post-Enron), stakeholders want to know a company's values when deciding where to work and do business. Cause marketing communicates and reflects the alignment of companies, causes, and stakeholder values and shows them in action.

Each phase has been affected by the shifting societal relationships, the changing way corporations and nonprofit organizations work together, and finally the growing positive reaction of the ultimate focus for cause-marketing programs, company stakeholders. Distinctive characteristics define each phase and show how the cause-marketing spectrum has grown and evolved since its original beginnings.

SALES PHASE

Cause marketing was launched in the early 1980s by American Express as a short-term sales promotion. Usually no more than three months in duration and designed to spike sales, the impact on either the organization's profile or reputation was fleeting. However, because of the novelty of early cause programs, they were high profile. But compared to later, more in-depth programs, these cause-marketing initiatives were still relatively low impact.

Cause-marketing programs were the first step in moving from passive support of nonprofit charities normally done through traditional philanthropic channels

AMERICAN EXPRESS AND SAN FRANCISCO ARTS FESTIVAL

Although its first national program was in 1983, American Express had developed an earlier regional program in 1981 to donate funds to a number of arts organizations through the San Francisco Arts Festival and in Dallas for local museums. In San Francisco a donation was made for every American Express card use and every new card member signed up during the promotional period. The locally based, short-term campaign generated over $100,000 for the work of the charities. Additionally use of the American Express card increased, and as an important side benefit, American Express improved their relationship with their local merchants.

to more active engagement. Businesses saw these promotions as a unique way to support nonprofit organizations that were part of their philanthropic commitment and obligation to the community. The early cause programs were the first integration of other business functions, specifically marketing into corporate charitable activities. These programs leveraged new resources and integrated value-added strategies that supported business activities and objectives.

For nonprofits the focus was on receiving financial and marketing support. As American Express CEO James D. Robinson III said, "This was a way to provide a much needed new source of funding for nonprofit organizations."[4] A spin-off effect, although usually short term, was that nonprofits benefited from direct donations made as a result of sales and from having their profile raised through the corporation cause-marketing program.

The relationship between the business and nonprofit organization was of short duration and driven by the business partner. Most nonprofits did not have the capacity or maturity to think of cause marketing strategically. Although they were responsive to the idea, they were passively involved in the strategy and execution of the program.

SCOTT PAPER/CHILDHOOD DISEASES, PEPSI/EASTER SEALS

Following American Express's lead, other companies got involved in cause marketing. In the mid-1980s, Scott Paper Company created a "Helping Hand" product line where purchases generated funds for childhood disease charities.

Another short-term promotional program saw Pepsi donating a dime to the Easter Seal Society for each Pepsi sold during the telethon period.[5]

The 1980s was the beginning of the end of big government. Many long-established nonprofit organizations had to adapt to the new reality of smaller government grants and the increased need for broader financial support. Numerous newly established community organizations set up to address community needs resulting from government cuts were still in the formation and even survival phase of their organizational life cycle. Nonprofits were struggling with these new realities, and because there were a relatively small number of cause programs, many considered cause marketing as a passing fad that over time would run its course.

At the same time, corporations were moving from a government regulated environment to a more voluntary approach. Relationships in the community were becoming increasingly important as companies realized they needed their support to operate effectively. Greater demands from nonprofit organizations for support added another pressure and the need to think creatively. The changing government environment, the need to visibly contribute to the community, and the desire to creatively extend limited corporate resources were initial cause-marketing drivers.

Cause-marketing programs did resonate with consumers and business partners such as retailers and suppliers. They were the main target for cause programs, and their positive response was a factor in its growth and development. Consumers were fascinated. Retailers saw the immediate benefit. Both sensed the approach was an innovative and unique way to support their community while satisfying their own needs and desires. Provided the cause program was transparent and sincere, they willingly participated in and supported cause programs.

The sales-focused approach continues to be used by business and nonprofit organizations, especially those just entering the cause-marketing field or looking for short-term sales spikes. Their growth can be seen in magazines, shopping malls, and store promotions. Some causes lend themselves particularly well to this approach, especially where there is an awareness week or month. October is

SUTTER HOME WINERY, BREAST CANCER CAUSES

In "Capsules for the Cure," Sutter Home Winery donated $1 per seal sent in to breast cancer causes to a maximum of $250,000. The company used this as the focus for their advertising during this time period. With October as Breast Cancer Awareness Month, it helped demonstrate their community commitment to a cause that has become better known through cause-marketing programs.[6]

Breast Cancer Awareness Month, and there is growing proliferation of cause programs dedicated to raising financial support and awareness for this critical health issue. Programs range from a donation for every wine cap sent in to donations from T-shirt sales at women's clothing stores.

Locally, a drive for the United Way or a local hospital campaign also stimulates sales promotion cause programs. A donation is made to a hospital campaign for every ice cream purchased at a local dairy in the summer of 2004; "Lattes for Literacy" were sold by Starbucks January 27, 2005 in support of Frontier College, a Canadian organization dedicated to literacy and learning for life. The impact of this approach is on short-term sales, community connection, and immediate but brief nonprofit cause financial support and profile building.

Today, sales-driven programs can be a great way to build an initial relationship with a corporate partner. They can demonstrate the benefits of the program and prove the nonprofit partner's ability to execute and add value to a marketing initiative. But like other aspects of cause marketing, they have grown in sophistication.

Although sales-based cause-marketing programs can be very successful because they only last only a few months, they offer limited opportunity to position the product or company and create enduring relationships with corporate stakeholders such as retailers, employees, or customers.

CUSTOMER LOYALTY PHASE

By the early 1990s, leading businesses and nonprofits recognized that cause marketing could provide greater benefits, especially if done through a more strategic, long-term approach. Well-executed, relevant programs could have a significant impact not only on sales, but also on customer loyalty and company reputation, which included retailers, suppliers, and consumers. In early research studies undertaken in 1993, results pointed out that more than 8 in 10 American consumers had a more positive image of businesses involved in cause-marketing programs. As well, companies were viewed as being more trustworthy if they supported a cause. This was a critical factor in attracting and retaining loyal customers in an ever more complex marketplace.[7]

Cause programs were moving from being one-off sales tactics to being part of companies' overall marketing strategy. Longer-term, deeper relationships were sought with nonprofit organizations with appropriate causes of interest and relevance to the corporate partner. The 1993 *Cone/Roper Cause Related Trends Report*, the first of its kind, found that

- Nearly two-thirds of Americans felt cause marketing should be a standard business practice.

- 80% of those surveyed in the 1993 study agreed that companies should be committed to a specific cause over a long period of time.
- 84% said they had a more positive image of a company engaged in making the world a better place.

Cause marketing was evolving from a tactical promotion meant to drive sales in the short term to a more strategic approach—one that saw it become part of a company's core business strategy and directly tied to a range of business functions. Cause marketing was also becoming more mainstream. A longer-term strategy could build greater customer loyalty, provide community assistance through a more strategic community investment approach, and build greater profile and reputation for partners involved in cause initiatives.

AMERICAN EXPRESS AND SHARE OUR STRENGTH

American Express and Share Our Strength, a leading antihunger, antipoverty organization in the United States, is an excellent example of the transition to a longer-term, deeper cause-marketing program.

The relationship first began in 1988 when American Express was one of the sponsors of the organization's Taste of the Nation, the biggest food and wine tasting event in the country. Inspired by the success of their original campaign, American Express developed in 1993 a new and longer program with an even closer strategic link with their business. At the time, they were experiencing some difficulties with their restaurant partners, who were challenging American Express's high fees and commitment to merchants and local communities. American Express needed to work with restaurants to rebuild existing relationships, establish new ones, and increase card member use.

Building on their previous success, they looked to build a cause program with a nonprofit that would help them build a stronger relationship with their restaurateurs. Recognizing a hunger cause could be a strong alignment, they approached their existing partner, Share our Strength, to develop a cause-marketing program. For a four-year period every November and December from 1993 to 1996, American Express donated 3 cents per card purchase from every single card member transaction to Share Our Strength's campaign to reduce hunger.

Program Approach and Focus

The program had a three-part approach to appeal to different constituents: card members through a donation for every use of the card during the promotion, merchants by providing opportunities to participate locally and benefit from additional sales, and employees' volunteer opportunities tied to the hunger cause.

Charge Against Hunger was launched with a $15 million advertising campaign, including television ads using Share our Strength founder Bill Shore to talk about hunger. Throughout the time the program was supported, American Express provided through a "Do More" theme, an opportunity for consumers to obtain more information on the program and to make their own contribution.

A number of American Express partners, including scores of restaurants and retailers such as K-Mart, Campbell's Soup, Williams-Sonoma, Hertz, and Delta, also combined donations to extend the value of the program. Charge Against Hunger decals were distributed by American Express to merchants who provided additional funds. Public relations were a major part of the program and even then–First Lady Hillary Rodham Clinton was involved in a nationwide breakfast event designed to start the 1994 campaign.

Results

American Express found that the program resulted in an increase in card use of 12% and improved the merchants' perception of the company. Merchants appreciated the program which encouraged greater acceptance of the card at the retail level. Cardholders expressed strong support for the Charge Against Hunger campaign and great satisfaction with American Express itself. In addition, thousands of company employees volunteered their time to the cause of fighting hunger, and the financial contribution to Share our Strength was millions of dollars. Employee pride and involvement was seen as a new and powerful benefit of cause programs.

Share Our Strength received over $21 million during the four-year program. In the first year alone, they received $5 million, 10 times the amount they had received through the American Express Taste of the Nation sponsorship.

Share Our Strength founder, Bill Shore, was dramatically affected by his cause-marketing experiences. The partnership transformed the organization and helped them to expand in new directions and to build new corporate cause partnerships. In his book, *The Cathedral Within*, published in 1999, he stated

> The potential now exists to transform the role that the civic sector plays in society, and to transform the way the nonprofit and corporate communities work together by literally creating community wealth through business enterprise, cause-related marketing partnerships, and licensing—directing profits back into the community. The challenge now is to advance this concept.[8]

Maturing Nonprofits

This program and other cause-marketing programs showed nonprofit organizations how significant they could be for their profile and ability to raise dollars. It also demonstrated the value of collaboration and they had assets that could be used in an entrepreneurial way to raise revenue, create awareness, and help achieve mission. Nonprofit organizations were reaching a new level of maturity and readiness in terms of their dealings with corporate cause partners. They were actively involved in building the cause strategy and implementing their end of the program. As well, leading nonprofit organizations were developing cause strategies of their own and actively seeking collaborations with corporations. With the changes to funding structure and the greater reliance on community support, nonprofits recognized the benefit of cause marketing to expanding traditional fundraising and marketing endeavors.

A number of nonprofit organizations launched their own "cause marketing" initiatives such as commendation or certification programs. Examples are the Arthritis Foundation's Ease of Use and the American Heart Association and Canadian Heart and Stroke Foundation's "Health Heart" and Heart Check programs. Some actively pursued cause-marketing relationships with corporations like the Canadian Parks Partnership and the National Park Foundation's program with Eureka Vacuum Cleaners, a program launched in the mid-1990s that had a portion of the proceeds going to support programs in National Parks in both countries. The program, although tied to product sales, was not short-term promotional in nature. Rather, a donation was made for every vacuum sold, and the commitment lasted over five years and was supported by a marketing campaign.

National events, where corporate cause partners were actively pursued, were another approach used by nonprofit organizations to extend their corporate philanthropic relationships and tie into a company's marketing program. Different from sponsorship, the events were used to engage a corporation in helping to deliver mission-oriented messaging and programs. The Arthritis Foundation's "Arthritis Walk" built an important cause-marketing relationship with Aleve. The American Heart Association's "Heart Walk" saw the development of an important cause alliance with Subway. The National Kidney Foundation and Novartis' Transplant Games was another such cause-marketing relationship that provided shareholder and social benefits (see Chapter 6).

Attorney General's Report

As cause-marketing programs grew in the 1990s, a number of cause-marketing relationships led to concerns about the arrangements between nonprofit organizations and business partners. Not all programs went off without a hitch, which resulted in a growing recognition of the need for guidelines, risk management, legal agreements, and generally greater sophistication in execution and public presentation.

Several cause-marketing initiatives, including ones with the American Medical Association and Sunbeam, the Arthritis Foundation and McNeil Consumer Products, and the American Cancer Society and Smith Kline Beecham Consumer Healthcare, lead the Attorneys General of 16 states and the District of Columbia Corporation Counsel to undertake a major study on "corporate-commercial/ nonprofit product marketing advertising of commercial projects."[9]

The purpose of the 1999 report was to explore guidelines and principles for agreements in which a nonprofit allowed its name and logo to be used in a for-profit entity's marketing and advertisement campaign in exchange for a fee from the for-profit. The report cited potential for misleading consumers and undermining public confidence in charitable institutions.

Guidelines, Policies, Regulations

The report set new expectations for nonprofits undertaking cause-marketing ventures and triggered a host of new guidelines, policies, and regulations. (For a summary of requirements see Chapter 7.)

Exclusivity and Endorsement

The report highlighted the need for nonprofits to avoid exclusive arrangements, unless they were time limited or tied to category exclusivity for a specific program. Avoiding endorsement or the appearance of endorsement was another recommendation. Nonprofits working in cause-marketing arrangements were doing so to advance their mission, not to sell a company's product, goods, or services.

Nonprofit Credibility and Trust

Another major result of the Attorney General's report was that the issue of trust and credibility around the new corporate–nonprofit relationships was being publicly discussed. The report highlighted the importance of nonprofits never violating the trust of the public, key to any nonprofit organization's reputation, fundraising, volunteer recruitment, staff retention, and overall good organizational health. Damage to a nonprofit's reputation was viewed as potentially devastating, and many with otherwise strong programs would have a hard time recovering from a reputation "hit."

AFP Response

The AFP responded to the report with recommendations for the nonprofit sector to create standards for cause-related marketing arrangements. Although the professional association felt no crisis existed, this form of corporate–nonprofit collaboration required new attention. The association did see the benefits through increased revenue and profile for the sector. It concluded: "Most cause-related marketing arrangements occur without incident."[10]

Growing Potential

By the mid-to-late 1990s, cause-related marketing was becoming a more commonly used practice by companies and nonprofits. The potential as a major marketing and philanthropic initiative was being realized. Longer-term programs had the greatest impact for companies, nonprofit causes, and stakeholders including employees, retail partners, suppliers, and consumers. In fact, research on cause-marketing programs confirmed that longer-term programs received the greatest approval from respondents. One-off programs were replaced by marketing commitments lasting at least one year, which convinced consumers a company was committed to impacting societal programs and that the efforts were sincere and credible.

Although a few programs led to the review of commercial–nonprofit relationships, consumers were participating in cause programs and viewing companies involved most positively. By 1996, 2 in 10 consumers had purchased a product or service that was associated with a cause or issue. The Cone/Roper Studies undertaken between 1993 and 1998 showed that

- Almost two-thirds of Americans agreed that cause marketing should be a standard business practice (63% in 1993, 61% in 1998).
- The same number reported they would likely switch brands or retailers to one associated with a good cause when price and quality were equal.
- Consistently 8 in 10 Americans had a more positive image of companies who supported causes.[11]
- 94% of influentials (defined by social activism and role as opinion makers and group leaders) were positive about cause programs and had a more favorable image of companies committed to a cause, up from 88% in 1993.[12]

Cause marketing was becoming mainstream and a component of leading business and nonprofit strategies. The approach integrated fundraising, marketing, and stakeholder connection and was proving to be a unique and effective way to support critical community causes that needed long-term and strategic commitment while simultaneously supporting business objectives. This approach continues to be used, especially by companies interested in using promotions and products sales to build customer loyalty.

BRANDING PHASE

By the mid-to-late 1990s cause programs were evolving again and moving to a new level on the cause-marketing spectrum. Cause-supported programs were a way to brand a company with a cause. Cause branding, a "strategic, stakeholder-based approach to integrating social issues into business strategy, brand equity, and organizational identity,"[13] is what Cone Inc. called the new deeper approach to publicly supporting a cause and demonstrating good corporate citizenship. This phase shifted the emphasis from product sales, where a consumer's purchase was the end result, to a cultural emphasis, publicly supporting a cause to enhance a company's brand, inner culture, and reputation in the community. Although the approach was different, the end result was the same: companies were deriving tangible marketing and business benefits for the cause alignment.

Less About Immediate Product Sales, More About Brand and Reputation

Leading companies were now beginning to make long-term commitments to causes and make them part of the business identity and culture. As well, cause marketing was moving away from being associated only with product sales or promotions and moving to engagement with cobranded events and programs. These cause-marketing initiatives were deeper, imbued the company culture, and provided a broader involvement of company constituents, especially employees.

Another key characteristic of the growth of cause-marketing programs was the acceptance of focusing on a broader range of causes, including ones originally considered taboo in a public-oriented program. Cause programs feature breast cancer, prostate cancer, AIDS/HIV, food banks, hospices, and literacy as well as the more traditional health, arts, and social service organizations. "Can you image five years ago breasts being talked about in such a public way?"[14] asks Carol Cone, of Cone Inc. The acceptance of so many issues makes cause marketing more available to a wide range of nonprofit organizations.

EXAMPLE: LEE JEANS AND SUSAN G. KOMEN BREAST CANCER FOUNDATION

The Lee Jeans "One Day, One Cause" program illustrates the changing nature of cause-marketing programs. In 1996 Lee Jeans was looking to do something unique to give back to the community. A group of six women in the company were talking about different causes that could be supported. Quickly, the discussion turned to breast cancer: every one of them had been touched by this disease, including two, both under 40, who had been diagnosed and undergone treatment for it.

The group suggested tying an event back to their business to "brand" it with the breast cancer cause and to make people feel good about the Lee brand. The goal was not immediate short-term sales, but in the long run to get their customers and key stakeholders, including their employees, to love the Lee brand and to emotionally connect with it, feeling it was more than just a business. The concept was a one-day event to be held on the first Friday in October (Breast Cancer Awareness Month), where people in the workplace would be allowed to wear denim if they donated $5 to the cause. "One day, once cause, one cure" was born.

Program Goals

Lee saw the program as achieving four key goals. First, they needed to differentiate their brand. This was a time when there was an explosion in the number of companies making and selling five-pocket jeans. There was a huge new level of competition as private labels and designer jeans were flooding the marketplace with essentially the same type of product sold by Lee. Second, Lee wanted to change the perception of wearing jeans in the workplace. In 1996, casual workplace clothing did not include jeans. Lee wanted to give people a reason to wear denim at work.

Lee also wanted to use the program to give something back to their target market, which was essentially women. Finally, they wanted a cause that would be relevant to people. Market research led them to realize the power and impact supporting breast cancer would have. One focus group comment particularly hit home for the Lee team. When one woman said she thought of breast cancer as an old person's disease, the young woman beside her passionately said, "Oh my god, I think about breast cancer every single day." Lee realized they had hit on something that resonated with their key audience and that people could be passionate about getting involved with.

First the Cause, Then the Charity

Once the cause was determined, the decision had to be made: How should the money get back to support the cause? The team at Lee met with several nonprofit organizations focused on the breast cancer issue, but decided on the Susan G. Komen Foundation. "There was an instant connection," stated Kathy Collins, Lee's Vice President of Marketing. "They were so passionate about the idea and loved tying it back to the workplace." At the time, breast cancer was an issue that wasn't talked about in the workplace. The Foundation saw this not only as a way to generate revenue for the cause, but also to get it out of the closet, to make it part of the mainstream discussions, and to encourage people to be aware and to regularly incorporate screening as a part of their health routine.

The Komen Foundation also has been a collaborative partner, giving Lee lots of flexibility and say as to where the money raised would go. The Komen Foundation has local affiliates, so the money has gone to those groups across the United States for research and programs. One year the event funded the development of a Web site for the organization.

Impressive Results

The program has grown ever since it began in 1996 with a total of $52 million raised by 2004. Each year, with the exception of 2001, has seen an increase in the number of participants and the dollars raised. A key feature of the program has been to put a public face on the event. Celebrity spokespersons, including two men (Rob Lowe and Charlie Sheen), have helped participants to connect to the cause and demonstrate that both men and women are affected by this cruel disease.

The program has become completely integrated into the company's operations. Both participants and employees feel a great sense of pride and ownership of the program. In fact, it has provided the greatest source of pride in the Lee organization and one that, even with fluctuating marketing budgets, will never be cut.

As Kathy Collins, VP of Marketing at Lee Jeans says, "Lee National Denim Day is my favorite day. It says more about the Lee brand than anything else we do and it's a day when everyone in our organization is so proud. It's a wonderful thing."[15]

Has the program helped sell more Lee Jeans? It's hard to know for sure. But what Lee does know is the importance of connecting the company and product with their employees and customers on a sophisticated emotional and values level. Today it's difficult to compete on product alone. As Kathy Collins says, "There are a million different jeans brands; we want to build a relationship beyond just sales and show that we understand and respond to their concerns." Another major benefit of the programs has been the effect on employee pride and commitment. The 165 employees at their head office in Kansas City, from the president to sewing machine operators, participate in the event and take great pride in its impact on breast cancer awareness and financial support to the cause.

CORPORATE SOCIAL RESPONSIBILITY PHASE

Recent corporate scandals, retaliation against business, and call for more ethics has transformed stakeholder expectations of business's roles and responsibilities. Post–September 11 has seen leading companies using cause-marketing initiatives as part of their corporate social responsibility palette.

Cause-marketing programs are being integrated as a critical component and the public face of corporate citizenship. The goal is to use these programs to connect with stakeholders, especially employees, to align with their views and values and to build a strong and emotional connection with them.

"Get to know who your constituents really are, what really matters to them, and show them that you feel the same way," stated Carol Cone in a discussion about the new phase in cause marketing.[16]

Communities are expecting more of corporations and demanding that they play a major role in community. From March 2001 to October 2002, Americans' expectations of a company having a responsibility to support social issues rose from 65% to 78%.[17]

In Cone's 2004 study, 90% of respondents said they would consider switching to another company's products and services, speaking out against the company (81%), and selling investments (80%) if the company was behaving illegally or unethically. In the same study, 92% of Americans have a more positive image of companies and products that support causes, significantly higher than figures preceding September 2001 (81% in March 2001, 83% in 1999, 85% in 1993). As well, 85% say a company's commitment to a social cause influences the decision of which companies could do business in a local community.[18]

The 2005 Cone Inc. national poll taken after two major hurricanes, further demonstrated this growing expectation.

- 87% of people surveyed expect companies to play an important role in re-building affected hurricane disaster areas.
- 62% said companies are better able to effectively respond to disaster than government.[19]

Deeper, sophisticated cause-marketing programs are becoming more common, and a multidisciplinary approach is being taken by many companies, incorporating philanthropy and community relations as well as marketing and human resources. Cause marketing is being integrated into the culture of a company and the visible component of its overall corporate social responsibility program. Leading companies recognize the positive effect on their brand, corporate image, consumer relationships, and the connection it helps them make with key stakeholders, community leaders, and their employees.

Changing Nature's Impact on Nonprofit Organizations

As cause marketing has moved away from being sales focused to more about building a company's culture, brand positioning, and demonstrating corporate values the scope of cause-marketing partnerships has broadened to include a greater emphasis on cobranding nonprofit programs, building joint signature events, and social marketing campaigns aimed at changing people's attitudes and behavior.

As cause marketing has become more tied to corporate social responsibility, one of the biggest challenges has been the blurring of lines between philanthropic giving and cause marketing. Many nonprofits are seeing an increase in financial gifts along with the expectation of significant promotion or advertising of the contribution by the company. For example, a law firm may donate to Habitat for Humanity, provide employee volunteers to help with the building, and then spend as much on billboards showcasing this support. Many corporations want to know the level of media partnerships and amount of coverage that will be secured. For nonprofits, this has created issues over tax receipting, what level of public recognition should be expected, and demands for value from corporate contributions.

Companies are also proactively taking out advertisements or doing a special advertising insert announcing their community support and featuring the nonprofit organization's logo, mission, and programs. Some nonprofits are calling this gift-based marketing. This can be a great benefit for nonprofits—a way to extend their reach with advertising that they could never afford on their own.

EXHIBIT 3.1   EVOLUTION OF CAUSE MARKETING

Sales-driven	Customer Loyalty	Branding	Social Responsibility
• Sales oriented →	• Loyalty and sales →	• Brand and loyalty →	• Value creation and value reflection
• Short-term profile →	• Profile builder →	• Branding tool →	• Corporate social responsibility tool
• Business/ nonprofit benefit →	• Community benefit →	• Societal impact →	• Leadership role in social issues
• Nonprofit participants →	• Partners →	• Integrated collaborations →	• Sophisticated positioning
• Engaged corporate philanthropy →	• Strategic community investment →	• Cause branding →	• Corporate social responsibility
• Financial support →	• Financial plus in-kind support →	• Multifaceted support	• Multifaceted, integrated support
• Consumers →	• Stakeholders and customers →	• Employees, stakeholders, citizens	• Employees, community
• Causes supported →	• Causes with focused area of interest →	• Causes aligned to business, broader range supported	• Causes aligned with values of key stakeholders
• Passive nonprofits →	• Proactive, entrepreneurial nonprofits →	• Positioning	• Sophisticated, proactive non-profits using branding approach
• Customers/ stakeholders interest →	• Acceptance →	• Embrace	• Expect

Nonprofit Driven Branding

One of the latest evolutionary trends in cause marketing is nonprofit organizations creating program platforms that position them to achieve bottom-line results and strengthen corporate partnership opportunities. To break through the clutter, the same effort to develop integrated reputation management and focused strategies undertaken by companies is happening in the nonprofit sector.

Nonprofits are recognizing and developing platforms that create a signature program and give their cause focus and greater corporate appeal that provides deeper level relationships. They are moving from traditional product and promotional-driven activities to a more focused social marketing, storytelling approach that makes it more appealing for companies to get behind. Organizations like the Susan G. Komen Foundation have successfully built a focused platform. "For the cure" became the succinct message that helped them build many successful relationships—"Cook for the cure" with KitchenAid; "Drive for the cure" with BMW; "Charge for the Cure" with American Express; and "Run for the cure" with Yoplait and other corporations.

"Cook for the Cure": KitchenAid and Susan G. Komen Breast Cancer Foundation

Launched in 2001, "Cook for the Cure" is a multifaceted cause-marketing program that features donations with purchase, special products, and even home grassroots fundraising events. In its first four years, the program raised more than $2 million for the Foundation.

Purchase Programs

During Breast Cancer Awareness Month (October), KitchenAid makes a donation to the Komen Foundation for the purchase of select KitchenAid major appliances at select retailers. To encourage active participation, a donation certificate form is mailed to KitchenAid to complete the support of the foundation.

Special Products

KitchenAid's pink stand mixer and pink coffee mill trigger donations with purchase. For the pink stand mixer, a $50 donation is made. The coffee mill generates $10 to the Foundation for each one sold.

Cook for the Cure Dinner Parties

KitchenAid, in collaboration with *Gourmet* magazine, created a Home Dinner Party Kit to encourage individuals to host dinner parties in support of breast cancer research. The kit included invitations, menu suggestions, recipes, entertaining tips, and an envelope and instructions for sending proceeds from the party to the Komen Foundation.

Other Programs

Another nonprofit pioneer in creating cause brands is the American Heart Association. Kathy Rogers, Vice President, Cause Initiatives and Marketing at the American Heart Association, took a leadership role in positioning the organization to be a charity of choice. "We had great success with corporate partnerships and building revenues. But we weren't getting anywhere with visibility. What our corporate partners were telling us was to give us a higher level of messaging, all you have is an event, we need a bigger message that we can get a hold of."[20] "Go Red for Women," a social cause-marketing platform focused on women and heart health, is the first initiative in their repositioning strategy (see Chapter 11 case study).

The American Heart Association is not alone in taking a more focused approach. The Arthritis Foundation is moving from their original corporate cause-marketing programs of commendation and events to a series of social marketing platforms focused on rheumatoid arthritis (alliance with the NFL), osteoarthritis, and juvenile arthritis (alliance with Radio Disney). The American Cancer Society has three social marketing programs that form the foundation of their cause-marketing activities: Great American Weigh-In (with Weight Watchers as a major cause partner), Great American Smoke Out (Nicotine Cessation), and the Great American Health Check (with Met Life). The National Trust for Historic Preservation is rebranding their program from the National Trust Home Furniture Line to National Trust, "Designed in America."

St. Jude's Hospital Foundation launched a fully integrated cause-marketing program, "Thanks and Giving." The inaugural Thanks and Giving campaign launched in November 2004 encouraged consumers to shop where the St. Jude Thanks and Giving logo was displayed in stores, malls, and online shopping sites throughout the holiday season; proceeds from designated purchases benefited St. Jude's. First Book is building platforms that focus on specific literacy programs geared to schools, preschools, and after school. It's another way for the organization to brand the cause and support children and literacy.

As cause marketing continues to evolve, so too will the public's expectations about how companies address social issues. There is no turning back now. Employees, investors, communities, governments, and consumers will demand to know what a company stands for and what its community citizenship is. With cause marketing falling at the intersection of business strategy and societal good, it is fast becoming a "must-do" practice for the 21st century. This too can be a great opportunity for nonprofit causes.

Conclusion

Cause marketing has evolved over four phases and is defined by Cone research as moving from sales focus to customer loyalty to deeper commitments that imbue the brand of a corporation with causes to being the public face of corporate social responsibility. Each is an evolution from the earlier, but change and development is not linear; there are aspects of each phase in the others, and all four phases continue to be seen in today's cause-marketing programs. The cause-marketing phases are

- **Sales phase:** an initial one-off promotion tactic meant to drive short-term sales while supporting nonprofit organizations efforts
- **Customer loyalty phase:** a more strategic, longer-term approach focused on building customer loyalty, reputation management, and extending broader support to the cause
- **Branding:** a deeper social commitment to build a company's brand and corporate identity tied to a cause
- **Social Responsibility:** the public face of corporate social responsibility to connect with stakeholders, especially employees, to align with their values and demonstrate what a company's stands for

Cause marketing has grown in sophistication and depth. The expectation of companies, consumers, and other stakeholders has grown as the programs have developed and evolved. Today, cause programs are becoming more and more complicated and nonprofit organizations have to have the capacity, assets, and ability to work in a corporate alliance at an advanced level.

Endnotes

1. *Cone/Roper Cause Related Trends Report*, 1999.
2. Ibid.
3. "Cause branding" was trademarked by Cone Inc. in 1999 *Cone/Roper Cause Related Trends Report.*
4. Sue Adkins, *Cause-Related Marketing: Who Cares Wins* (Boston: Butterworth-Heinemann, 1999), 14.
5. Ibid.
6. "Capsules for the Cure," as seen in *Real Simple*, October 2004 (promotion ran between August, 1, 2004 and December 31, 2004).
7. "The Evolution of Cause Branding," 1999 *Cone/Roper Cause Related Trends Report.*
8. Bill Shore, *The Cathedral Within: Transforming Your Life by Giving Something Back* (New York: Random House, 1999), 143.
9. *What's in a Nonprofit's Name? Public Trust, Profit and the Potential for Public Deception*, Office of New York State Attorney General Eliot Spitzer, April, 1999.
10. *What are the concerns around cause-related marketing*, April 6, 1999, press release, AFP Web site: www.afpnet.org/tier3_cd.cfm?content_item_id=1096&folder_id=907.
11. 1999 *Cone/Roper Cause Related Trends Report.*

12. Cone/Roper Study, 1997.
13. Cone Corporate Citizenship Study: The Role of Cause Branding, 2002 (Executive Summary), 2.
14. Interview, Carol Cone, October 5, 2004.
15. Kathy Collins, Cause Marketing Forum Teleconference, October 2004.
16. Interview, Carol Cone, October 5, 2004.
17. 2002 Cone Corporate Citizenship Study.
18. Cone Corporate Citizenship Study, 2004.
19. National Poll by Cone Inc., Sept. 23, 2005.
20. Interview, Kathy Rogers, January 24, 2005.

PART II

Cause-Marketing Initiatives

The Seven P's: Best Practices Case Studies

OVERVIEW

This section looks at the different types of cause initiatives and presents best practices case studies in each area. Cause-marketing's seven *P*'s fall into three major categories: **products**, **promotions**, and **programs**. Each of the practices is presented in three separate chapters that look at the characteristics of each, how it works, benefits, and challenges.

A small sampling of best practices case studies are provided, and suggestions are made as to the type of nonprofit best suited to this form of cause marketing and the elements needed for successful implementation. The cases presented represent a cross section of cause-marketing initiatives and are by no means meant to be an exhaustive list; more exist in every sector of the nonprofit world and at every level—national, regional, and local. I hope this will stimulate thought about cause-marketing possibilities for your organization.

Chapter 4: Products

Cause-marketing products are sales driven and transactional based. This form of cause marketing is linked to sales of product and generates revenue and awareness for a nonprofit and its cause. The products can be directly tied to a nonprofit's brand through a percentage of sales going to a cause or by facilitating giving at point of sale.

- *Product Purchases: Doing Good by Buying Goods*

  Often considered to be the classic form of cause-related marketing, cause purchases allow consumers to do good while buying goods. Product cause purchases have three characteristics: they are transaction based; they involve a portion of the proceeds, from the sale of a specific product or use of a specific service, going to a nonprofit cause; and finally they involve consumer participation.

- *Purchase Plus: Facilitating Gifts*

  Almost everyone has experienced a company facilitating a donation to a specific cause. One of the most common ways is to add a donation onto purchases at the cash register. Add $1 or more to support the local hospital campaign, send unprivileged children to summer camp, or contribute to the food bank. This form of cause marketing is easily implemented at any level, including for local nonprofit organizations and businesses.

- *Licensed Products: Using Nonprofit Logos, Brand Identities, and Assets*

  In this type of cause marketing, a nonprofit organization licenses its name and/or logo to a business for use on products in return for a fee or royalty. Product licensing is a way for nonprofit organizations to market their brand equity and turn it into revenue and awareness through product sales. Described as an agreement whereby a for-profit business (the licensee) uses the equity (logo, brand identity, or assets such as images and photographs) of a nonprofit organization (the licensor) to create a link between the sale of the licensed product and the cause.

Chapter 5: Promotions

Cause-marketing issue promotions involve businesses supporting a nonprofit cause by using their brand, marketing, and promotional resources to actively engage in raising awareness of a nonprofit cause.

- *Issue Promotions: Cobranding Through Issue Promotion*

  A cause promotion relationship sees a corporation using promotional activities to raise awareness of a societal issue. The promotion involves disseminating information on a cause's mission and activities through advertising, contesting, and other promotional activities such as product hangtags, media efforts, and in-store posters. Often the company developing the promotional campaign will include a direct donation to the charitable cause as their way to demonstrate their commitment.

Chapter 6: Programs: Cobranded Programs and Events; and Social Issue Marketing

This area of cause-marketing practices is one of the deepest forms of support. A specific program or cause message aimed at having an impact on or changing behavior and attitude is the focus of this cause-marketing support.

- *Cause Promotional Events: Cobranding for Active Engagement*

  Cause event support is specifically designed around an event to raise awareness and/or funds for a cause as well as to engage people in supporting the organization. The event is cobranded with the company and the cause. The company provides the power of their brand, marketing might, and people to advance the cause's mission by supporting the event. The event demonstrates their commitment to a cause, involving company employees, and provides assistance to facilitate its organization and implementation.

- *Cause Programs: Cobranding Through Program Collaborations*

  Cause program relationships involve corporations stepping up and actively partnering with nonprofit causes to support, through their brand, marketing, and people, a specific cause program. The cause program involvement and support is used as a signature piece to build the company's name, brand, and reputation while helping the nonprofit organization advance their mission.

- *Public Service Cause Marketing: Encourage Behavioral Change*

  This form of cause marketing builds an alliance between a nonprofit organization's cause and a company or media outlet to promote a public service message to encourage or change attitude and behavior. Commonly known as social marketing, public service marketing takes the cause beyond awareness to impact the way people act and think while building brand equity and brand preference and being the public part of a company's social corporate responsibility commitment.

EXHIBIT P.1   HIERARCHY OF CAUSE-MARKETING INITIATIVES

Programs: Promotional Events, Programs, Social Marketing
- Fewer, deeper relationships
- Focused on impacting behavior
- Greatest opportunity for messaging and revenue

Promotions: Issue Promotions
- Second most common form of cause marketing
- Focus on issue promotion — awareness
- Higher level of messaging possible

Products: Product Sales, Purchase Plus, Licensed Products
- Most prevalent form of cause marketing
- Donation tied to product sales
- Lower opportunity for messaging and lower donation

CHAPTER 4

Cause-Marketing Products

This chapter looks at the three forms of cause-marketing products: product sales; purchases plus, also known as facilitated giving; and product licensing. Cause-marketing products are consumer driven and transactional based, are linked to sales of product or service, and are usually meant to **drive sales** and **build customer loyalty**. Revenue is generated for a nonprofit and its cause through a percentage of sales going to a cause or by facilitating giving at point of sale and awareness created through associated promotional support material. Working best for companies that have a direct link to consumers, this form of cause marketing can work for national and local nonprofits.

PRODUCT SALES

Product sales programs are most commonly associated with the term *cause-related marketing* and were the first type of cause programs. Donations are made to a nonprofit cause based on transactional sales and are usually meant to drive sales and build customer loyalty. In a product purchase, a contribution is made for every sale of a product, a percentage of the revenue is donated to a cause, or the use of a coupon or opening of an account triggers a donation. Product sales programs encourage passive consumer participation and most often are offered for a defined period of time and tied to a specific product.

This form of cause marketing is strongly driven by the marketing and sales department, which has specific sales targets and objectives for a program. The program uses the cause to drive sales, differentiate a product, and appeal to a new audience. In the fall 2004 Cone Inc. survey on corporate citizenship, 86% of those surveyed said they were very/somewhat likely to switch from one brand to another that was about the same in price and quality, if the other brand was associated with a cause.[1] As a side benefit and secondary focus, cause sales programs can enhance corporate reputation.

Nonprofit causes receive direct financial contributions and awareness creation of their organization and cause. Product sales programs can also be used to disseminate information about the charitable organization.

How Does It Work?

- Cause product sales programs can support a wide range of causes and benefit national, regional, or local nonprofit organizations.

- Most programs guarantee a financial minimum contribution and will set a maximum amount of support to the cause. This allows nonprofits to gauge the potential financial benefit and companies to limit their financial risk.

- Either partner can initiate the idea for a cause product sales program; however, the company drives the decision and implementation. A company's marketing and sales department takes the lead on this type of cause-marketing program.

- The company defines the product that will be tied to the cause sales and establishes the time frame and donation that will be made. A full marketing plan is developed for the initiative that includes all aspects of the marketing mix.

- The cause and cause partner is chosen, and it is highly recommended that a formal agreement be drawn up to outline the terms of the program, tracking of sales, the financial contribution, use of the nonprofit's logo, name and brand and sign-off, and promotional and advertising support. The agreement will ensure clarity around roles, responsibilities, expectations, and execution.

- The support can be directly to an individual nonprofit organization or indirectly to a number tied to the cause chosen for support.

- The program is launched and run for the determined time frame.

- Sophisticated companies and nonprofit organizations will have an evaluation of the program that will analyze what worked and what didn't work.

- Leading companies and nonprofits are using product sales programs as part of an annual ongoing program and developing it as a strategic initiative, often part of a larger initiative rather than a tactical one-off program.

What Are the Benefits?

- Nonprofit organizations generate revenue and increase awareness for their organization.

- Awareness can lead to further donations from individuals participating in the product sales that might be inspired to continue their support to other corporations and foundations made aware of the organization.

- Revenue generated is rarely designated to a specific program or activity and can be used for operational support.

- Corporate benefits include attracting new customers, increasing product sales, product differentiation, positioning the brand, building positive brand connection, and communicating values through community support.

What Are the Challenges?

- Programs must be sincere and transparent. Consumers are ever more sophisticated and want to know that the donations will make a difference to the cause, not just the corporation.

- Nonprofit organizations should insist on minimum fees for participation and use of their name, logo, and reputation, otherwise the revenue generated rarely can justify the work involved in developing and implementing these types of cause-marketing relationships.

- The connection between the company and product must be consistent with the cause and their values if it is to be well received.

KaBOOM! AND BEN & JERRY'S KABERRY KaBOOM! ICE CREAM

KaBOOM! "A great place to play within walking distance of every child in America" KaBOOM! has used cause marketing as their main fund development strategy by building a model that allows efficient and easy access for corporations to put their marketing power behind the cause, engage their employees, help sell their products, and create an integrated investment in a cause. "It helped us to achieve our mission and get further, faster to our end goal," states Carrie Suhr, Vice President of Corporate Development at KaBOOM!

Ben & Jerry's, a leader in corporate social responsibility, developed a cause-marketing partnership that involved their consumers, retail partners, and employees in the creation of playgrounds in neighborhoods where they were most needed. The program resonated with consumers, grocery and convenience store partners, and employee volunteers alike.

Background and Alignment

KaBOOM! is a nonprofit organization dedicated to building a great place to play within walking distance of every child in America. Established in 1995, cause-marketing relationships have been a leading KaBOOM! development strategy in their first decade of operation. "Over 90 percent of our revenue is fuelled by corporate partnerships, many of which have been cause marketing driven. Ka-BOOM! works closely with corporate partners to build playful, impactful initiatives that use private sector strategies for the public good. We understand the power of play and have built a range of partnership opportunities that help our corporate partners leverage this compelling issue to build brands, strengthen employee teams, celebrate corporate milestones, launch new products and drive sales through programs that advance our mission,"[2] says Carrie Suhr, Vice President of Corporate Development at KaBOOM!

Ben & Jerry's is founded on and dedicated to a sustainable corporate concept of linked prosperity. Their mission consists of three interrelated parts: product, economic, and social mission. Central to this is the belief that all three parts must thrive equally in a manner that commands deep respect for individuals in and outside the company and supports the communities of which they are a part.

Both organizations share values and beliefs in taking an entrepreneurial approach to supporting community and engaging the public.

Program

In 2000 and 2001 Ben & Jerry's created the first-ever ice cream flavor named after a nonprofit organization. "This was a cause-marketing relationship that was proactively pursued by our Co-Founder and CEO, Darell Hammond," states Carrie. "His big ideas and energy for the cause are legendary in the halls of Ben & Jerry's. Our organizations became huge mutual fans and friends."[3]

Ben & Jerry's developed a kid-oriented flavor of blueberry, strawberry, and a crackling candy and named it Kaberry KaBOOM! The packaging had Ka-BOOM!'s name and logo attached and included a consumer call to action message to encourage involvement in the organization's mission of creating great play spaces. This was especially appealing to KaBOOM! to connect consumers directly with their mission.

KaBOOM! earned a licensing fee for use of the KaBOOM! name and marks, as well as a percentage of sales for each pint sold. The cause-marketing program earned unrestricted dollars for KaBOOM! and dollars to support the construction of playgrounds in local markets.

In addition, KaBOOM! and Ben & Jerry's developed a full marketing activation program to drive sales of the ice cream flavor and advance the Ka-BOOM! mission by getting consumers involved in creating great new playgrounds in their communities. The marketing of the program included a feature in Ben & Jerry's Chuck Mail, their e-mail direct marketing tool, being the featured flavor during Ben & Jerry's Free Cone Day and getting KaBOOM!

staff to serve along with the Ben & Jerry's staff. Ben & Jerry's cofounder, Jerry Greenfield, participated in the KaBOOM! University of Play and other events, which provided great exposure for the flavor and helped encourage hundreds of communities to rally their neighborhoods to create great new playgrounds for kids.

Goals

Ben & Jerry's goals were very clearly defined from the outset: to achieve incremental sales, get prime shelf space and point-of-purchase signage, and to build relationships with their key retailers including Jewel-Osco, 7-Eleven, QFC, and others. They were also adamant in making this a true collaboration in every respect; they didn't want it to be the Ben & Jerry's playground program. They wanted to have a genuine role in contributing to the cause and moving toward a solution to the serious social issue of a lack of playground facilities.

Results

Like many of the leading cause-marketing arrangements, the program also featured more than just the sale of a product. It actively worked to help KaBOOM! fulfill its mission of building playgrounds while involving local retailers in playground builds in their community. It also assisted Ben & Jerry's in building stronger retailer relationships.

In specific markets, buying a pint of the ice cream triggered a donation to build a local playground. Ben & Jerry's offered the retailers in these markets the pass-through rights to a turnkey, ready-to-go, high-profile, high-impact community affairs day where the employees could come out and join neighborhoods in building a KaBOOM! playground from the ground up in a single day. Retail staff at Jewel-Osco or 7-Eleven, for example, along with Ben & Jerry's employees, came out to lead the construction program together with KaBOOM!

The two-year program was a win for KaBOOM!, a win for Ben & Jerry's, and a win for the local retailers. All three partners achieved key goals, and anecdotally the program was considered to be a huge success.

Equally important was the impact on consumers. Consumers enjoyed a fun, new flavor, and their purchases contributed to the construction of playgrounds in their communities.

"The power of this partnership was its authenticity. The Ben & Jerry's guiding principle in designing the partnership with us was to 'lead with the cause,' and the result was a partnership that changed the landscape of play for thousands and thousands of children across the country,"[4] explains Carrie Suhr.

LANCE ARMSTRONG FOUNDATION AND NIKE

The cause-marketing sensation of 2004, the Yellow Bracelet campaign spawned a whole series of similar bracelets featuring different colors from a National Wildlife Federation (NWF) produced environment-friendly, evergreen-colored band to the Crohn's & Colitis Foundation of America "Got Guts" blue wristband. Cause marketing allows for its participants to publicly communicate values—*the bracelets let people support a good cause, while proclaiming they are doing just that.*

Background

The Lance Armstrong Foundation provides information and support to young cancer survivors and their families. With a mission that believes in the battle with cancer, knowledge is power and attitude is everything. From the moment of diagnosis, the Foundation provides practical information and tools to "live strong."

In spring of 2004, when the Lance Armstrong Foundation launched a yellow bracelet with the phrase "Live Strong" stamped on it, little did they realize they would unleash one of the hottest products and cause-marketing initiatives of the year.

Program

"Live Strong" is the foundation's motto, and yellow reflects the color of the lead rider's jersey in the Tour de France and symbolizes for Lance hope, courage, and perseverance. The $1 cost of the bracelet went to the nonprofit charitable organization of the world's greatest cyclist and famous cancer survivor, Lance Armstrong.

In a cause-marketing partnership, Nike underwrote the production and distribution of the entire five million first run, ensuring that 100% of the proceeds went directly to the foundation. To show their full support of the initiative and the Foundation, Nike contributed an additional $1 million. While Nike partnered on the cause product initiative, their swoosh was nowhere to be seen. Their involvement extended to sales of the bracelet in Niketown outlets. They were also available at Foot Locker stores and various independent retailers.

Goals

Revenue generation, consumer engagement, and awareness of the cause and the organization were key goals for the Foundation. Nike's support extended their ongoing relationship with Lance Armstrong and provided an interesting cause product for their stores. Nike supported the campaign with the goal of helping the Foundation raise $5 million. By Christmas 2005, revenue generated was four times that amount.

Results

Purchases were recorded as strong right from the very beginning of the launch. But it was during the Tour de France that sales really began to take off. Armstrong and his whole team wore the wristband from the start of the Tour de France. As the competition continued, all the competitors and even officials started wearing it. With Armstrong's sixth consecutive record-setting Tour de France victory, everyone got bracelet fever, and suddenly they could be seen everywhere. A cause-marketing phenomenon was born.

The original five million bracelets sold out quickly; after another four million more were made and sold, two million more were produced. By December 2004, they were nowhere to be found in retail outlets. Even on the Foundation Web site, supplies were nonexistent. "There is currently a three- to four-week shipping delay on *all* orders. We appreciate your patience & support,"[5] stated the front page of the Web site. A secondary market popped up on eBay. Fashion trend, support for a cause, or both? Either way, the impact was the same: commitment to the Foundation's mission made famous by its founder and a fashionable, visual symbol of the wearer's concern and loyalty to Lance and his cause.

THE AMERICAN RED CROSS AND THE HOME DEPOT

Ready Gear, Emergency Kit
The development and sale of Ready Gear kits by The Home Depot creates a unique alliance with the Red Cross to support its mission of helping people prevent, prepare for, and respond to disasters and life's emergencies. The relationship extended to provide additional support during the Hurricane Katrina Disaster in 2005.

Background

The American Red Cross is a nationwide network of nearly 900 field units dedicated to saving lives and helping people prevent, prepare for, and respond to emergencies. In 2004, the American Red Cross and Home Depot, the world's largest home improvement retailer, launched Ready Gear, an emergency kit containing essential, lifesaving items recommended by the American Red Cross.

A study conducted for the American Red Cross in July 2004 indicated that 67% of Americans feel it is very important to be prepared for catastrophic events, yet only 22% of those surveyed feel they are very prepared. "Build a kit" is one of the five simple but important steps the Red Cross recommends people take to be better prepared for emergencies. Although the Red Cross sells its own preassembled kits through local chapters and online, recent research suggests that many shoppers prefer to make their purchases in a traditional retail store environment so they can see, feel, and inspect the product before they buy it.

Program

In 2004, an unusually severe hurricane season and other weather-related disasters along the east coast of the United States punctuated the importance and urgency of being prepared. The Home Depot donated nearly $4 million to numerous nonprofit organizations to assist with the repair and rebuilding efforts throughout the impacted area. In addition, the company mobilized supplies and associates to meet the needs of its customers.

As an extension of this support The Home Depot created a unique alliance with the Red Cross to support its mission of helping people prepare for disasters and life's emergencies by developing and selling a Ready Gear kit. The contents of the kit were recommended by the Red Cross and could provide two adults support for the 72 hours during or immediately following a disaster or emergency. Ready Gear was introduced at a time when emergency preparedness was at the top of the mind for Americans. Its retail price includes a $10.00 donation to the Red Cross. The Home Depot sells the Ready Gear kit in their stores in selected coastal and "high-threat" markets.

No one has more credibility when it comes to disasters than the Red Cross, and The Home Depot looks for adjacencies to extend the cause relationship and align the products with a public messaging program. "If the partnership is only about a product, the mission focus can be lost. So we look for other facets and cause-marketing tools that allow us to get the message and mission out into the public in stores,"[6] explains Kevin Martinez, Director, Community Affairs at The Home Depot.

Relationship Extended

Direct education programs have been added to the cause-marketing program through in-store clinics. The clinics provided customers with information on how to be prepared for potential disasters such as hurricanes, tornadoes, or wildfires. They also allow individual Home Depot stores to work with community-based Red Cross chapters and engage their store associates in the program.

"As a retailer, we want to get as close to the consumer as possible," says Kevin Martinez. "When we undertake programs in stores it engages our associates and allows them to commit to the mission and cause marketing message. The clinics provide additional support to the local chapter and can give them strength that they never had before. This can be a capacity building tool, which is also what cause marketing should do. We struggle as to where to place our dollars, at the national or local levels. We want to be supportive of both, so if an organization has a strong brand, national and local presence we can do both."[7]

PURCHASE PLUS: MAKING GIVING EASY

Purchase plus involves corporations facilitating giving to a nonprofit cause by promoting and encouraging an add-on financial contribution from their customers at their retail or service locations, usually at the point of purchase. A wide range of organizations can be supported, and the means by which this can be implemented are equally broad.

This form of cause marketing is a variation on the traditional charity donation boxes in stores. The main difference: the boxes were driven by the nonprofit organization with secondary support from the retailers. Boxes at checkout counters were easily available to pop in loose change left over from purchases. Charities were responsible for distributing the boxes to stores and collecting them regularly. The main contribution from the retailer was the space.

Purchase plus involves the company facilitating and collecting the donations and submitting the contributions to the nonprofit cause. Advertising and promotion around the program is common and another contribution made by the partner company. These types of cause programs involve the consumer donating and receiving some form of recognition that is placed in the store, communicating individual values while showcasing the contribution of the company.

Purchase plus cause marketing, like other product-based programs, is transactional and consumer driven. Companies that deal directly with consumers and who have retail points of contact can establish these types of programs. They can be implemented by national, regional, or local companies and accompanying nonprofit organization. The cost is nominal while the benefit to the corporation and nonprofit organization can be significant.

Interestingly, even though the donations are made by consumers, the corporations get a halo effect from a program. They are seen as being good corporate citizens through their association and willingness to facilitate consumer support.

How It Works

- Cause-marketing purchase plus can support a wide range of causes and benefit national, regional, or local nonprofit organizations.
- Either partner can initiate a program, but the driver will be the company who must execute the program.

- Once a program is in place, the company determines the method of collecting, donation at the cash register, add-gift with payment of statement, or collection of change, and the process by which the donation will be collected and recorded.

- Sophisticated computer scanning and bar coding makes it easy for the company to keep track of and report donations.

- Promotional material is developed including point-of-purchase advertising, donor recognition, and broader advertising of initiative.

- Program is implemented and donations collected and submitted to the charitable partner.

- A letter or memorandum of understanding is beneficial to clearly outline processes and procedures for execution of program and use of the nonprofit organization's logo and word mark.

Benefits

- Is relatively easy to implement once the processes and procedures are put in place.

- Encourages individual charitable giving and makes it easy for people to give.

- Connects more people with a specific nonprofit cause and broadens awareness of a nonprofit organization and specific cause.

- Positions corporate partner as good citizen and actively engaged in the community supporting relevant issues.

- Provides unrestricted funding for nonprofit organizations.

- Is a simple program that can be undertaken at the local or national level.

Challenges

- Execution processes and procedures must be clearly outlined in advance of program implementation to ensure accurate recording and distribution of donations as well as approval procedures for advertising materials developed using the nonprofit's logo and word mark.

MISSIONFISH, EBAY GIVING WORKS AND THOUSANDS OF CHARITIES

The first major cause-marketing initiative using the Internet, this program has the potential to significantly increase individual giving while enhancing sales for eBay vendors and positioning eBay as a good corporate citizen.

Background

MissionFish and eBay joined forces to develop an innovative purchase plus facilitated giving program that provides buyers and sellers on eBay the opportunity to support their favorite causes. Using the power of the Internet and eBay's marketplace, the program provides a win–win–win tool that benefits sellers, buyers, and charitable organizations and eBay.

Program

eBay Giving Works was developed in response to a demand from eBay sellers who wanted to support charitable organizations through their sales. The program provides support to charitable organizations through community sellers and through direct nonprofit sales.

MissionFish, a nonprofit service of the Points of Light Foundation, was invited in 2003 by eBay Giving Works to act as the conduit between eBay users and charitable organizations by being the dedicated solution provider of the online listing tool for eBay Giving Works. MissionFish, committed to building a marketplace for change, provides nonprofit verification, donation collection and disbursement, and donation processing and tracking. They issue the tax receipts and assist with customer care.

The two partners work together to combine strength to operate an important service for sellers and the community. Here's how it works.

Community Sellers

Community sellers simply select their favorite charity from a list of approved and validated nonprofit organizations and designate the percentage of proceeds they will donate for each listing. eBay provides community sellers with a distinctive Giving Works icon, a blue and yellow ribbon displayed in the title bar of the listing that signifies to buyers that proceeds will benefit a nonprofit. As well, eBay lists the donation information, percentage, and recipient nonprofit prominently in the listing to build buyer confidence and confirm that the listing is a legitimate charity listing. Enhanced search functionality by category, keyword, mission, and nonprofit name allows buyers to find sellers' items easily. Finally, eBay provides a centralized tax management reporting tool that tracks sellers' charitable contributions throughout the year. This helps sellers optimize and manage their eBay charitable tax deductions in one place.

Nonprofit Sellers

Nonprofit organizations can also benefit from the service by listing items for sale on eBay. Often nonprofits will receive the offer of goods that they can't use.

Because selling had been time consuming and cumbersome, many nonprofits were unable to benefit from these donations. Now through eBay nonprofits have an avenue to sell products directly, collect the proceeds from the buyer, and issue a tax receipt for the donated goods, if applicable. eBay Giving Works taps into a new source of unrestricted funding for nonprofits, adds names to their donor base, and reaches millions in the eBay Marketplace with messages and information about their cause.

Goals

eBay's goal was to use its Internet auction powerhouse to assist the community and provide a value service to its users all in the interest of "making the world a better place through trading." As they state on their Web site, "Giving Works is the dedicated program for charity listings on eBay, offering a marketplace for compassionate commerce—buy items and support worthy causes at the same time!"[8]

MissionFish's goal is to ensure that the program works for donors and non-profit organizations by acting as the conduit and ensuring the best service to the sector and donor. Both partners are committed to building the program. A special icon is now put on the products featuring donations to charities.

Results

Launched in November 2003, the first 15 months of operation saw the program raise over $3.8 millions for American charities. Over 4,300 organizations listed during this time and they span the gamut from the largest, like Red Cross, to small groups like the Pig Placement Network, a one-person organization dedicated to finding homes for Vietnamese potbelly pigs, and everything in between.

Cone's research shows that consumers will purchase a product that supports a charity, price and quality being equal, over one that doesn't. This has definitely held true on eBay Giving Works. On average, items that support a charitable or-

AMERICAN CANCER SOCIETY AND WALGREENS

Hope Blooms for You

A longtime purchase plus program, these easy-to-develop and implement cause-marketing arrangements can build customer loyalty and help to brand the company as a good corporate citizen.

ganization have 20% more bids and sell at a higher price than those that don't.[9] For eBay sellers who are trying to differentiate themselves in front of millions of buyers and develop buyer loyalty and repeat business, the additional benefit of charitable support has made it even more compelling for sellers.

Background

The American Cancer Society is the nationwide community-based voluntary health organization dedicated to eliminating cancer as a major health problem through research, education, advocacy, and service. Walgreens, a retail pharmacy, is dedicated to offering customers the best drugstore service in America.

Program

Since 1996, Walgreens has run a purchase plus promotion, Hope Blooms with You, to benefit the American Cancer Society's breast cancer research. The program is held every May for the full month. During that time they offer customers the opportunity to support the cause of breast cancer research while encouraging women to take care of their breast health by visiting their doctor and doing self-examination. A simple bar code system on a paper bloom facilitated customers' donations of $1, which can be added to a Walgreens customer's purchases.

Walgreens pays for the promotional material and ads and trains their staff to participate in the program, a critical component to the overall success of the program. Donations come from the customers; Walgreens' promotion and the use of their customer channel is their donation to the program.

Goals

American Cancer Society's cause-marketing program goals are twofold: income development (fundraising) and mission accomplishment. "When we go in the door to talk about a possible cause-marketing program, we start talking mission first," explains Cynthia Currence, National Vice President, Strategic Corporate Marketing Alliances for American Cancer Society. "We want to change consumer behaviors and this program provides us with an opportunity to get our message out. We look at how much it would cost us to get into the marketplace and what they put into promoting this program and the earned media value is more than we could ever afford to buy."[10]

As a major pharmacy retailer, Walgreens sees the program as a way to align itself with a cause relevant to their business. Equally important is the opportunity to engage their employees and customers in taking action to promote good breast health and supporting the work of the American Cancer Society.

Results

In 2004, the program generated $2.2 million to support the American Cancer Society. As Cynthia Currence explains, "Equally important for the organization is the 2.2 million that saw the message and were encouraged to take action." For American Cancer Society, their cause programs including the one run annually by Walgreens are not just a revenue strategy, but a key mission strategy: a way to fulfill their education mandate and goals. The messaging that is tagged with the Walgreens program is a central part of all of American Cancer Society's cause-marketing relationships. The earned media value of the relationships has been estimated at over $8 million.

Walgreens' commitment to the program is driven by its success. Although details of sales impact haven't been revealed, they feel their customer base looks forward to the promotion and that it definitely builds traffic for them. Employee involvement and pride in the program is another strong feature that makes it a success for the company.

In addition to their facilitated giving program with the American Cancer Society, Walgreens gives customers the opportunity to donate directly to other worthwhile organizations through Take Heart and Give (American Heart Association) and the Buy a Sneaker for a Dollar (Juvenile Diabetes Research Foundation). Along with the American Cancer Society program, these promotions generated over $5.2 million in 2004.

McKinley Masters Custom Homes and Hospice Calgary

Facilitating giving can work well for local organizations and support a wide range of causes. The case of local Calgary, Alberta, Canada home builder McKinley Masters Custom Homes supporting Hospice Calgary demonstrates the simplicity and effectiveness of these types of cause-marketing relationships.

Program

McKinley Masters' show home was the focal point for the facilitated giving program. A voluntary donation of $5 a person was suggested to visitors of the show home with the proceeds going to Hospice Calgary, a local grief and bereavement and palliative care nonprofit. The organization was suggested by a partner of the company who had previously been a Hospice board member and volunteer.

Hospice Calgary was given the opportunity to have information at the show home on their organization and programs. They provide specialized, professional care for dying individuals and counseling and comfort for bereaved family and friends. The company featured the program and Hospice Calgary in a number of their promotional ads. On-site signage also introduced the organization. McKinley Masters organized and paid for cost of signage and advertising.

Goals

McKinley Masters' main goal was to create goodwill for their company in the community. "We wanted to make people realize that we are community oriented" said marketing manager Ken Hubert. "So doing something visible for a local charity was a good way to do this."[11]When approached, it was clear Hospice Calgary would be a good fit. Their services had benefited many local Calgary families, and the organization was always looking for community support and profile.

The local building company had contributed to nonprofit organizations before, but this was the first time they had taken a more public approach to their charitable giving. A secondary goal was to use the donation like an admission charge, which had been proven to result in visitors showing more respect for show homes.

Generating awareness and revenue were the key benefits for Hospice Calgary. "We were delighted with the program. McKinley Masters had signage about the program, and staff went an extra step and asked for a donation to the hospice right at the door,"[12] explained Karen Bronstein, Hospice Calgary's director of marketing and development.

Results

The award-winning show home had over 4,000 people tour through during the run of the cause program. Although the donation was voluntary, over $10,000 was raised for Hospice Calgary (see Exhibit 4.1).

Hospice Calgary volunteers and staff were delighted with the exposure and financial support. Their enthusiasm spread to family and friends, who came to see the show home to say personal thanks. A lot of people came because of the Hospice Calgary connection, according to Marketing Manager, Ken Hubert. "Their supporters thought it was a good gesture and they wanted to support us too. It was like an endorsement; although not a goal for our company it was certainly one of the spin-off benefits."

The positive response success and simplicity of the program has encouraged McKinley Masters to consider doing a similar program with the Hospice. Are there changes that would be made? Maybe a slight refinement, but keeping it simple was a great tenet for the home builder and the charity.

EXHIBIT 4.1 McKINLEY MASTERS

LICENSING: USING NONPROFIT LOGOS, BRAND IDENTITIES, AND ASSETS

Licensing is a business that grants the right to use a legally protected trademark, name, graphic, logo, slogan, likeness, or other similar intellectual property in conjunction with a product or service for a royalty or fee. A formal licensing agreement outlines the prescribed amount of time the license is granted, the specific geographic area, tracking of sales, marketing and distribution vehicles, and dates royalty payments will be made. In exchange the nonprofit receives payment in the form of a royalty, usually a percentage on the product sales.

There are four types of nonprofit licensing:

1. Brand extension, products that are a natural extension of the nonprofit organization's identity (e.g., Save the Children's line of products that features artwork produced by children)

2. Promotional products, the organization's logo or trademark put on promotional type products such as T-shirts, mugs, ball caps, or credit cards

3. Certification or commendation (e.g., an arrangement in which the nonprofit organization recognizes that a product or service of a company com-

plies with established standards they have developed, such as the American Heart Association's Heart Check Program)

4. Intellectual property or information (e.g., National Geographic licenses the use of its internationally recognized photograph for commercial use)

How Does It Work?

- A licensing program begins by a nonprofit organization determining the assets it has that could be licensed. Name, logo, credibility, and intellectual assets are the most commonly licensed property.

- Organizations with strong brand-name awareness, a perceived quality, and loyalty to the name and organization and intellectual property have valuable assets for a licensing program.

- Nonprofit organizations can have other assets such as images that are unique or proprietary to the organization.

- Licensing is based on a contractual agreement, which gives formal permission to a company (licensor) to use the nonprofit's asset subject to certain terms and conditions. This can include such things as for a specific purpose, a defined geographic area, a finite time, and royalty payments.

- Licensing does not require nonprofit organizations to make any investment in product development, production, or marketing. By partnering with a licensor, they get the benefit of their product expertise and built-in marketing and distribution channels.

What Are the Benefits?

- Licensing offers mutual opportunities and benefits to both the owners of the properties as well as the manufacturers of the goods or services.

- Nonprofit licensing helps the manufacturers use the brand identity to create immediate consumer awareness and add value to the product. A nonprofit licensing program helps to distinguish products, makes a regular product unique, and links the product and manufacturer with a "good" cause or the credibility of the organization.

- For nonprofit organizations a product is linked to brand extension and the enhancement of brand image and goodwill at a consumer level without having to develop, produce, or market the product themselves. Licensing is low risk for nonprofits, with no upfront capital needed to develop products.

- Using a licensing arrangement, the nonprofit benefits from the capabilities and connections of the business licensor and avoids having to build a structure and staff with these types of skills.

- Licensing brings a nonprofit and its message into the retail environment, a nontraditional venue for reaching consumers. Frequently, other promotional material and advertising vehicles are incorporated into a program, which also helps expand marketing and message reach.

- Nonprofits receive legal protection because licensing a brand for use in certain product categories prevents potential competitors from legally using the brand name to enter those categories.

- The economic advantage for the nonprofit organization lies in the profits from royalty payments. In financial terms, a nonprofit usually receives an average royalty payment between 5% and 10% of the wholesale price of each sold product.

- Revenue generated is usually nondesignated and can be used for operational support.

What Are the Challenges?

- Licensing takes time, and perseverance is important. A licensing program is a long-term proposition. Building up a stable of licensed products is important to seeing a solid financial return, but this doesn't happen overnight.

- Quality products representing quality organizations are an important consideration for nonprofits. Name, brand, and reputation need to be protected in a licensing program.

- Although licensing limits a nonprofit organization's need for upfront capital investments, a program does need adequate resources if it is to be successful.

- The competition in the licensing area is fierce, and market interests and demands can change rapidly. Although the risk is limited, the return might not be as great as originally expected if products don't do well.

- Licensing is one of the most time-consuming forms of cause-related marketing and often provides a low return compared to resources invested. Regular cost/benefit analysis is important to ensure most productive use of a nonprofit's resources.

- It is important to ensure the organization receives a guaranteed minimum royalty to make the program more than self-supporting. This encourages the licensee to properly market the licensed products or services and ensures, even as a minimum, a set amount of revenue from the endeavor. A percentage of this guarantee is normally paid as an advance.

- Legal agreements must be in place that outline the terms and conditions of the program in addition to how sales will be recorded and when payment will be made.

Brand Extension

Licensing is big business in North America, and the availability of licensed merchandise has proliferated over the last decade. Well-known nonprofit trademarks are licensed as a cost-effective means of brand extension, additional consumer awareness, and revenue. For the manufacturer, the popularity and familiarity of trademarks can help an otherwise undistinguished product stand out from the crowd.

The 2003 LIMA Licensing Industry Survey estimates retail sales of licensed merchandise to be $110 billion for North America alone. In 2003, over $5.8 billions dollars in royalty payments were made.[13] The lion's share of the revenue generated goes to well-known commercial trademarks and brands in entertainment, sports, and art. Licensing is most often associated with the latest Hollywood blockbusters, sports, or even cartoon characters from popular TV shows like *The Simpsons*. But nonprofit organizations have valuable assets that can be brought to bear in a licensing program.

Nonprofit organizations are turning to licensed products as a way to use their brand recognition and assets to generate revenue and create awareness for their cause. And the value to nonprofit organizations is growing. Royalties paid in 2003 from this source of cause marketing were approximately $40 million dollars, up by $1 million from the previous year.[14] Product licensing is initiated by nonprofit organizations proactively taking a strategic, entrepreneurial approach to raising revenue and building awareness.

NATIONAL TRUST FOR HISTORIC PRESERVATION AND THE VALSPAR CORPORATION

American Traditions Paint

Nonprofits have many assets that can be used in cause-marketing arrangements, including their name and mission. This is an excellent example of a product that is built on the organization's good name, its mission, and its hundreds of historic places.

Background

The National Trust is a private nonprofit organization established in 1949. With more than 200,000 members, the National Trust provides leadership, education, advocacy, and resources to save America's diverse historic places and revitalizes communities.

The National Trust's licensing program has evolved since it was first launched in the mid-1990s. At that time, the focus was on building a line of gifts and collectibles based on historic reproductions and inspired by the National Trust collection. Early in 2000 the program was revived and refocused on two core areas: home furnishing and home renovation. The goal of the program was to develop products that had broad appeal and mass market with distribution channels that could reach a greater number of Americans and generate more revenue for the National Trust. One of the highest profile licensing programs was developed in 2001 with the Valspar Corporation, a major paint company.

Program

American Traditions Paint is a unique collection of historic paint colors created by the Valspar Corporation with the National Trust and inspired by their historic places. The American Traditions palette, sold exclusively at Lowe's Home Improvement Warehouses nationwide, has been ranked number one by a leading consumer magazine for two years in a row. Valspar supports preservation by paying a royalty, a percentage of every sale to the National Trust, and by supplying paint to National Trust Historic Sites and Associate Sites.

Valspar has developed a full-color brochure for the paint programs that gives the National Trust an opportunity to educate the public about their mission of preservation and to introduce the spectrum of historic places under the care of the National Trust. This is one of the biggest benefits of the program. The program reaches a whole new public not traditionally touched by National Trust messages. For Valspar, the connection provides an authenticity and connection that could not have been achieved without the National Trust relationship. It also allows support of an important national institution vital in maintaining historic homes. Regular meetings and conversations have been critical in keeping the lines of communications open between the two partners.

The program goals are twofold: to increase visibility for both brands—National Trust and American Traditions (Valspar); and to increase sales because of the co-branded differentiation in the marketplace. The five-year agreement began in 2001 and expires in 2006 with an anticipation of renewal.

Results

The American Traditions relationship has provided a substantial undesignated revenue stream for National Trust. Equally important has been the increased awareness and visibility for the organization's name and mission. Valspar's American Traditions has helped create a unique and differentiated product line. For both partners, the relationship has helped build an emotional connection to consumers.

The relationship continues to grow with fresh ideas and opportunities to keep the program relevant and to connect consumers directly to the cause and National Trust organization.

Promotional Licensed Products

Promotional products use the logo and name of a nonprofit organization tied to a specific promotional product. Affinity credit cards are one of the most popular forms of promotional licensed products.

THE NATURE CONSERVANCY AND MBNA AFFINITY CARD

Based on connecting to nonprofits' loyal donor and membership base, the cards provide an opportunity to contribute to a cause in which they believe, while doing something they do anyway.

Background

The Nature Conservancy's mission is to preserve the plants, animals, and natural communities that represent the diversity of life on Earth by protecting the lands and waters they need to survive. Through a strategic, science-based planning process, called Conservation by Design, The Nature Conservancy identifies the highest-priority places—landscapes and seascapes that, if conserved, promise to ensure biodiversity over the long term to achieve meaningful, lasting conservation results.[15] MBNA is the largest independent credit card issuer in the world and the leading affinity marketing credit card issuers with relationships with over 5,000 organizations.

Program

In 1995, MBNA and The Nature Conservancy joined forces in a cause-related marketing arrangement to provide a no-annual-fee credit card to Conservancy members. The customized Nature Conservancy cards feature the red-eyed tree frog, great blue heron, and sea otters. The card generates royalty payments for the Conservancy for each new account, renewed accounts, cash advances, and purchases.

The card is marketed exclusively by MBNA to Conservancy members. Marketing and promotion are essential for cardholders to apply for the card and encourage them to use it. Because of unrelated business tax, The Nature Conservancy currently does no direct marketing of the card.

Goals and Results

The Conservancy developed the program to generate vital operational funding for their programs. It was also a simple way to connect with their members and provide them with a service and an additional way of contributing.

MBNA has built its business by leading the affinity credit card area. Connection with a well-respected national organization like The Nature Conservancy adds credibility to the program and extends its credit card reach.

By far the most lucrative cause-related marketing program the Conservancy has undertaken, the program generated more than $5 million in undesignated financial support in the first 10 years. The program has provided additional visibility for the organization and added another tool for members to easily contribute to the work of the Conservancy.

The relationship between The Nature Conservancy and MBNA has extended to include support for the Conservancy's conservation program of the St. John's River in Maine and as a sponsor of their "In Response to Place" exhibition.

Certification Programs

Certification programs have been established by nonprofit organizations to lend credibility to products or services that meet certain established standards. Manufacturers submit an application and provide information for products or services they would like entered in the program. If they meet the specific category criteria, manufacturers will then agree to the program requirements (such as promotional issues and logo use guidelines) and provide the required licensing fee. Manufacturers may then display the program logo on their licensed products and advertising and promotional materials if they so choose. The manufacturer pays a specific fee. Most programs are at least self-supporting through levies on participating manufacturers. Some programs generate additional funds, which are reinvested in the organization.

EASE-OF-USE PROGRAM: ARTHRITIS FOUNDATION

One of the first of its kind, the ease-of-use program launched the Arthritis Foundation's corporate cause-marketing initiatives. A leader in the field, a research study by the Foundation proved that corporate-funded activities are the primary drivers of the Arthritis Foundation awareness and strengthen perceptions about the Foundation.

The Arthritis Foundation launched its ease-of-use program in the early 1990s, the first of its kind in North America. Consumer research reveals that nonprofit organizations are perceived to be an independent and respected third party that brings an unbiased approach to the development of an on-pack identification program.

Program

The program was launched when Tide approached the national nonprofit to approve its new easy-to-use packaging. Recognizing that the foundation could both achieve its mission to help those living with arthritis and generate revenue for its ongoing operation, the program was created to encourage manufacturers to design with ease-of-use in mind.

"It's important to note that this was not an endorsement of the product," stated Harry Abel, former vice president at the Arthritis Foundation, who oversaw the launch of the program. "What we were doing was endorsing the packaging and its ease of use."[16]

Products and packaging are submitted for review to an independent panel of people with arthritis and health professionals. If approved after extensive testing and research, they can receive a favorable review for ease-of-use. These products carry the Arthritis Foundation Ease-of-Use Commendation Logo. The makers of these products pay for the testing and make an annual contribution to the Arthritis Foundation in support of the mission.

Goals

The commendation program has provided an additional way to support those living with arthritis and extended the name, logo, and message of the organization.

Although the program has generated revenue for the organization, the Arthritis Foundation has keep its certification fee low to encourage manufacturers to develop ease-of-use products and to apply for use of their certification logo. The challenge for all nonprofits using certification programs is how much to charge. The benefits for companies gaining the rights to the ease-of-use logo are tangible and can be seen in increased credibility and sales. But the foundation wants to keep the programs accessible and encourage manufacturers to make products that are beneficial to its clients.

Results

The program has grown by leaps and bounds, and more than 10 years after it was launched over 25 products have received the ease-of-use commendation. The types of products run the full gamut from vacuum cleaners to gardening tools to golf products.

The certification program helped the foundation build its corporate partners program. The foundation worked with a range of corporations—some that would not normally partner with the organization, such as Folgers Coffee, and others that allowed a broader and deeper relationship to be built. Tylenol came on board with their easy-to-open cap and have moved into being the title sponsor for the Foundation's Joints in Motion marathon.

Using the commendation program as the base, the Arthritis Foundation has continued to build corporate relationships. Although some concerns were raised by volunteers about the impact they might have on the organization's image, research, in fact, proved the opposite to be true. The public's perception and understanding of the organization had been enhanced by the corporation partnerships, and those surveyed saw them as a positive and effective way to get the message out.

Intellectual Property Licensing

Licensing of knowledge or technology is another form of licensing. Here charities license their tangible knowledge or intellectual property to generate revenue, achieve their mission by partnering with a commercial venture, and extend the impact of their work.

GLENBOW MUSEUM AND KEY PORTER BOOKS

Built on the premise that the Museum is an expert on content development and the publishing firm is an expert in editing, publishing, and marketing of books, this alliance resulted in four major publications from 2001 to 2005.

Background

Glenbow Museum, one of Canada's top 10 museums, is based in Calgary, Alberta, with a mandate that includes preserving and presenting the heritage and culture of Western Canada. One of Canada's most prominent publishers, Key Porter Books Limited, is known internationally for its high-quality illustrated books and in Canada for its broad range of books of national interest. Founded in 1979, Key Porter Books publishes about 100 titles per year and has over 500 titles in print.

Program

Glenbow Museum annually produces research and writing on topics relating to the history, art, and culture of western Canada, a core part of its mandate and mission. Providing broad dissemination of that information is important for the institution to have the greatest impact. Glenbow Museum's publications program was developed to record and share the history, art, and culture of Western Canada. Previous to 1999, most of the publications were self-published, with the museum taking on developing the content, designing, printing, and marketing their own publications. Recognizing that the strength of the institution lay in curatorial knowledge and content, the museum developed a publications program that saw it license the content and partner with a commercial publisher to benefit from their expertise in editing, design, printing, marketing, and distribution. Key Porter Books has become the main publishing partner, producing all but two of the past seven books.

Goals

Key Porter Books saw the opportunity to access Glenbow's knowledge, tie into its credibility, and extend their market through Canadian museum gift shops, including Glenbow's.

Glenbow recognized the potential to create a commercial licensed publication program that would provide a vehicle to share new information and broaden the dissemination of information.

Results

From 2001 to 2005, four publications were developed in collaboration with Key Porter Books, including two major art publications and two first nations focused books. Each publication was tied to a major exhibition, several of which traveled nationally and internationally, providing a further market for Key Porter Books.

Glenbow Museum has benefited from Key Porter's expertise in editing, design, and book printing, and by partnering with a major commercial publisher it saw wide distribution of the publications, including in the United States and Britain. A small royalty payment has been earned along with profit from book sales in the institution's Museum Shop. The program helps Glenbow reach out beyond its four walls and share its work with everyone from scholars to the general public to schoolchildren.

CONCLUSIONS

There are three forms of cause-marketing products: product sales, purchases plus, also known as facilitated giving, and product licensing. Cause-marketing products are consumer driven and transactional based that are linked to sales of product or service and are usually meant to **drive sales** and **build customer loyalty**. Revenue is generated for a nonprofit and its cause through a percentage of sales going to a cause or by facilitating giving at point of sale and awareness created through associated promotional support material. Working best for companies that have a direct link to consumers, this form of cause marketing can work for national, regional, and local nonprofits.

ENDNOTES

1. 2004 Cone Corporate Citizenship Study.
2. Interview, Carrie Suhr, February 2, 2005.
3. Ibid.
4. Ibid.
5. Message on Lance Armstrong Foundation Web site on December 22, 2004 (www.laf.org).
6. Interview, Kevin Martinez, March 30, 2005.
7. Ibid.
8. http://pages.ebay.com/givingworks/.
9. Interview, Clam Lorenz, MissionFish, February 17, 2005.
10. Interview, Cynthia Currance, American Cancer Society, January 25, 2005.
11. Interview, Ken Hubert, McKinley Masters, April 25, 2005.
12. Interview, Karen Bronstein, Hospice Calgary, July 29, 2005.
13. LIMA—Licensing Industry Survey, 2003.
14. Ibid.
15. www.nature.org.
16. Interview, Harry Abel, January 27, 2005.

CHAPTER 5

Cause-Marketing Issue Promotions

This chapter looks at cause-marketing issue promotions. This form of cause marketing allows for a deeper relationship and more opportunity for broader messaging and active engagement of constituents. Both involve businesses supporting a nonprofit cause by using their communications, marketing, promotional, and operational resources to actively engage in creating public awareness and concern about a social cause and to encourage support by purchasing, donating, or volunteering. Cause promotions touch all three realms of cause-marketing relationships from **sales to customer loyalty to branding to social responsibilty**, but have a heavier emphasis on the latter two.

Issue promotion sees a company, in collaboration with a nonprofit partner, create a promotional campaign to create public awareness of a social issue. This form of cause marketing is driven through the marketing department with support from community relations. The campaign uses the company's marketing and advertising resources to develop promotional material and uses their distribution system to reach consumers and other stakeholders, including their employees, suppliers, and investors. Longer-term relationships help the issue to become tied to the corporate name and brand and position the company in the community and with their employees and other stakeholders relative to the cause.

FINDING THE SYNERGISTIC FIT

The fit between a cause and a company has to be synergistic to work and to be sincere and authentic. Promotional material is jointly developed, with the nonprofit organization providing the information and the company developing promotional vehicles and ensuring distribution. Some cause-marketing promotions will also include the distribution of the charity's own promotional material.

Most programs also include a call to action that will encourage individuals to find more out about the cause, make their own personal contribution, financial or otherwise, or to volunteer. Most often the financial support provided through issue promotions is not tied directly to product sales, but is made as a straight financial contribution.

How Does It Work?

- A company and nonprofit cause develop a collaborative arrangement to create a communications program around a societal issue. Some companies will launch their own issue awareness cause-marketing promotions. Dove is an example of a company that initiated a cause-marketing promotion, which in this case focuses on women and beauty.

- Cause-marketing issue promotions can be developed at the local, regional, or national level and can relate to any type of issue.

- Either a nonprofit or company can initiate a joint issue promotion, but both have to be equally involved to make it work. Companies with direct access to consumers are most interested in this form of cause marketing.

- Issue promotions are focused on building awareness and concern about a social issue, encouraging people to learn more about it, to donate money or other nonmonetary resources, or to volunteer their time in support of the cause.

- Unlike product-based cause-marketing initiatives, the donation is not exclusively tied to product sales.

- Although most companies will include a donation to support the cause, the main contribution from the corporation is in building awareness and in the call to action. It can be difficult for nonprofit organizations put a dollar value on the awareness contribution.

- Promotional material includes posters, print advertising campaigns, brochures, Web sites, and printed material.

What Are the Benefits?

- For nonprofit organizations, it provides them access to a broader audience beyond anything they could achieve on their own.

- It creates positive connections, access to additional human resources, and operational support.

- For corporate partners, cause-marketing promotions help build a company's brand, improve corporate image and customer loyalty, and create employee pride and involvement.

What Are the Challenges?

- Nonprofit organizations must do their homework and make sure that the cause partner fits with their culture and is committed to a partnership of equals.

- Sincere, authentic promotions must be developed to maintain the integrity of the issue, cause, and partners.

SUSAN G. KOMEN FOUNDATION AND YOPLAIT®

"Save Lids to Save Lives" Breast Cancer Awareness Promotion

The first case study looks at long-term issue promotion that was launched in 1997 between the national organization Susan G. Komen and General Mills' product Yoplait®. The promotion runs in store during a three-month period in the fall and has had a significant impact on raising awareness of the issue of breast cancer.

Background and Alignment

The Susan G. Komen Foundation is a global organization focused on breast cancer. The Foundation was established in 1982 by Nancy Brinker to honor the memory of her sister, Susan G. Komen, who died from breast cancer at the age of 36. It provides breast cancer research grants and community outreach programs. Today, the foundation has more than 75,000 volunteers working through a network of affiliates and events to eradicate breast cancer as a life-threatening disease by advancing research, education, screening, and treatment.

Yoplait® is a yogurt brand of its parent company, General Mills. For 17 years, a major commitment of the brand has been to women's wellness—breast cancer, heart health, osteoporosis prevention, and fitness, with a goal of making a healthy difference in the lives of its consumers.

Program

"Save Lids to Save Lives" was launched in 1997. The promotion built on Yoplait's® existing relationship with the Foundation, which had begun through cause sponsorship support of Komen's annual "Race for the Cure" event. "Save Lids to Save Lives" is a consumer-activated promotion that results in a donation of $0.10 to the Susan G. Komen Breast Cancer Foundation for each pink lid mailed. The General Mills Foundation also commits to making a donation to the Foundation.

Here's How It Works

The program aims to demonstrate the value of the individual and the dynamic force of many. "One person alone sending in a lid might not seem like a lot, but there are over 11 million people sending in lids—that a powerful collective,"[1] says Cindy Schneible, VP, Cause-Related Marketing and Sponsorship.

The promotion reaches and connects with a broad audience. More importantly, it actively engages people and stimulates them to think and talk about breast cancer. E-mails triggered by the program tangibly demonstrate the impact it has had: Women have been stimulated to get a mammogram; fathers have used it to have a difficult conversation with children about their mother's illness, and children have sent them in because they lost a teacher to breast cancer.

Results and Learning

For Yoplait® the program has branded their commitment to women's health and publicly communicated theses values to their employees and consumers. Consumers have come to look for the promotion—an important customer loyalty benefit. Since the beginning of the program, Yoplait® has met their financial contribution goals. It has also helped them reinforce the position of their brand as a healthy product and support to a cause that their employees and consumers care about. The promotion helped put breast cancer on the radar screen and stimulates conversations and personal action about breast health.

Komen sees the clear benefits of the program in advancing breast cancer awareness, support of their outreach mission, meaningfully engaging the public in direct action around breast health, and raising revenue in support of their cause.

Yoplait's® signature pink-lid promotion, Save Lids to Save Lives, marked its seventh anniversary in 2004. Consumers collected and sent in the pink lids in October, Breast Cancer Awareness Month, and Yoplait® committed up to a $1.2 million contribution to the Susan G. Komen Breast Cancer Foundation. Combined with the General Mills Foundation guaranteed donation of $900,000, the program raised more than $2 million for breast cancer research. General Mills and its Foundation have donated over $14 million to the breast cancer cause in the first seven years of the program.

Some controversy surrounding the impact a 10-cent donation per lid could have has brought to light the importance of transparency and open communications. "If there is one learning, we realized consumers are very savvy. They want to know exactly how the program works, what the details are, and what the benefits are to the charity," says Cindy Schneible. "Making a commitment to full disclosure and transparency in any cause program is essential. The program has offered something of value to corporate supporter, to consumers, employees who support the initiative and the return to Komen has to be significant."[2]

In 2003, General Mills and the Komen Foundation received Golden Halo Awards for outstanding leadership and achievement from the Cause Marketing Forum, an association of marketers and charities who come together to share best practices.

AMERICAN CANCER SOCIETY AND FLORIDA DEPARTMENT OF CITRUS

"Healthier Living" Promotion

This issue promotion was one of the American Cancer Society's earliest cause-marketing relationships. The promotion with the Florida Department of Citrus, which grows and provides the majority of the fruit juice in the United States, lasted over five years and was focused on the benefits of fruits and vegetables to reduce the risk for cancer.

Background and Alignment

The American Cancer Society is the nationwide community-based voluntary health organization dedicated to eliminating cancer as a major health problem by preventing cancer, saving lives, and diminishing suffering from cancer, through research, education, advocacy, and service.[3]

The National Center for Health Statistics reported that 48% of Americans eat less than a single serving of fruit on any given day, whereas 10% eat less than a serving of vegetables. Only 23% of Americans eat five or more servings of fruits and vegetables each day. The American Cancer Society recognizes that one-third of all cancers may be diet related. Adding fruits and vegetables to the diet may help reduce the risk of developing certain cancers.[4]

The Florida Department of Citrus (FDOC) is an executive agency of the Florida government charged with the marketing, research, and regulation of the Florida citrus industry. Its mission is to help grow the demand for Florida citrus products by positioning orange juice as one of the most nutrient-rich beverage choices.

In 1996, the American Cancer Society and the Florida Department of Citrus established an alliance with the goal of educating Americans about the importance of good nutrition in preventing cancer and encouraging them to consider citrus juice as a part of the campaign. The relationship began as a result of a decline in the number of Americans who were drinking orange juice.

Program Goal

The American Cancer Society and the Florida Department of Citrus aligned to educate Americans about the importance of good nutrition in preventing cancer.

Greater awareness of the link between diet and cancer could have a long-term impact on the number of lives saved from cancer. A key message was to help consumers realize that each person has the power to reduce the risk of certain types of serious cancers by the diet and lifestyle choices made.

Program

The campaign featured a nationwide education campaign carried out in grocery stores and other venues. The promotions featured the American Cancer Society logo and messaging on all the ads and directly on orange juice containers. The campaign was supported by approximately $10 million in national and local advertising and promotion, which gave the Society the ability to reach millions of people with its message about the importance of a balanced diet. It also created awareness of the link between diet and cancer and its long-term potential impact on the number of lives saved from cancer.

Tennis star Pete Sampras was featured in one of the public service announcements urging viewers to reduce their risk of developing cancer by eating more fruits and vegetables. The spot also showed a table of cancer-fighting foods and Sampras drinking a glass of orange juice.[5]

Results and Learning

The American Cancer Society measures their cause-marketing relationships in mission outcome as well as revenue generated. The issue promotion was a great mission win for the American Cancer Society. Marketing research showed that the campaign resulted in 69% recall of the health message of the campaign. It wasn't just about encouraging people to drink more juice, but that juice is a part of a healthy diet that can reduce your risk of cancer. The relationship also resulted in a significant financial contribution to the Society.

One of the earliest cause-marketing relationships for the American Cancer Society, they learned a lot about the importance of understanding what the or-

CHEERIOS® (GENERAL MILLS) AND FIRST BOOK

"Spoonful of Stories" Literacy Promotion

The promotion, geared to raise awareness of the issue of literacy and to encourage children to read, is a great example of a long-term commitment to a cause and the impact it can have for both the company and the cause.

ganization could bring to an alliance and what they could achieve from promotional issue–based cause-marketing programs.

Background and Alignment

General Mills has long been involved in numerous major cause-marketing campaigns, both corporatewide and through its individual brands. Cheerios® has adopted reading and childhood literacy as its cause. "Spoonful of Stories" was launched by Cheerios® in partnership with First Book, with the goal of "encouraging kids to read" and supporting literacy. Between 2001 and 2004, Cheerios® annually put five million quality children's books in cereal boxes for a total of 15 million books in the first three years of the program.

An acknowledged leader in the field of social enterprise, First Book is a national nonprofit organization founded in 1992 with a single mission: to give children from low-income families the opportunity to read and own their first new books. Cause marketing has been a primary source of funding for the organization; since its inception First Book has used cause marketing as a powerful tool both to generate operating revenue and to be a driver for implementing their mission-based programmatic activities.

Program Goals and Execution

Cheerios® made a commitment to childhood literacy with a goal of reaching out to kids by putting great books directly in their hands. Annually, Cheerios® places one million high-quality copies of each of five celebrated children's books free inside specially marked boxes. The books are printed to conform to the size of the boxes and include the entire content and illustrations.

The goal of the program is to go beyond the cereal boxes, and that's where First Book is a critical partner. Cheerios® donates $500,000 annually to First Book to support the organization putting books in the hands of kids through their network of 27 local affiliate organizations. As well, beginning in 2002, a form was put on Cheerios® boxes to encourage consumer donations directly to First Book and its ongoing mission. Donations are then designated by First Book to serve children in the region nearest the donor.

Additionally, through its Web site, Cheerios® offers parents tips on reading to children and encouraging children to enjoy reading. Each year additional features are added to the program. In 2003, Cheerios®, First Book, and John Lithgow, actor and children's author, developed a public service announcement to encourage parents to read with their children. To engage local TV stations, each time they broadcast the PSA during the promotional period, Cheerios® and First Book donated 500 books to the First Book Advisory Board in the region, up to a maximum of 7,500 books.

At selected NASCAR races, Jeff Green, driver of the number 43 Cheerios® Betty Crocker Dodge, kicked off a books-per-lap donation by reading to kids, through the Cheerios® Spoonful of Stories program. For every lap Jeff Green completed, Cheerios® and First Book donated books to children in the local area. In the first two years of the program more than 100,000 books were provided to children. Green has "raced for reading" from Kansas to California.

Results

Since the program's inception, 15 million books have been distributed through Cheerios® boxes, and more than $1.5 million has been donated to First Book. Through the NASCAR component more than 100,000 books have been donated to help First Book achieve its mission.

Equally important have been the efficiencies achieved as a result of the partnerships. Every $1 contributed in cash to First Book has been leveraged to yield over $11 in retail value of books to children in need. First Book donation forms and information have appeared on over 100 million boxes of Cheerios®.

Kyle Zimmer believes that "Spoonful of Stories" is a "breathtaking program. Cheerios® has made an exceptional effort to support and encourage childhood literacy. Consumers have responded with great enthusiasm and every year a new component is added to make the program fun and engaging."[6]

The First Book team has seen the benefit that cause promotions can bring to both partners. "Our four year relationship with Cheerios® has resulted in millions of books going to children and they deserve a lot of credit for the major commitment they have made to literacy and to executing such a broad ranging integrated program. I am so impressed with the care and investment of our corporate partner to the program. When I hear them worrying about the quality of books and how to most effectively implement the program I know they're not in it for themselves. It is very heartening to see corporate people deeply concerned about substance the way the Cheerios® team is."[7]

INVESTORS GROUP (ATLANTIC CANADA COMEDY TOUR) AND 14 LOCAL FOOD BANKS, "FOOD FOR THOUGHT" PROMOTION

Cause marketing can happen at any level, local, regional, and national. This case study is an example of how national support for the cause of hunger through Food Banks was successfully taken and implemented in a regional issue promotion that was good for the cause, the company, and the client base.

Background and Alignment

Investors Group (IG) is a Canadian-based investment company providing individualized financial advice and services for over 75 years. A founding member of Imagine Canada, a national program to encourage corporate giving, Investors Group is designated a "Caring Company" through donating at least 1% of their average annual pretax income to support the community.

Investors Group has a national partnership with the Canadian Association of Food Banks (CAFB) and their member food banks across the country in the fight against hunger and poverty. Each year, through the Food for Thought campaign Investors Group underwrites the cost of a national media campaign to raise awareness of the needs of Canadians, particularly children and families, living in poverty. Local IG offices across the country partner with their local food banks to raise funds and food through a variety of events and activities. Because Investors Group does not have retail presence, their promotion of an issue is tied into client events.

Challenge/Opportunity

As part of IG's marketing efforts, each region regularly invites clients to an evening event usually focused on investment speakers. Designed to provide information and to connect the IG consultants with their clients, the turnout had never been stellar in Atlantic Canada. Recognizing it was time to try something different, the Atlantic Canada office's research lead them to create a comedy tour event to be held in their major centers.

At the same time, the company regularly held community events to support a host of organizations, helping lots of groups but not really having a dramatic impact on any. With such strong interest in the tour, the Atlantic office realized there was an opportunity to attach a community cause to the tour, and local food banks were chosen.

The national partnership with the CAFB helped the Atlantic Canada IG office to consider food banks. But additional research showed the significance of food banks to Atlantic Canadians. Nationally, 41% of Canadians know someone who needs the services of a food bank. But in Atlantic Canada, that figure was 10% higher, with more than half the population touched by a food bank user.

"Everyone was really excited about the comedy tour and we recognized there was a great opportunity to marry our event with community support, really let people know about an issue and actually have an effect on people's behaviour," explained Drew Robertson, Atlantic Canada Area Marketing Manager. "We already were supporting food banks, but not in a very visible or leveraged way.

When we realized we could use a single platform to do both jobs and do them better, we were underway."[8]

Program Execution

IG consultants invited clients to the various events held across the region. Tickets were sent to those who confirmed, and they were encouraged to bring a donation for their local food bank. All of the print collateral material mentioned the food bank support, encouraged food bank contributions, and positioned the event as a way to give while having fun. In 2004, 12 performances were held and in 2005, 14, with cities ranging in size from 15,000 to 300,000 people.

The first year of the event, Investors Group committed $25,000 to the 12 local food banks, with a goal of matching that with leveraged in-kind food contributions. The second year, the contribution was doubled.

The evening began with a reception an hour before the comedy event started. "We wanted our guests to be able to enjoy refreshments and the company of their friends and to give their food bank donations before the event," said Drew Robertson, "The amazing thing was that people showed up well before the event started and the first thing they asked wasn't where's the bar, where do I sit, or where's my consultant, but where should I put this food bank donation. There was something tangible about having the food bank donation. They really felt they were contributing and the response was overwhelming."

Before the event started, an IG consultant presented a check to the local food bank representing the company's cash donation. Their representative was given an opportunity to thank IG and the people in the audience for their support and to speak about the food bank in the community.

Results

The results were dramatic, and the marketing team attributed a lot of the success to their "cause overlay." Anecdotally, Investors Group staff had people say they came to the event to support the food banks, but really enjoyed the comedy component. In terms of participation, the event had a whopping 90% attendance rate. In the past, events held by IG were more likely to have a 66% rate.

Although no business was discussed or information distributed at the event, it did result in a positive connection between the client and IG consultants. Many felt the event contributed to building a stronger relationship with their customer base, and some even secured new business.

For the food banks the impact was positive. To have a fun event attached to their cause gave them an opportunity to move away from talking about doom and gloom of people starving. It gave them a forum to thank the audience for the donations and talk about their cause in a positive and upbeat environment. Many of the local food banks are in small communities and are largely run by volunteers or part-time staff, and they are not sophisticated marketers or used to leveraging donations. The cash and food contributions along with the additional marketing and focus on the food bank brought their cause to the forefront at a time of the year that is usually a slow time for donations.

After the event was over, letters of thanks attributed the event to creating a swell of new support for several weeks for the local food bank. Not only did people bring something to the event, many were also moved enough to commit to doing something the next day or week.

Learning: Sincerity Key to Success

The success of the event lay in the sincerity of contributing to the food banks. As Drew Robertson affirmed, "If a company wants to do something like this, they need to want to have an effect on the charities' bottom line. It's easy to say you care, but you need to have something you feel strongly about and show them how to get the most out of these events. We encouraged them to speak because it had so much more impact coming from them. Lots don't want to, but it makes a huge difference. This year we had one lady stand up and say if it wasn't for this event and all the donations that were piled up out front there were probably about 40 families that would have gone hungry the next week."[9]

The sense of pride in the success of the event is clear. But the impact of the food bank support is even stronger for the IG staff. Drew summed it up, "Here I am the Investors Group Marketing Manager for Atlantic Canada and for a small portion of the year, I feel like the marketing advisor for the food banks. It makes me feel good to coach them and help them see we were giving more than money."[10]

UNICEF AND IKEA

"The Right to Play" Issue Promotion

Any issue can be part of a cause-marketing issue promotion with the right fit between corporate partner and nonprofit representing the cause. Raising awareness about the right to play combined with a product sale is a multilayered cause-marketing issue promotion initiative. The relationship began with IKEA working with UNICEF to improve child protection and education, then developed into sales of the UNICEF greeting cards and finally merged with a cause-marketing piece. Many cause-marketing initiatives are built out of long-term relationships.

Background and Alignment

UNICEF is committed to the advancement and support of children around the world. Through their health, education, equality, and protection programs, they aim to support the advancement of humanity. A major initiative for the international organization is giving every child the right to playtime in a safe environment. To play is not a bonus for children but a fundamental right, enshrined in the 1989 Convention on the Rights of the Child that states, "Every child has the right to play time in a safe environment."[11]

The IKEA group is the biggest group of franchisees, operating over 100 IKEA stores globally. They have been a UNICEF supporter since the mid-1990s. IKEA supports UNICEF in the belief that every child has the right to playtime in a safe environment, something that millions of children around the world are deprived of because of war, disease, and exploitation, including childhood labor.

Initial Alliance: Out of Challenges Comes Good

In 1994, a TV documentary, "Mattan," about the carpet production in Pakistan, named IKEA as one of many Western companies that buy carpets from the production facilities with "brutal production structure based on the debt slavery and child labour." The IKEA management responded quickly with the statement that they did not know how the rugs were produced, and they asked organizations like UNICEF and Save the Children Sweden to help the company gain better knowledge and understanding about human rights issues.

UNICEF agreed to work with IKEA to help address the child labor issue. This was the beginning of a relationship that would expand and extend into a long-term commitment to UNICEF. Starting from a mission-driven perspective, UNICEF worked closely with the company to help them to address allegations of child labor at manufacturing and sourcing and to develop some policies and procedures. Because the child labor problem was not a problem that would vanish from Pakistan if IKEA pulled out their business operations from the country, a recommended solution was to provide schooling for children in the area where the carpets were being made.

IKEA donated five million SEK in the UNICEF project to provide education for 5,000 local children. IKEA also developed a document called "The IKEA Way of Purchasing Home Furnishing Products" to explain that all IKEA's suppliers have to take care about issues such as working conditions, child labor, environment, and forest.

Integrated Program, Including Cause-Marketing Issue Promotion

UNICEF and IKEA had developed a number of issue promotional pieces on the effects of children and war, child soldiers, the importance of childhood education, and the right to play. A cause-marketing platform was created in 2003 with the development of the IKEA Brum bear, with the proceeds of about $2 do-nated directly to the UNICEF (two euros, or approximately US$2) "Right to Play" project in Angola and Uganda. In the first year, more than 500,000 bears were sold. Each bear carried a message about the right to play.

"This is a really very good example of where the Corporate Social Respon-sibility commitment of a company meshes with UNICEF's," explained Anne-Marie Grey. "We have been able year after year, to develop new integrated ways of raising awareness of UNICEF's work as well as generating resources for our program."[12]

Results

Through the promotion, hundreds of thousands consumers have learned more about UNICEF and their "right to play" program and have directly engaged in supporting that work. IKEA continues to help the company to present its com-mitment to children and human rights issues. The funding has enabled UNICEF to work with the Angolan Education Ministry to set up outreach centers target-ing 1.3 million children who do not attend school and some 80,000 street chil-dren. In Uganda, the support has helped train youth peer educators to teach at-risk adolescents about the dangers posed by HIV/AIDS.

The relationship between UNICEF and IKEA extends beyond "the right to play" initiative. The retail provides ongoing corporate grants to the organization and is a major seller of UNICEF cards. In 2004, IKEA responded to the needs of the tsunami-affected countries by donating some 250,000 much-needed quilts and bedsheets valued at more than US$813,000 to UNICEF in Indonesia and Sri Lanka.

UNICEF and Corporate Cause Programs

The mission, values, and alignment match is critical to every cause-marketing arrangement UNICEF does. UNICEF is very careful with its brand and credi-bility, and the international organization has established guidelines for their na-tional committee that outline how they will work with the corporate sector. They also use an independent third-party consulting firm to help screen companies.

An overarching principle for any cause-marketing relationship is that it has to be tied to the organization's mission. When done right, the programs can get in-formation out to new audiences. "When we can tie a corporate promotion to our mission and advocacy it's an opportunity to touch people we wouldn't nor-mally be able to reach to make them aware of our work and key issues. It also allows companies, consumers, shareholders feel real connection with work we do,"[13] says Anne-Marie Grey of UNICEF. The organization is committed to making the relationship beneficial for the businesses, and they work closely with every partner to assist with leveraging all programs.

KaBOOM! and Stride Rite

Promoting Children's Right to Play

Launched in late 2004, this multilayered promotional partnership features an in-store component and out-of-store playground build, all focused on promoting the issue of fun, safe play spaces for children.

Stride Rite and KaBOOM! combined forces to raise awareness and public support for play and playgrounds nationwide. In the first year, the integrated multilevel cause-marketing partnership included three playground builds, a national advertising campaign, Life's Waiting, Let's Go, public relations support, and the launch of a new shoe: the ultimate playground shoe. The Jungle Gym playground shoe collection was designed especially for the program. Stride Rite donates $1 from every sale to support the work of KaBOOM! up to a maximum of $200,000. The shoes are available at Stride Rite stores and have been designed as the ultimate playground shoe for babies, toddlers, and youth. The first playground build took place in Boston, Massachusetts, at the St. Ambrose Family Shelter in the fall of 2004.

The relationship started out as a fully activated, integrated campaign, something that KaBOOM! traditionally expects after several years of working with a partner. The program was rolled out in Stride Rite stores, and company employees participated by wearing buttons and lanyards. In-store advertising displays (see Exhibit 5.1) included a call to action to Stride Rite consumers to get engaged with this cause, either by creating a new play space in their own neighborhood, writing an elected official about the state of play space in their neighborhood, or donating to the KaBOOM! cause to make playgrounds possible in neighborhoods where they are needed most.

CONCLUSION

This form of cause marketing allows for a deeper relationship and more opportunity for broader messaging and active engagement of constituents. Both involve businesses supporting a nonprofit cause by using their communications, marketing, promotional, and operational resources to actively engage in creating public awareness and concern about a social cause and to encourage support by purchasing, donating, or volunteering. Cause promotions touch all realms of cause-marketing relationships from **sales to customer loyalty to branding to social responsibility**, but have a heavier emphasis on the latter two.

EXHIBIT 5.1   IN-STORE POSTER FOR THE KaBOOM! PROMOTION

The "Ultimate Playground Shoe" is here. Introducing the lightweight, flexible and breathable Jungle Gym Collection from Stride Rite. For every pair sold, Stride Rite will donate $1 to help KaBOOM!, a nonprofit organization dedicated to building more playgrounds in play-deprived communities all across the country. For more information on KaBOOM! and to learn how you have the power to change a child's world, log on to www.kaboom.org/striderite.

Playgrounds are waiting. Let's go.

ENDNOTES

1. Interview, Cindy Schneible, January 24, 2005.
2. Ibid.
3. www.cancer.org/docroot/NWS/content/NWS_5_1x_Sampras_Lobs_One_In_for_ACS.asp.
4. Ibid.
5. Ibid.
6. Interview, Kyle Zimmer, November 4, 2004.
7. Ibid.
8. Interview, Drew Robertson, Investors Group, April 25, 2005.
9. Ibid.
10. Ibid.
11. www.unicef.org.
12. Interview, Anne-Marie Grey, UNICEF, April 5, 2005.
13. Ibid.

CHAPTER 6

Cause-Marketing Programs

This chapter looks at the three forms of cause-marketing programs: cobranded events and programs and public service or social marketing programs. All aim to have a significant impact on people's attitudes and to change or encourage behaviors.

Cobranded events, programs, and public service marketing campaigns are most commonly associated with **branding** and the **corporate social responsibility phase of cause marketing**. These relationships are deeper and broader and traditionally don't involve direct consumer purchases of products or services to generate revenue for the nonprofit. This form of cause marketing is driven through the marketing department working closely with community relations, and often human resources, and the executive suite. The programs are not only used for external branding and reputation building, but as part of the palette of a company's corporate social responsibility. These programs are also used to engage employees and strengthen employee pride and loyalty and build and share skills. Cause program marketing support has more intangible marketing objectives such as a focus on market positioning, building reputation or stakeholder relationships, and differentiating or branding the company tied to a cause issue. Companies derive the most tangible marketing benefits if the cause fits its core markets, goods, and services.

Nonprofit causes receive direct financial contributions (sometimes referred to as gift-based cause marketing), awareness creation of their organization and cause through their corporate partner's marketing support, and additional human power from corporate employees.

COBRANDED EVENTS

In cause-marketing events, companies engage in providing promotional communications, marketing, and operational support for a nonprofit organization's event. Cause-marketing events are designed to involve individuals in participating in a walk, run, bike, or other activity that raises revenue, creates awareness, and connects people on an emotional, social, and personal level with the cause. Cause-marketing events provide an avenue for direct employee involvement and put a company's values in action. Unlike straight sponsorship, cause-marketing program support has the company taking an active role as a partner promoting not only the event or program, but also the cause itself.

How Does It Work?

- Once confirmed as a partner, a company will advertise and promote the event and encourage participation. They are committed to advancing the goals of the nonprofit partner and ensuring success.
- Often companies will provide a range of additional support services, including registration information at their retail locations, in-kind product donations, and a connection to their customer and employee base. A legal agreement is recommended.
- Most events actively engage company employees as volunteers.
- Usually a donation is made by the company, but the real value comes from the promotion, awareness raising, and additional resources that their involvement provides.
- In exchange, the nonprofit usually provides a range of benefits, including on-site promotion, product distribution, and extensive publicity coverage.

What Are the Benefits?

- Cause-marketing relationships provide a whole host of promotional and other resources that a nonprofit could never afford to purchase or secure without the corporate partner.
- Revenue generated by the event has the chance to be higher with corporate cause partner's involvement.
- Cause promotional events can be local, regional, or national and can support any type of nonprofit cause.
- These relationships allow for active involvement by employees and other company stakeholders.

What Are the Challenges?

- National organized events with local execution can be a challenge. They require local group or chapter buy-in and local delivery on recognition commitments.
- Not all local chapters will receive the same benefits, as some companies will not have local offices that can work with each individual chapter affiliate.

- The program must provide appropriate recognition while ensuring that the nonprofit organization name and message doesn't get lost.

- One of the biggest challenges in most cause-marketing arrangements, especially events, is pricing. How you do put a dollar value on their connection to the organization while recognizing the nonmonetary support provided?

CANADIAN BREAST CANCER FOUNDATION AND CIBC

Cobrand event: "Canadian Breast Cancer Foundation CIBC Run for the Cure"
This is Canada's largest single-day fundraising event dedicated to breast cancer research, education, and awareness. The Canadian Breast Cancer Foundation CIBC Run for the Cure is also one of Canada's most prominent cause-marketing arrangements. The Canadian Breast Cancer Foundation actively pursues cause marketing and has over 70 cause relationships.

Background and Alignment

The Canadian Breast Cancer Foundation is the leading national organization in Canada dedicated to creating a future without breast cancer. The Foundation works collaboratively to fund, support, and advocate for relevant and innovative research, meaningful education and awareness programs, early diagnosis and effective treatment, and a positive quality of life for those living with breast cancer. The organization's signature fundraising initiative is the "Canadian Breast Cancer Foundation CIBC Run for the Cure," a one-day event started in 1992 by a small group of volunteers to raise awareness and funds for the cause (see Exhibit 6.1).

CIBC is a leading North American financial institution comprising three strategic business lines: CIBC Retail Markets, CIBC Wealth Management, and CIBC World Markets. CIBC provides financial services to more than nine million clients, including retail and small business banking clients as well as corporate and investment banking clients and is one of Canada's largest banks.[1]

CIBC joined forces with the Foundation in 1997 to become title sponsor of the "Run for the Cure" event and since that time has actively grown its involvement. Like a number of prominent cause-marketing initiatives, its initial support was driven by an employee who was involved in the run. Combined with their employee demographic—more than 75% of their employees were women—the event lent itself well to CIBC supporting a cause that most directly affects women and their families.

EXHIBIT 6.1   CIBC Run for the Cure Poster

"CIBC supports causes that are important to its staff and customers. Breast cancer is one such cause and there is huge support at all levels of the Bank," says Mark Hierlihy, National Director of Development for the Foundation. "Over 10,000 of their employees participate in the Run every year, in addition to the cash and in-kind support of the bank. In the last couple of years, CIBC has undergone a rebranding strategy and they are now using a tag line "For What Matters." "This is meaningful to them," explains Mark Hierlihy. "They are a philanthropic company that understands that the Run helps strengthen their brand, but they do it for the right reasons as well."[2]

Being marketing driven has meant that CIBC continually analyzes its involvement to make sure the cause is aligned and helps achieve its goals. In 2004, CIBC undertook a study that backed up all the intuitive reasons for supporting the event. The research showed breast cancer is a leading health issue in lives of Canadians. The mandate of the Canadian Breast Cancer Foundation fits with CIBC's charitable interests and the demographic of its employee group perfectly.

Major Employee Involvement and More

The relationship is deep and has come to mean much more than direct corporate financial support for the Run event. Across Canada, CIBC employees have adopted breast cancer as one of their most strongly supported causes. In 2004, Team CIBC had more than 10,500 participants in the event and raised over $2.5 million in support of breast cancer research.

Throughout the year, the employees are actively engaged in fundraising for the Foundation through a number of cause-marketing product sales. CIBC employees sell the Circle of Strength necklaces, and in 2004 they sold over 20,000 bags of pink jelly beans, all to benefit the cause. In 2003, CIBC also encouraged use of its new EMT (electronic mail transfer) system by making a $1.50 donation to the CBCF for every transaction made for a three-month period.[3]

Cause-marketing support isn't measured by the Canadian Breast Cancer Foundation only in dollars. The additional support CIBC provides the Foundation is generous and helps create awareness. The bank provides major advertising support for the event through print and television media.

A Strong and Evolving Relationship

After almost 10 years, the relationship has expanded and evolved. The event, growing over the past several years at a rate of 30% annually, is providing both partners with greater benefits than when they started working together. As a result, support has continued to grow from CIBC, and the two organizations have developed strong planning, marketing, and communication links.

CIBC has made a major investment in the event and has a strong interest in many aspects of the Foundation's work. The two organizations have a very detailed contract that outlines the relationship, how both brands are used, how marketing and creative materials are developed, and the activities around the event, all things carefully negotiated and approved by the Foundation. "We enjoy the collaborative relationship," states Mark.

One of the challenges for any cobranded event or program is the potential for the nonprofit to get lost. There are many people who believe that the event is an initiative of CIBC even though it is the Foundation's signature special event. The event is called the Canadian Breast Cancer Foundation CIBC Run for the Cure and the Foundation name is there to ensure that both the Foundation's and sponsor names are recognized. This title helps to tie the event back to the founding organization, which in the end executes the intended outcome of the event—support for a breast cancer cure. The Bank knows it's important for the public to know where the money goes. This "end state" is what matters to both partners.

Elements of Success

The key elements of success lie in having clear expectations, clear deliverables, and then a plan for implementing them. Mark is a firm believer in the phrase "promise what you can deliver and deliver more than you promise." This means having solid processes and strong planning in place to make sure the work gets done on time and on budget.

Strong personal relationships have been critical to the success of this long-term cause relationship. Central to this is good communications. Any challenges have almost always come from miscommunications. In any good cause relationship, you can't drop the ball on communications.

NATIONAL KIDNEY FOUNDATION AND NOVARTIS

U.S. Transplant Games

A long-term cause marketing promotional event has helped change the way people view and understand transplants. After the event there is a marked difference in organ donation referrals.

Background and Alignment

The National Kidney Foundation's mission is to prevent kidney and urinary tract disease, improve the health and well-being of individuals and families affected by these diseases, and increase the availability of all organs for transplantation. Novartis is focused on enhancing the quality of life for transplant recipients through the development and introduction of novel drugs and technologies. As the leader in the field of transplants, Novartis is also committed to educating the public about the urgent need for organ donation and the lifesaving potential of organ transplantation.[4] The two organizations have developed what they describe as a best-in-class relationship to support shared objectives such as organ transplant education and awareness.

Cause Event Relationship

In 1990, Sandoz (Sandoz merged with Ciba in December 1996 to form Novartis Pharmaceuticals Corporation) approached the National Kidney Foundation with the idea of collaborating on an event to promote transplant awareness. Recognizing the potential for messaging around organ transplants and celebrating both recipients and donors, the Foundation agreed. Novartis Pharmaceuticals Corporation has been the primary cause partner since the U.S. Transplant Games were founded in 1990.

The U.S. Transplant Games is a biennial, four-day athletic competition among recipients of organ transplants. Competition in the U.S. Transplant Games is open to anyone who has received a lifesaving solid organ transplant—heart, liver, kidney, lung, and pancreas. Bone marrow recipients are also eligible to participate. As much as the Games are an athletic event that calls attention to the success of organ and tissue transplantation, it is also a celebration of life among recipients, their families, and friends. Novartis supports the event by providing a financial contribution up front to help with its operations, marketing support, and providing local employees as volunteers.

Goals and Objectives

The National Kidney Foundation and Novartis worked closely on identifying objectives for the event, which are

- To demonstrate to the public the collective and individual successes of the life-restoring therapy of organ transplantation
- To use the mass media to promote the success of organ donation and transplantation and to call attention to the need for organ donation through events and support activity before, during, and after the event

- To contribute to the successful rehabilitation of the nation's transplant patient community

- To involve the entire transplant community—including physicians, allied professionals, patients, donor families, and related organizations—in a collaborative effort for the benefit of organ donation

- To provide an opportunity for these goals to be achieved locally by NKF affiliates and other participating organizations[5]

Program Execution

The event provides the National Kidney Foundation with other types of education tools. A video of the event is produced and put in the hands of the transplant community. A very powerful communications and public education vehicle, it brings the philosophy and excitement of the transplant games to a broader audience. People can see participants of all ages swimming, running, and biking, and it helps to demonstrate the benefits of transplants and organ contributions.

The event also produces a calendar that features profiles on athletes and information on transplants and making organ donations. The piece is distributed widely by both partners, including to doctors' offices and hospitals.

This event is not about selling a product, but about helping the transplant community and communicating the value and importance of transplants. Novartis is prominently featured on all promotional and educational material. While getting out in front of key decision makers is a benefit, it was not the core objective of the cause-marketing relationship.

Results

The event has achieved the goals established and has provided strong outcomes for each partner. The Kidney Foundation has used the games to develop highly effective communications tools that are widely distributed, significantly increasing their education message and outreach goals. Statistics show that after the event, there is a marked difference in organ donation referrals and awareness of the need and importance.[6]

Novartis has developed a strong positioning as a major supporter of organ transplants. When Novartis went out to the transplant community and asked what they thought the company was doing in the community, the number one response was the Transplant Games. That's important among their key target audiences: patients and physicians. Although there is altruism in the arrangement, Novartis still has a responsibility to find value for its shareholders.

Employee engagement and pride is another spin-off benefit not originally anticipated. "I can't imagine walking away from the games," states Barbara

Tombros, Director, Alliance Development at Novartis. "It gives our employees such a sense of pride and that's important."

Elements of Success

Perhaps equally important is the impact the cause promotional event has had on solidifying their relationship. "We have a phenomenal relationship with NKF. I can pick up the phone anytime and we can make decisions that don't take 17 months to do. Kidney is also related to diabetes and hypertension, which has allowed us to extend our relationship into other therapeutic areas."[7] says Barbara Tombros.

The relationship is one of mutual respect, trust, and open communications that extend to contacting each other to exchange information or looking at ways to work together to get out important messages relating to kidney disease. "It's always about the core message—how we can work together to get out information, to create awareness and even change behaviour, how we can help the patient," states Gigi Politoski, Vice President of Programs for the National Kidney Foundation. "That integrity is important to us both. Each year, the Foundation develops plans for the year and outside support is sought. But because of the strength of our relationship any National Kidney Foundation program relating to transplants is presented to Novartis first."[8]

COBRANDED PROGRAMS

How Does It Work?

- Cause cobranded programs can support a wide range of causes and benefit national, regional, or local nonprofit organizations.

- Most programs provide a straight donation (gift-based marketing) and are not geared to generating support through product or promotional sales.

- Either partner can initiate the idea for a cause cobranded program.

- The program's name is tied directly to the corporate partner. They use the program to promote the company or brand and as a marketing/communications tool. The program has very specific business goals, often not to drive overt sales but to position the company in the community to demonstrate values and build reputation and brand of the company.

- There is usually a time limit on the naming of the program.

- Sophisticated companies and nonprofit organizations will have an evaluation of the program that will analyze what worked and what didn't work.

What Are the Benefits?

- Nonprofit organizations generate revenue, increase awareness for their organization, and achieve key mission goals.

- Nonprofit gets support beyond just dollars. Corporate partners bring valuable expertise and support that significantly extends the benefits of the cause-marketing relationship. Unlike straight sponsorship, cause-marketing program support has the company taking an active role as a partner promoting the program and the cause itself.

- The focus of the cobranded program is on the corporation working to help the cause partner achieve its mission while achieving their own branding and reputation goals with a longer-term goal of increased business.

What Are the Challenges?

- Programs must be sincere and transparent.

- Nonprofit organization must make sure that the financial support more than covers the costs of the cause-marketing execution.

- The connection between the company and program must be consistent with the cause and their values if it is to be well received.

- A formal agreement is highly recommended to ensure clarity around roles, responsibilities, expectations, and execution.

LONDON REGIONAL CHILDREN'S MUSEUM AND 3M, CANADA

3M Science in Your World Gallery

This cobranded science gallery was a perfect fit between the museum's mission and vision and 3M's desire to achieve profile, engage employees, and build their brand and reputation tied to science and innovation.

Background

The London Regional Children's Museum was Canada's first-ever children's museum. Established in 1975, it attracts over 100,000 visitors annually. The Museum decided to add a science gallery focused on infants to 12-year-olds with an emphasis on providing hands-on science experiences and demonstrating to young children that science is all around us.

3M Canada's head office is based in London, Ontario. Known for products and ideas that solve problems and make lives easier, 3M has more than 55,000 products, 30-plus core technologies, and leadership in major markets served worldwide. Strongly science based, 3M develops ingenious solutions to meet varying needs and is best known for its 3M brands—Scotch, Post-it, Scotchgard, Thinsulate, Scotch-Brite, Filtrete, Command, and Nexcare.

Both partners believed that good science education for young people was important. Jointly, the museum and 3M were committed to developing a gallery that made science interesting, relevant, and fun and that would inspire young people to get involved in science.

Alignment

London Regional Children's Museum is a nonprofit that must raise financial support in the community to undertake capital work. Although the museum's staff has strong expertise in museum gallery development and knowledge of how to translate concepts into interactive and educational exhibits, they benefited from the science knowledge of the 3M staff.

3M is not a direct retailer, although their products are well known. The company was looking for a longer-term engagement that would assist with specific marketing and business objectives. With London as their Canadian head office, they are a major local employer and an important corporate citizen. Partnering on the science gallery was seen as a way to achieve several softer marketing goals: raising their profile in the community, positioning the company as tied to science and education, demonstrating the company innovates through science, and building their brand from the inside out through employee engagement. Another objective was seen to be building a workforce of the future. Good science education supported by 3M could inspire young people to study science and potentially be future 3M employees.

Program Execution

As the largest project at the time in the museum's history, the kind of financial resources were central to the development and construction of the science gallery. But equally important was the expertise and knowledge the 3M scientists brought to the planning and concept development of the gallery. They worked closely with museum staff to look at learning objectives and then identified science concepts and accompanying activities and experiments that would explain and enhance the various gallery areas. The 3M scientists continue to be involved by presenting "really cool" science demonstrations and by participating in "Meet a Scientist" Day.

The gallery was cobranded with the 3M name tied directly to the gallery inside the London Regional Children's Museum. In addition, all the advertising featured 3M as the copresenter of the gallery. Their name and logo appeared on all the letterhead, promotional material, and exterior and interior signage at the museum.

"We were lucky to have each other," states current Executive Director, Tammy Adkins, "As partners it was a perfect fit between our mission and vision and their desire to achieve profile, engage employees and build their brand tied to science and innovation. What they did for the museum was so much more than their financial support. Their staff expertise propelled the museum and the exhibit's development."[9]

Results and Key Learning

3M's name and connection to science is seen by over 100,000 targeted visitors annually. Although their direct involvement has decreased, their employees' connection to the museum as both visitors and volunteers built pride in the company and a sense of ownership in "their" museum.

The project highlighted the importance to this regionally based museum of having clear guidelines on how to work with corporate partners. "It was really important to do our homework and make sure that their objectives fit ours. We must maintain the integrity of Children's Museum and a corporate collaborative partnership needs to help us achieve our objectives, fit with our mission and our vision of the institution. In this case it really did,"[10] says Tammy Adkins. Although the museum retained creative and content control, their expertise and ideas were critical in the success of the gallery. 3M shared the same commitment to making it truly an exceptional educational experience and ensuring that the information was well presented and exciting.

The museum's fund development committee played a major role in the development and execution of the corporate collaboration. The committee was charged with prospecting, cultivating, and stewarding partners. Before the company was approached, a lot of research went into finding out 3M's marketing objectives and determining if there could be a fit.

The London Children's Museum subsequently undertook another smaller cause-oriented collaboration with local corporate partners. Recently, they developed a new gallery focused on introducing children to where they live. The gallery's design incorporates a streetscape and a number of community partners, including a credit union, grocery store, car dealership, and McDonald's restaurant, have supported the work. As the gallery is meant to represent a city street, it was appropriate to have that kind of signage within the space, and for the museum, the support received from the corporate partners was critical to being able to develop the gallery. The museum is concerned to make sure the galleries don't look commercial, and the community's response has been largely supportive, recognizing that good quality learning experiences benefit from support by the corporate community.

BURNET, DUCKWORTH & PALMER LLP AND THE EPCOR CENTRE FOR THE PERFORMING ARTS COBRAND PROGRAM: BD&P WORLD MUSIC SERIES

Recognized with a national award from Business and the Arts in Canada and a local award from the Association of Fundraising Professionals this co-branded program has not only helped to engage lawyers and clients and build the brand and reputation of this law firm, but it has also helped develop an audience for the program and an appreciation for the arts in the city.

Background and Alignment

Burnet, Duckworth & Palmer LLP is a law firm known as a community leader in combining its marketing and charitable budgets to realize the firm's values and build its business and reputation as leaders in enhancing the local community. With 125 lawyers and 175 support staff, BD&P is Calgary's largest independent, single-office law firm.

EPCOR Centre for the Performing Arts is located in the heart of downtown Calgary. The Centre attracts almost 300,000 people yearly at 1,700-plus performances and events, including live theatre, dance, spoken word and readings, children's events, arts education activities, and a range of music from symphonic concerts to jazz, folk, blues, world, and rock.

The BD&P World Music Series was launched over five years ago, and the law firm has been the cobranded named supporter since the beginning (Exhibit 6.2). The music series aims to ignite imaginations and inspire wonder as it explores the rhythms, traditions, melodies, and movements that make up the rich cultural mosaic of the globe.

When the World Music Series at the EPCOR Centre for the Performing Arts was first launched in 2001, it was a BD&P lawyer, a board member at the Centre that brought it forward for support from the law firm. "Most of our community involvement is driven by our lawyers' own commitments," said Jamie Niessen, Marketing Director for BD&P. But the series, an innovative, cutting edge presentation of music from around the world, was a perfect alignment. "When we

EXHIBIT 6.2   POSTER FOR THE MUSIC SERIES

did research and heard the EPCOR Centre describe the series with words like innovative, cutting edge, we were sold. Those are the words we use to describe ourselves: contemporary, innovative and creative."[11]

Support Beyond Just Financial

The EPCOR Centre works with a number of companies in the community, many of whom contribute critical financial support. "BD&P has provided a uniquely integrated, multi-level support that includes a direct financial contribution, purchase of a significant number of tickets and additional dollars for outdoor advertising. In 2004, the firm had 828 guests attend the 6 concerts," says

Laurie Leier, EPCOR Centre's Manager, Resource Development. "Their on-going commitment of financial, promotional and audience development resources has grown the attendance and audience awareness for the series."[12]

Results and Learning

BD&P undertook a client survey to gauge response to their involvement in the innovative music series. The astonishing 44% return rate, more than 10 times a survey average response, showed there was nearly universal praise for the quality and selection of the concerts and BD&P's involvement in making them happen. Many clients took the time to write personal notes thanking the law firm for its support and indicated that they had purchased additional tickets to other concerts after having attending as a guest of one of the firm's lawyers—something they said they would not have done without BD&P's exposure to the series in the first place.

The EPCOR Centre is very conscious about making the program work for the law firm. "We are very thoughtful about recognizing their involvement and making sure they get mentioned throughout the Series presentations. Out of respect for the relationship, we also nominated them for the AFP Generosity of Spirit Award and the Business and the Arts Award," says Laurie Leier of the EPCOR Centre.

The firm also understands the value of communicating their community support and puts an emphasis on promoting the organizations that receive BD&P's signature investments. Another example of their cause-marketing support is their campaign featuring their involvement with Habitat for Humanity. Over the past several years, the firm's marketing campaigns have included a bus wrap and a single billboard campaign, prominently located in the downtown core. The impact has raised the level of the BD&P brand and its reputation in the community. "When one of our staff members was sitting in his backyard and his neighbor yelled over the fence, "Why aren't you out building a house for Habitat," we knew our work and reputation for community support was getting out," said Jamie Niessen, BD&P's Director of Marketing. "And then when the mayor of Calgary said to one of our lawyers during the AFP awards ceremony, 'What is your next billboard campaign?' we thought, wow, unaided, unprompted recall of a message in a room full of our business colleagues. *And*, they knew exactly what he was talking about."[13] BD&P is proud of its help in raising Habitat's recognition in the community. "I'm told they get calls saying we want to be like BD&P," says Niessen with pride.

The music series is entering its fifth year in 2005 and continues to grow both in terms of audience and the level of music presentations. Has their support made a difference? "Without a doubt,"[14] says Lehr. BD&P has received broad recognition and awareness of its work in the community. Has it helped build business? Feedback shows the firm has gained a reputation as leaders in community support. Clients say they and their staff are proud to use a firm so active in the community.

SOCIAL (PUBLIC SERVICE) MARKETING PROGRAMS

Social marketing is emerging as the way to gain a marketing edge while supporting a cause. Leading nonprofits are building social marketing platforms as a way to engage corporations in their organization at a higher and deeper level. Social marketing uses marketing principles and techniques to foster behavior change in a targeted audience, achieving societal goals while building brand equity and brand preference benefits and demonstrating a company's values. It can often involve a multiple level of partners including other nonprofits, government agencies, and several corporations, all working for a common goal of impacting behavior and being a real catalyst for change.

How Does It Work?

- Social marketing campaigns can be developed for many issues where behavioral change will improve society. Health issues, such as heart disease and injury prevention, emergency preparedness, environmental issues like water conservation, or broad community issues like getting out the vote are examples of the range of social marketing campaigns that can be undertaken.

- Social marketing campaigns can be national, regional, or local in scope.

- Either a company or nonprofit can initiate a social marketing campaign.

- Determine a clear campaign purpose, message, and target audience and prepare internally. Build the marketing and execution plan and look for partners.

- Once cause partners are secured, a formal agreement must be drawn up to outline the terms of the program, roles, responsibilities, use of brand elements, etc.

- Execution requires all partners' active engagement. Significant and genuine commitment is needed to be effective, be sincere, and have impact.

What Are the Benefits?

- Social marketing campaigns are longer, deeper relationships where meaningful change can occur.

- These relationships allow for active involvement by employees and other company stakeholders.

- Social marketing campaigns can provide superior marketing benefits for all partners. If done right, they can build a company's brand equity and increase brand preference with the targeted audience, and a nonprofit can build profile and relevance in the community.

- With proper alignment of cause and company, social marketing can result in either people needing the product or in saving the company money.

- Social marketing campaigns do the greatest good for the cause and the company.

What Are the Challenges?

- There must be good alignment between the cause and the company, where the associative links are clear.

- Desired outcomes are rarely immediate. It might take years to see the real results.

- These deeper, longer relationships require active involvement from all partners to have the greatest impact. All the partners must be prepared to commit for a long period and put adequate resources behind the cause to be effective.

- Not all nonprofits can implement social marketing campaigns. Food banks, for example, can't change the behavior of those needing their service.

BOYS AND GIRLS CLUBS OF AMERICA AND CREST

Crest Healthy Smiles

The Boys and Girls Clubs of America collaborated for a social marketing campaign, "Crest Healthy Smiles," with Crest toothpaste. The multimillion-dollar program focused on improving the oral health of 10 million children by 2010. As part of this alliance, the Boys and Girls Clubs have become "Cavity-Free Zones" where good oral health is a priority.

Background and Alignment

"A silent epidemic of oral disease in America" was the way the surgeon general, Dr. David Satcher, described what he saw as a critical concern, especially among low-income children. The report catalogued the concerns—poor children were more likely to have cavities than other children, miss school because of dental-related diseases, and have a higher risk of gum disease. The surgeon general challenged the private and public sectors to work together to end this disparity. Inspired and driven by the report, Crest, in collaboration with the Boys and Girls Clubs of America developed a social marketing campaign to create a "cavity free-zone" in each of their 3,400 clubs. The multifaceted program provides oral health education, tools, and access to underserved families.

Crest had the commitment, resources, and reputation. Boys and Girls Clubs of America (BGCA) were serving the group that was targeted in the report. As the "The Positive Place for Kids," BGCA is a national network of neighborhood-based facilities that serve over four million young people principally from disadvantaged backgrounds. Boys and Girls Clubs emphasize character, leadership and career development, and health and life skills.

Program Execution and Results

Crest has donated millions of tubes of toothpaste and toothbrushes to club members. Donations are made on an ongoing basis. Crest also funded construction of six full-service in-club dental clinics where volunteer dental professionals from the community will provide affordable care to club members and their families. A major print and television advertising campaign, above and beyond the support to Boys and Girls Clubs, raises public awareness of oral health issues and highlights Crest's role in combating it.

By early 2004, consumers who were aware of the program showed an increase in intention to purchase Crest toothpaste. Research by Crest demonstrated an incremental increase in sales through a promotion with Walgreens, in which in-store signage featured Crest's work with the Boys and Girls Clubs.

Longer-Term Benefits

Social marketing campaigns are longer-term efforts that are aimed at changing behaviors rather than focused on immediate sales. Most social marketing cam-

BOYS AND GIRLS CLUBS OF AMERICA, DEPARTMENT OF HEALTH AND HUMAN SERVICES, THE COCA-COLA COMPANY AND KRAFT FOODS: "TRIPLE PLAY"

Launched in early 2005, this social marketing program focuses on encouraging healthy lifestyles for young people and encouraging them to make informed decisions about their physical, mental, and social well-being. It's an excellent example of multisector partners coming together around a cause.

paigns will change behaviors that eventually can turn into increased sales. For the nonprofit, these initiatives are directly focused on assisting groups in need.

Background and Alignment

An epidemic of obesity and related health and lifestyle issues is a major crisis in North America. The Boys and Girls Clubs of America, The Coca-Cola Company, and Kraft Foods developed, in collaboration with the U.S. Department of Health and Human Services, an initiative to empower young people to make informed decisions about their physical, mental, and social well-being through a program offered at Boys and Girls Clubs.

Program Emphasis

"Triple Play" is a five-year $15 million commitment from The Coca-Cola Company and Kraft Foods and is the largest health and wellness endeavor undertaken by the Boys and Girls Clubs of America and the first of its kind developed in collaboration with the U.S. Department of Health and Human Services (DHHS).

The program encompasses three components:

1. Mind—Developing knowledge to acquire healthy habits, such as making smart food choices, understanding appropriate portion sizes, and creating fun and healthy meals
2. Body—Becoming more physically active through daily fitness and fun, including activities to get kids active and moving
3. Soul—Strengthening character and reinforcing positive behavior with social recreation activities designed to improve confidence and develop interpersonal skills[15]

Every Boys and Girls Club is able to participate in Triple Play. Staff of BGCA received training and information about the program. The organization's president, Roxanne Spillett, stated their interest in the campaign, "By addressing mind, body and soul, we're taking an integrated approach to helping young people help themselves. Learning to eat right, keep fit and behave respectfully creates a holistic approach to healthy living that will benefit youth throughout their lives."[16]

Evaluation and Measures

Triple Play has established a number of measures, including an increase in the amount of time each day Boys and Girls Club members engage in physical activities and their enhanced awareness of healthy habits relating to fitness, nutrition, and self-esteem.

WWW.BULLYING.ORG AND FAMILY CHANNEL (CANADA)

A growing form of cause marketing relationships is partnerships with media companies. This is part of a larger trend that sees nonprofits understand the importance of marketing beyond traditional nonprofit forms such as newsletters and brochures as a way to reach their target audience.

Background and Alignment:

Established in 2000, nonprofit organization www.bullying.org is a social marketing campaign dedicated to changing attitudes and behaviors toward bullying. Using the World Wide Web as its main connection vehicle, the site allows people, especially youth, to connect in a safe, moderated online community where they can share their stories, poetry, drawings, music, animations, and videos.

A team of volunteer reviewers moderates replies and the original submissions. Visitors to the Web site can also use the worlds' largest online database of helpful resources on www.bullying.org to find information about bullying. www.bullying.org is now one of the world's top-rated Web sites about bullying. www.bullying.org has become the most visited Web site in the world on the topic of bullying with nearly ¾ of a million hits in one month alone.

Bullying.org Canada developed a partnership with Family Channel, a Canadian television programmer that is received in nearly five million homes throughout Canada.

Program Goals and Focus:

Together www.bullying.org and Family Channel partnered to create a very effective national anti-bullying "Take the Pledge" campaign.

Results:

The partners created and distributed thousands of Pledge posters to schools across Canada. A Public Service Announcements (PSAs) video was developed and run on Family Channel as well as on the www.bullying.org Web site. In May 2005, the Canadian Public Relations Society recognized this campaign with an "Award of Excellence." In November 2005, a DVD with the video PSAs and an accompanying Teachers' Guide was mailed to over 10,000 schools across Canada thanks to the support of Family Channel.

Background

American Cancer Society, a leader in cause marketing, developed a series of social marketing campaigns around the theme "Great American" and have focused

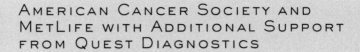

AMERICAN CANCER SOCIETY AND
METLIFE WITH ADDITIONAL SUPPORT
FROM QUEST DIAGNOSTICS

Great American Health Check

The third piece in the American Cancer Society's social marketing platforms (Great American Weigh In, Great American Smokeout), the Great American Health Check is a campaign to encourage testing for cancer. Early prevention is critical to the fight against cancer.

it on three factors that can impact cancer—a person's weight, whether a person smokes, and if a person gets regular testing for cancer. Each campaign is geared to impacting and changing behavior to help achieve its mission: eliminating cancer as a major health problem by saving lives, diminishing suffering, and preventing cancer through research, education, advocacy, and service.

Each of its social marketing platforms is done through an alliance with a major corporation. The Great American Health Check has two key partners. MetLife is the lead partner and is a leading provider of insurance and other financial services, serving approximately 13 million households and 37 million employees and family members through their plans. Additional support is provided by leading diagnostic testing provider, Quest Diagnostics Inc.

Program Goals and Focus

Great American Health Check is a campaign to raise national awareness about the importance of early detection in the fight against cancer and change behavior. The initiative involves a major public outreach campaign to encourage Americans to get tested for the disease. An online assessment tool (www.cancer.org/healthcheck) is designed to be easy, confidential, and help individuals understand which early detection tests they should take to find cancer early when treatment is more likely to be successful or to render it preventable altogether.

According to American Cancer Society statistics, fewer than 50% of all adults get all the early detection tests they recommend. Cancers detected earlier by following the Society's guidelines account for nearly half of all new cancer cases. Survival rates have improved over the past two decades due in large measure to early detection testing.

Corporate Alignment and Mutual Benefits

The National Institutes of Health estimated the annual costs of cancer to be nearly $190 billion in the United States. As the leading provider of employee benefits, MetLife is committed to fighting cancer to reduce the financial burden of cancer-related illnesses to its customers by preserving good health.

Diagnostic testing plays an important role in the campaign, which will include posters and patient literature both in physicians' offices and in the nearly 2,000 Quest Diagnostics Patient Service Centers.

When the cause needs the product or helps save money, it highlights the superior marketing power of social marketing alliances. In this case, both companies can see dramatic benefits from using marketing dollars that are good for the American Cancer Society and good for them.

Conclusions

Cobranded events and programs and social marketing programs aim to have a significant impact on people's attitudes and to change or encourage behaviors. These cause-marketing initiatives are most commonly associated with **branding** and the **corporate social responsibility phase of cause marketing**.

The relationships are deeper and broader and not focused on direct consumer purchases of products or services to generate revenue for the nonprofit or the company. Financial contributions are made to the charity for the association and alignment with the cause and to help implement specific initiatives. Cause program marketing support has more intangible marketing objectives such as a focus on market positioning, building a reputation, or stakeholder relationships and differentiating or branding the company tied to a cause issue and demonstrating a company's values. Companies can derive tangible marketing benefits if the cause fits its core markets, goods, and services and encourages uses of the product as part of the program or behavioral change.

Endnotes

1. www.cibc.com/ca/inside-cibc/quick-facts.html.
2. Interview, Mark Hierlihy, July 29, 2005.
3. IEG Sponsorship Report, December 22, 2003.
4. www.kidney.org.
5. Ibid.
6. Interview, Gigi Politoski, Elizabeth Hackbarth, NKF, and Barbara Tombros, Novartis, January 29, 2005.
7. Ibid.
8. Ibid.
9. Interview, Tammy Adkins, London Children's Museum, April 13, 2005.
10. Ibid.
11. Interview, Jamie Niessen, BD&P LLP, August. 10, 2005
12. Interview, Laurie Leier, September 12, 2005.
13. Interview, Jamie Niessen, August 10, 2005.
14. Interview, Laurie Leier, September 12, 2005.
15. Press release, Boys and Girls Clubs of America, April 28, 2004.
16. Ibid.

PART III

Getting It Right:
Framework for Success

Any new movement has to "Get It Right" or it will quickly disappear. There are three very simple but essential components to achieving success in cause marketing. First, it must clearly define its goals; second, design the means to deliver them; and finally, develop criteria to measure success.

With more corporations entering the cause-marketing arena and an increase in dollars being spent, nonprofit organizations are recognizing the potential to generate dollars, enhance their mission, generate awareness, promote issues, and change behaviors. Tied to this is an increase in competition in the field and an environment where nonprofits have to raise their standard of expertise and delivery.

Cause marketing doesn't require grandiose plans or a big bureaucratic structure to make them work, and small beginnings can turn into significant programs. But getting a cause-marketing relationship right takes thought and a strategic approach. As the field matures and both sides become more savvy and experienced, sophistication and knowledge are needed to build cause-marketing programs.

Nonprofits don't have to be well-known or large organizations to get into the field. As we've seen from the cause initiatives presented, cause marketing involves every size of organization from small, local organizations to large, national organizations with extensive memberships and affiliated local offices. They can be developed in any charitable sector from health to environment to education to social services to the arts—and everything in between. Whatever the size or type, setting up cause-marketing programs involves key steps. Unlike traditional philanthropic relationships, cause-marketing arrangements involve an exchange of value combined with philanthropic intent. This takes a different approach and strategy to implement and get right.

Nonprofits wanting to proactively build cause programs need to know their mandate and goals, evaluate their assets, and understand how to position themselves to represent their cause. In the cause-marketing field, corporations want partners who can align with their goals, have the capacity to undertake cause programs, bring tangible assets, and are ready to collaborate. Whether nonprofits are actively seeking cause-marketing relations or reacting to approaches, they must be innovative, flexible, and most importantly marketing and results oriented. They must understand how cause-marketing programs work. Presented in this section of the book are the seven components of a cause-marketing framework. The seven C's: cause readiness, collaborative fit, combining assets, creating value, executing the program, communicating values, and achieving corporate and community goals are the foundation of any successful cause-marketing program. Cause collaborations can be designed, structured, nurtured, and maintained in a manner that enables both partners to contribute to solving pressing social problems and to fulfilling important strategic objectives for companies and nonprofits. Knowing and understanding these seven steps will help guide nonprofit organizations through their cause-marketing planning, development, and execution.

The Seven Steps in Building a Successful Cause-Marketing Program

1. **Cause:** Prepare internal readiness by linking organizational goals and assets to position organization, look for associative links, and then prepare internally.

EXHIBIT P.1   CAUSE-MARKETING FRAMEWORK 7 C'S

Achieve cause goals and mission

Implement cause-marketing program

Build cause-marketing program

Create cause-marketing orientation

Achieve cause goals and mission
- Community and corporate outcomes

Implement cause-marketing program
- Communicate
- Execute

Build cause-marketing program
- Create value
- Combine assets
- Collaborate

Create cause-marketing orientation
- Cause

2. **Collaborate:** Seek out an aligned partner and build a strategic collaboration that focuses on what each can bring to the relationship rather than nonprofit need.

3. **Combine Assets:** Combine your assets with your partner and use for maximum benefits.

4. **Create Value:** Determine how you will create value for both partners up front through joint planning. Maximize your value and underpromise and overdeliver.

5. **Execute:** Set up the structure to execute and deliver on commitments, then go the extra mile.

6. **Communicate:** Communicate values, get out key messages to your internal and external audience, and articulate what you both stand for.

7. **Community and Corporate Outcomes:** Cause marketing is about win-win-win for the nonprofit, community, and corporation. Celebrate, evaluate, and build on what has been achieved.

An Overview of "Getting It Right"

The "Getting It Right" framework is presented in three chapters. Chapter 7 looks at **Creating a Cause-Marketing Orientation**. For business, cause marketing is first and foremost about the cause, then the nonprofit organization. Causes are chosen for their alignment with company brands or products that are meaningful to their key constituents and that tie into their marketing and business goals. Nonprofits are chosen for their ability to represent the **cause**, the assets they can bring to a cause-marketing arrangement, and their readiness to be partners in a mutually beneficial relationship. This chapter looks at how to proactively develop a cause-marketing orientation and focus by creating a program that aligns organizational with goals and assets, builds the "10 second elevator message" to succinctly position the organization, and prepares the organization internally with a structure that facilitates cause-marketing collaborations.

Chapter 8, **Building the Cause-Marketing Program**, begins by proactively seeking a strategic **collaboration** where there is partner alignment and the focus is on what each can offer the other, not nonprofit need. The purpose of the cause-marketing arrangement must then be built so that it **combines assets** and **creates value** for both partners. Tying it all together is an agreement that outlines the goals, roles and responsibilities, decision-making process, and structure for the cause-marketing program.

Chapter 9 looks at **Implementing the Cause-Marketing Program**. The success and long-term sustainability and growth of the collaborative cause-marketing alliance is achieved by successfully **executing** the cause alliance. The final piece of partner satisfaction and implementation is **communication**, consistently getting the word out about the program and the collaborative alliance, and demonstrating the values inherent in a cause program. Communications must move from the inside out and be consistent, clear, and regular. The final step in the cause-marketing framework is **achieve cause goals and mission. Community and corporate outcomes** that benefit the community, nonprofit organization, and the corporation are the final goal of any cause-marketing program.

CHAPTER 7

Creating a Cause-Marketing Orientation: Cause Preparedness

For business, cause marketing is first and foremost about the cause, then the nonprofit organization. Causes are chosen for their alignment with company brands or products that are meaningful to their key constituents, from employees, to communities, suppliers, and consumers, and that tie into their marketing and business goals. Nonprofits are chosen for their ability to represent the cause, the assets they can bring to a cause-marketing arrangement, and their readiness to be partners in a mutually beneficial relationship.

With hundreds of thousands of charities in North America, corporations seeking cause-marketing arrangements have lots of choice. And of course, few would argue that almost all of them are good and worthy of support. So what does a nonprofit need to do to become a cause of choice? First, they must begin by proactively developing an internal cause-marketing orientation that

- Identifies goals, defines brand and assets, and looks for associative linkages
- Builds a positioning focus and determines potential corporate targets
- Prepares the organization internally and establishes a structure that facilitates cause-marketing collaborations

DETERMINING ORGANIZATIONAL GOALS AND ASSETS

Identify Goals for Cause-Marketing Program

An organization must have clear goals they want to achieve with a cause-marketing program. Generating revenue and raising organizational awareness are the cornerstones of a cause-marketing collaboration. Cause collaborations can help achieve an organization's mission, promote issues or increase awareness, and change behaviors. Other goals that can be achieved include building deeper corporate relationships, engaging employee volunteers, accessing new supporters, and building connections to new corporations. The Food Bank of New York City's cause program's goal was to reposition themselves in the community so they could access new corporate supporters, extend their awareness reach, and obtain more food—their central mission.

It's helpful to consider your definition of success, goals to be achieved, and how outcomes will be measured. A cause-marketing program will likely be driven by the fund development and/or marketing teams in a nonprofit organization. Senior management needs to be consulted and buy in to the idea of a cause-marketing program at this phase.

Define the Cause Brand and Assets and Look for Associative Links

The next step is to define the cause. Many nonprofits are so focused on—and competent at—service delivery that they've never given much thought to creating an identity for their organization that is easily explainable to external audiences or even themselves. For example, if your nonprofit staff were asked, "So, what does your organization do? How is it different?", could they clearly state their cause mission position, or would they be tongue-tied when giving a response?

Cause marketing requires nonprofits to be very marketing and externally oriented. Building a brand identity and tight brand position statement will establish distinctiveness, relevance, and passion for a charitable cause. Used well, branding makes it clear what an organization does, what they are about, and how these characteristics make them different in a very competitive marketplace. It also helps to begin the process of considering associative links.

A number of nonprofits are rethinking their brand position to make themselves more attractive as cause partners. A national hunger organization is repositioning itself with a focus on childhood hunger to make the cause more about a public health issue than a welfare issue. Other nonprofits are building new position platforms to create more of a hook and focus for their organization and potential cause partners.

For corporations, brand position statements are important for three reasons. The Home Depot is a leader in cause-marketing relationships. Kevin Martinez, Director, Community Affairs, explains the reasoning from the corporate perspective. First they quickly boil down a nonprofit's resonance to potential partners and are the first step in looking for an alignment fit. As Kevin states, "In that 10 second piece my CEO, our employees and my customers will know what the organization is about and understand why we are connecting to it."[1]

Second, Kevin says it must stir an emotional response and be a cause that reflects a company's own passion and values. A brand positioning that captures your mind changes behavior. A brand that captures your heart gains commitment.

Cause marketing is about helping a company connect at an emotional level with their constituents that include their employees, suppliers, and customers. It is also about value reflection. All charitable organizations are passionate about what they are achieving, whether it is an environment, children, or health issue. The passion must come through in the brand positioning statement and express that emotional and value connection.

Finally, potential corporate partners need to have simple tight messages that can be quickly communicated and understood in their cause-marketing material: in-store, at the checkout counter, in advertising, or presented by employees. Kevin states, "If the company is going to achieve any kind of organizational awareness for the nonprofit partner, they must have tight communications that can be used throughout the cause marketing process."[2]

Build a Brand Positioning Statement: The "Ten-Second Elevator Message"

Building your positioning statement will require some degree of internal reflection and external positioning. Gather your leadership and go through the introspective process of clearly defining who you are and what you do. Use your findings to create a "positioning" or "identity statement" that can be stated succinctly and is understandable to internal and external audiences.

Brand positioning is all about laying claim to a particular piece of rational and emotional turf. The rationale part of the positioning statement must answer four questions: What is the purpose of the organization? What differentiates that purpose from others in the market? Who is the target audience? What is the benefit to the audience? The emotional side must breathe life into the organization and elicit a human response. How is the organization making a difference? What is the passion that inspires those working for the charity? Find a powerful way to communicate that emotional content of your cause.

For many organizations, identifying their brand position may not be easy. Often there are many competing interests that need to be sorted out before a consensus is reached. As well, some nonprofits have an unreal sense of their own virtue and importance, and this can be distorted by spin artists. Trying to put a brand face that is aspirational, not built on truth, never works. Nonprofits must bring candor and objectivity to the table if they are to authentically define and position who they are and what they do.

The time and effort invested in the process will be worth the result. Nonprofit organizations actively seeking or being sought out as cause partners must understand and be able to concisely communicate their cause brand position. The final statement must be concise and passionate. It needs to describe your organization with ration and passion in 10 seconds or less—the ultimate elevator message.

KaBOOM!, First Book, and Children's Hunger Alliance

KaBOOM!: "A playground within walking distance of every child in America" speaks to the cause of children, play, and physical activity. The emotional connection? All children deserve to have a place where they can play and be active. The cause has lent itself to alignments with builders (The Home Depot); children's activity wear (Stride Rite), and even food for children (Ben and Jerry's). As their leadership states, "The partnerships we're really pursuing are the ones we see the greatest fit of the brand DNA between KaBOOM! and the corporation."

First Book: "Giving children from low-income families the opportunity to read and own their first new books." The cause alignment: children, literacy, education; the emotional response: the importance of books in the lives of children; the potential partners: Universal Studios (children's movies—Dr. Seuss' *Cat in the Hat*); Cheerios® (children and literacy). Cause marketing has enabled First Book to tap into corporate funding on a broader scale, to achieve their mission, and to extend their promotional reach.

Children's Hunger Alliance, Columbus, Ohio: "Breaking the cycle of child-hood hunger" focuses on children, hunger, and action. The emotion: hungry children. This positioning has led to corporate cause-marketing partnerships with local restaurants, including Buckeye, where "Every Friday and Saturday enjoy the Buckeye Hall of Fame's multimillion dollar game room, ice cream, door prizes and more from 5–10 p.m. Children 12 and under can get unlimited game play cards for only a $5.00 donation to Children's Hunger Alliance!"[3]

Define Assets and Resources That Could Be Used

The next piece in preparing a cause for collaborations is an analysis of the assets and resources a nonprofit can bring to a cause-marketing relationship. Increasingly nonprofit organizations recognize the value of their assets and resources. But in thinking about them for cause-marketing partnerships, nonprofits must be prepared to view them from an external perspective and then think of associative links. How could the assets and resources you have benefit a corporate partner? The Canadian Parks Partnership and Parks Canada catalogued our assets when building our cause marketing and looked at everything from photographic collection to in-park opportunities and expertise to connections with high-profile historic sites and landmarks. It's important to be creative: you're a food bank and you are operating in the financial capital creates an associative link and resulted in the Food Bank of New York City's Bank-to-Bank program.

Although most nonprofits' equity is nonfinancial, they provide the focus and meaning for any cause-marketing partnership. Nonprofits have intangible assets that can align with a corporate partner in a cause-marketing arrangement: mission, brand, reputation, and community connections; and tangible assets of programs, events, and social campaigns. Assets are used to create cause-marketing partnerships. Nonprofits also have resources that can be used to add value to assets. They include promotional material, marketing and media partnerships, testimonials from users, and volunteer opportunities to engage employees. The more a nonprofit can contribute, the richer and deeper the relationship. Reviewing and building a list of these assets and resources is important in preparing the organization for cause-marketing collaborations.

Intangible Assets

- *Organization's brand, logo, and goodwill:* A nonprofit organization's brand and logo is one of its most valuable assets and the foundation for a cause-marketing relationship. Credibility and trust factors are the pillars of most nonprofit organizations' strength and essence. This is what most companies are interested in when building cause-marketing collaborative arrangements. For companies to tie their name and products to an organization with a strong brand and logo provides something that cannot be purchased: credibility and goodwill in the community. Protecting a brand and logo are important, and nonprofits should ensure their logos are trademarked and that they have established guidelines for use of their brand and logo. Brand is a key asset of the Boys and Girls Clubs, explains Kurt Aschermann. "In the 1990s we had 14% awareness. Now it's at 80% plus and our board was ranked as one of the top boards by *Worth* magazine in the country. Companies want to work with us because, one we're everywhere and two the brand is so strong. We say every time we do a partnership, we are a sub of their brand and vice versa."[4]

- *Who you serve:* Who is the organization serving? Although many nonprofits might not consider this to be an asset, client reach is an essential consideration for potential corporate partners. Arts organizations, for example, tend to have well-educated members; a health organization could specifically target men; a literacy organization could serve children. Corporate partners can use a cause-marketing relationship to associate with a specific market segment and often a highly qualified audience, something of great value to corporate marketers.

- *What you do:* Create associative links looking at what you do and the appeal that might have to a corporate partner. AIDS/HIV became the cause of the fashion industry because the industry had a higher percentage of AIDS sufferers. Literacy organizations have a high affinity with the publishing world because there are natural links.

- **Where you do it:** Who are the main corporations in your city or region can also be an asset that nonprofits can use to their benefit. For example, New York City has a major film industry, which resulted in the Food Bank for New York City creating the "Cans Film Festival." How can you link your organization and message with major players in your city or region?

- **Impact:** Being able to quantify your impact for potential partners can enhance the opportunity to form cause-marketing relationships. For example, knowing that 50% of Atlantic Canadians knew someone who used a food bank was a powerful motivator in Investors Group building cause partnerships with local food banks in the region. American Cancer Society has a 98% name recognition factor, and when it built a cause-marketing alliance tied to a nicotine therapy replacement product, reputation and impact was critical. The company wanted to be associated with the number one trusted cancer entity and the accompanying science.[5]

Tangible Assets: Programs

- **Programs and program concepts:** Nonprofit programs and program concepts can be attractive assets to a corporate partner. More and more cause-marketing collaborations are focused on programs. Rather than building their own cause programs such as Liz Claiborne's "Love is not abuse" program (see following), they can partner and get the benefits without the responsibility of implementation and execution. The programs can be supported by corporations and used to publicly promote their support of a relevant community cause. KaBOOM!, for example, has programs focused on building playgrounds. Companies can customize their involvement— from Ben and Jerry's selling a specialty ice cream and using the proceeds and local retailers to help with the playground construction to The Home Depot building their brand by creating civic engagement and volunteer activities for their employees by constructing playgrounds in local communities.

- **Events:** Nonprofit events that can engage company constituents are important assets that can be used to build cause-marketing partnerships. The Canadian Breast Cancer Foundation's Run for the Cure and CIBC have partnered since 1997 in this national event. Each year thousands of Canadians, current and potential CIBC bank users and employees, run in support of a breast cancer cure. CIBC's goal is to build brand image, and demonstrate its values all the while supporting this important community health issue. Across Canada, CIBC employees have adopted the Run as one of their most strongly supported causes. In 2004, Team CIBC had more than 10,500 participants who raised over $2.5 million for the Run.[6]

- *Marketing campaigns:* Nonprofit social marketing campaigns can provide a focus for corporate cause-marketing support. As discussed earlier, leading nonprofits are creating branded programs and social marketing campaigns to build a focus and to extend the number and types of companies, many of whom would not traditionally have been a fit. The American Heart Association launched a national awareness and social marketing campaign on women and heart health, Go Red for Women, in early 2003. The program clearly provides the organization the opportunity to broaden their corporate reach to companies targeting women. For example, in the first year of the program they were able to secure a new type of cause partner, a retailer. Macy's came on board as a lead cause supporter with a commitment of $6 million over three years. Macy's launched a whole series of in-store cause promotions and products to support the campaign. Equally important was the reach their cause relationship has allowed them through the Macy's stores nationwide, helping them to achieve a critical mission win—creating awareness of the vital issue of women and heart health.

Resources and Benefits

- *Community connections:* Nonprofit organizations bring privileged access to relationships with community leaders, their donors, members, volunteers, other partners, government agencies, and even celebrities. Connecting through nonprofit partners lends a level of credibility to any corporation. Share Our Strength's largest asset is their connection to a network of chefs and restaurateurs—something that has great appeal to companies working with restaurants and chefs. Each year the group organizes the "Great American Bake Sale" involving corporate media partners, *Parade* magazine and ABC News, and the Betty Crocker division of General Mills. Each partner has different goals, from driving sales for Betty Crocker products to watching the network news to reinforcing advertising relationships. All benefit from the organization's connections in the community, the Girl Scout troops, college students, and others who do the baking, generating significant dollars and awareness for Share Our Strength and the corporate partners.

- *Corporate employee volunteer opportunities:* A new area of interest for corporations is the opportunity for employee volunteerism at the nonprofit organization. In fact, some cause-marketing relationships are developed specifically with this in mind. The Home Depot and KaBOOM!'s ongoing cause-marketing initiatives exemplifies employee civic engagements as a key driver of their cause relationships. Employees can be a great benefit to the nonprofit, especially in executing programs or events. Some cause-marketing arrangements get started because of company volunteers who become internal advocates for the organization.

- *Media and marketing relationships:* Media partnerships are an important part of most nonprofit organizations' communications plans and outreach. Cause partners look to see how nonprofits will promote the cause initiative and by extension their support. Media relationships can include everything from special features to access to special advertising rates to privileged coverage of nonprofit events and activities. All have the potential to enhance a cause-marketing relationship and add credibility to a cause partner's support. Marketing partnerships for execution of a cause-marketing alliance can also be a critical resource that adds value to a cause-marketing relationship. The Food Bank of New York City's Bank-to-Bank cause-marketing promotion sees financial services and banks in the city being food drop-off locations during the holiday season. They promote the program and their involvement and have helped to strengthen donations at this critical time of the year. To make the program work, the Food Bank secured UPS as a marketing partner to pick up food donations and deliver them to their food depots. Savvy nonprofits bring all their partners together to share information, celebrate success, and help build connections between partners that share values and commitment.

- *Communication tools:* Access to a nonprofit organization's communications tools including Web sites, brochures, and newsletters can bring additional resources to a cause relationship. Communicating a company's support when done by a credible third party, such as a nonprofit organization, lends great value to the way their support is viewed in the community.

- *In-house expertise:* Nonprofits can bring recognized authorities and experts to a cause-marketing collaboration that adds important value and credibility. This can include scientists or medical people in the case of a health charity. Environmental scientists, authors, illustrators, or education experts can provide authority and integrity to a cause-marketing campaign. PNC developed a cause partnership with Children's Television Workshop, the nonprofit educational organization behind Sesame Street, because of the expertise they could bring to their PNC "Grow Up Great," a program to help prepare preschoolers for kindergarten.

- *Testimonials:* Testimonials add passion to a cause program in the way that in-house expertise adds credibility. Testimonials can be provided by clients, or people who have been touched by the work of the nonprofit organization. They can be powerful tools for a cause-marketing relationship.

- *National organizations with local chapters:* A major asset of national organizations is their ability to provide local connections and grassroots execution. Local organizations can be great allies in cause-marketing arrangements. The American Heart Association generates 90% of their leads from local offices.[7] The challenge? Making it work and delivering on commitments consistently. It is critical to have local buy-in and support for any cause-marketing arrangements. Making sure there is strong and effective communications and template promotional material provided helps. Some national organizations use creative ways to ensure strong local execution. First Book provides financial incentives for local organizations and has found this to be effective in strengthening local delivery.[8] At the American Heart Association the national office keeps in close communications with the executive VPs of each affiliate office as marketing partnerships are developed. Once agreement is reached on a cause-marketing partnership, it is that group who has local responsibility for making it happen. Each local affiliate has a separate volunteer committee that approves all relationships, and having this process has really helped the organization along the way.[9]

A Few Important Considerations . . .

• *Integrity and reputation assets:* A nonprofit organization's integrity and reputation are its most important assets. Every nonprofit understands that these are key to fundraising, volunteer recruitment, staff retention, and overall good organizational health. Damage to a nonprofit's reputation can be devastating, and many with otherwise strong programs would have a hard time recovering from a "hit." Nonprofit after nonprofit professional stressed the importance of ensuring the organization's reputation was never violated. "Never align yourself with a product that is not good for you or the public, or your donors will not trust you again," was stated by a number of cause marketers. Others highlighted that the vast majority of nonprofits' revenue comes from individuals, and if an organization does a cause program just for monetary purposes, not mission-related purposes, then authenticity and reputation of the program and the organization would be jeopardized. Nonprofits must recognize that they may be guilty by association if a corporate partner comes under fire or the cause program is viewed negatively.

• *Exclusivity and devaluing assets:* A note of caution: nonprofits must choose their partners carefully, but also be conscious of how many they have and avoid having so many partners that they all get lost. Too many partners tagged to one program or organization can devalue their asset's worth and its effectiveness for corporate partners. Companies want to have their brand identifiably linked with an organization and cause. Although they cannot "own" nonprofits, sensitivity around category exclusivity tied to a specific program or during a specific period or for a particular component of the cause initiative is important.

- *Assets that can't be used:* What assets can't be tapped also needs to be clearly understood. For example, many corporations are looking for direct access to mailing lists, clients, or nonprofit supporters. In some instances this can work; in others it won't. Cause-marketing partnerships between schools and businesses provide an example of when tying into the organization's client base, in this case students, can be a challenge and nonstarter for nonprofits.

PLATFORM: THE BIG SIMPLE IDEA

Knowing your goals, assets, and brand positioning will provide the framework for moving forward. The next step is to take the information and turn it into a platform for the organization that will take concepts and turn them into something real.

A key learning from other successful cause programs: A simple big idea can have massive impact and is easier to sell to potential partners. Why? It's easier to communicate, link to corporate objectives and products, explain to staff, and then execute. Think about the power of Nike/Lance Armstrong Foundation's Live Strong yellow bracelet campaign or the Susan G. Komen Race for the Cure, simple concepts that captured the public's imagination. The American Heart Association's "Go Red for Women," the Food Banks for New York City's Bank-to-Bank and "Cans" Film Festival, First Book's "The Cat in the Hat Challenge," and British Columbia and Yukon District of the Canadian Cancer Society's "Daffodil Campaign Products Sales" are the big simple ideas featured in the Making It Happen section of the book. A simple idea can start small and grow as the relationship builds and success is achieved.

The second key learning: An execution plan must be part of the plan, and it has to be simple, turnkey. Nonprofits need to show how the program will work for the company by reaching their core audience, aligning with their brand, and meeting their marketing needs and objectives.

A consideration for nonprofits is the objectives of the program. A focus on revenue generations will provide a different approach than one that aims to raise an organization's profile, change behaviors, or implement a specific program. The latter likely would look for a smaller number of deeper relationships, the former, as many as possible to raise the profile of the organization and cause message.

Some organizations are moving away from the one-off cause relationships or ones that provide a small return that are the hallmark of many young programs. Instead, they are looking to build a few deeper programs that are longer term and provide bigger benefits. UNICEF is an example of this approach. In the early 2000s many of the arrangements were one-offs. Now they are annually aiming for two to three new partners who will develop a long-term multiyear integrated program. KaBOOM! is another nonprofit whose focus has switched to a strategy of fewer, bigger, more-activated leveraged partnerships. Many of their relationships start with an 18-month to two-year pilot phase. If it works for both partners, a bigger, more leveraged program is developed.[10]

DETERMINE TARGETS FOR CAUSE-MARKETING APPROACH

Knowing its cause positioning and assets the nonprofit can then develop a list of potential partners. What types of partners will help achieve your mission and messaging? Where might be alignment and a fit? Don't ignore already established corporate relations; these usually will be excellent prospects that know, appreciate, and understand your organization. However, one of the benefits of cause marketing is it provides an opportunity to create new collaborations that might never have occurred using a traditional corporate philanthropic approach.

When Looking for Alignments, Consider the 60-30-10 Rule

All great marketing organizations follow the 60-30-10 rule. This rule suggests that approximately 60% of all marketing resources be dedicated to current customers, 30% to defined prospects, and 10% to the universe. The logic behind this focus is that it is more efficient to keep a current customer than to secure a new one. Existing supporters who are already engaged and excited about your organization can be the most effective cause-marketing partners.

Many cause-marketing relationships are built from existing relationships where there already is a high level of mutual respect and trust. The Nike/Lance Armstrong Foundation had an established partnership before launching the "Wear Yellow, Live Strong" cause collaboration. Investors Group was already working with food banks in Canada before they launched their cause Comedy Tour program. American Red Cross and The Home Depot had worked together on several disaster-related projects. The presentation to this group has to be a different conversation that focuses on marketing, not community investment or the foundation focus.

Many cause-marketing relationships are regularly developed with new corporate partners. Many examples demonstrate this point. Most will start small and build as trust is established and a nonprofit proves itself to be an effective cause-marketing partner.

Brainstorm for New Partners Using the Alignment Pyramid

It is important to look beyond existing corporate partners to build a new list of potential relationships where a cause marketing collaboration might be possible. One of the benefits of cause marketing is that it will often open up possibilities to work with corporate partners whose philanthropic giving focus might not fit an organization, but whose marketing needs could. A simple but effectively process developed by Kristian Darigan of Cone Inc. looks at analyzing alignment and brainstorming potential partners, in a three-level pyramid shape of high, medium, and low.[11]

- *High alignment:* Kristian defines these as companies where there is an obvious and clear fit. This tends to be a smaller group, but very apparent. Examples include a health charity aligning with a pharmaceutical company; an environmental group aligning with an eco-tour business; a food bank with a restaurant. Appearance of endorsement because of the clear connection must be watched. It could be very easy, if not handled with care, to give the impression that the charity's involvement with the company is as good as saying their product, service, or brand meets their standards. Regardless of level of alignment, if the cause program is tied to a product or promotion, following the Better Business Bureau's guidelines and ones established by your charity are critical for the integrity of the relationship and the cause-marketing program. (See following for the guidelines.)

- *Medium alignment:* In the middle of the pyramid are a greater number of companies that are moderately aligned to your mission and brand position. These are companies where a connection could be made. "An example," explains Krirstian, "is a health charity and a sport shoe company. Being active is good for your health and therein lays the fit. It is also highly unlikely that a person purchasing the shoe is going to do so because of a perceived endorsement."[12] However, nonprofits do have to scrutinize these potential corporate partners to ensure that there is no appearance that the nonprofit is approving, in this case, the shoe. Another example of medium alignment is an environmental group who partners with a catalog retailer. The retailer makes a donation for every product sold during a certain time period. The environmental group uses the support to plant trees. Here the fit relates to the use of paper to produce the catalogues and the retailer's desire to give back and present themselves as environmentally responsible.

- *Low alignment:* These are alignments where the fit is not initially obvious. Only further investigation brings the alignment to light. Examples include a health charity partnering with a retailer. The health charity focuses on issues relating to women's health. The retailer's employees and customers are largely women—the alignment becomes clearer. Another example is a recreation nonprofit aligning with a car company. The car company's main clients are hikers and outdoor enthusiasts. Because the connection is less apparent, there is little likelihood of implied endorsement. Sometimes the connection isn't even apparent—a literacy group partnering with a coffee company. The connection relates to the company's commitment to the community and the fact that a senior executive is on the board. The benefit of these alignments is that often these companies would not normally support this type of charity. This is also an opportunity to use the relationship as a way to change the way people perceive the nonprofit organization and to reach a whole new audience of potential supporters.

LOW BUT HIGHLY EFFECTIVE ALIGNMENT: UNICEF AND INTERCONTINENTAL HOTELS GROUP

Over the past 25 plus years, cause-marketing support has ebbed and flowed, following societal needs, interests, and commitments. Many of the early cause programs focused around top of mind and consumer friendly issues: children, education, and health care. As these cause fields attracted more support and cause programs, they have become so cluttered that is it difficult for companies to stand out. Issues like breast cancer, for example, have attracted over 300 companies to this cause.[13]

The result? Companies are seeking less-traditional causes and innovatively presenting the alignment fit. InterContinental Hotels Group and their cause event, Designs of Hope, in support of UNICEF's AIDS/HIV program, is a good example. (See Exhibit 7.1.) AIDS and HIV in Africa is a major issue and one that people are not talking about. Vicki Gordon, IHG's Senior Vice President, Corporate Affairs, recognized the potential benefits and alignment for both the cause and the company. "We were looking for a fit and we wanted a nonprofit organization and cause that had name recognition and a scope that was comparable to ours. The InterContinental brand was founded in 1946, the same year as UNICEF. We have hotels in 100 countries around the world. We have a major presence in Third World countries, where UNICEF also has a huge presence and where AIDS/HIV is a crisis issue. For us it was a good fit, there was name recognition in all the areas where we work and our employees around the world all know UNICEF."[14] For UNICEF, this event has helped reach out to a young target audience, those 25- to 45-year-old fashion-aware people who enjoy art and fashion. This example shows that today almost any community issue can find a home in a cause-marketing arrangement.

EXHIBIT 7.1   DESIGNS OF HOPE INFORMATION

Caring is the new black.

When a fashion show raises money for kids affected by HIV/AIDS, everyone looks good. By 2010, over 18 million children in sub-Saharan Africa will be orphaned by AIDS. InterContinental hotels in Atlanta, Chicago and Houston are presenting Designs of Hope fashion shows to raise money to help UNICEF care for them. And you can be part of this important effort. Visit **designsofhope.org** to learn about fashionable ways to show your support. You'll be helping to make the world just a little more beautiful.

A Lucky Few

Some nonprofits have brands that are so well known they are regularly approached for cause-marketing relationships. The World Wildlife Fund (WWF), with its famous panda logo, is the eighth-most-trusted brand in the United States and the second-most-trusted brand in Europe.[15] WWF has the powerful combination of a well-known brand and a cause environment, wildlife, wild places, that appeals to a range of companies (Back to Nature Organic Food, Bank One, credit cards) targeting environmentally conscious consumers.

But just because your organization is not well known doesn't mean you can't benefit from the power of cause marketing. KaBOOM! and First Book are examples of brand new nonprofits that through a lot of creativity, hard work, and perseverance built their organizations on cause-marketing arrangements.

Even for organizations that are prominently and regularly approached to participate in cause relationships, having a disciplined approach, set of actions, execution, and evaluation will ensure that the organization gets the most benefit out of cause-marketing alliances. Don't just assume you will always be in a position of prominence; make sure you earn it.

Internally Prepare and Align the Organization

To participate in cause relationships, nonprofits must have internal culture, capacity, and structure in place. Cause-marketing programs involve business objectives such as additional sales, expanded markets, brand positioning, or creating employee pride as a key focus. Although their community investment, public relations, and even human resources colleagues might be involved in the relationship,

American Express, Home Depot

As pioneer American Express explains, nonprofit partners must have the capacity and skills to undertake a program. They rarely take on more than a couple of cause-marketing programs at any time, and because significant resources are dedicated to make a program work, strong, capable partners are essential.

Kevin Martinez, Director, Community Affairs at The Home Depot agrees. "I am a firm believer that cause marketing is not an entry level position for any new partnership you have. A nonprofit partner has to earn it. They have to purvey a responsible partnership that will work directly with our culture and operations. If the wrong cause partner is picked, it will fall on deaf ears internally. I have to find the right partnership that will easily move our system."[16]

business objectives are drivers of a program. This requires nonprofits to be more business focused and to understand marketing language such as "target market," "employee engagement," "demographics," "ROI," "traffic," and "response rate" to assure potential partners that the organization is responsive to their bottom-line needs. Businesses have concrete objectives, and nonprofits must recognize the need for a different and more entrepreneurial approach to gain this corporate support.

Ensure You Have Senior Leadership Buy-in

Because cause-marketing programs are deeper, more engaged, and often have a commercial element, it is critical to have buy-in from the senior leadership, in-cluding in some cases the board of directors. For a cause-marketing partnership to succeed, senior leadership must be supportive and committed to cause-marketing arrangements. They must demonstrate their support through action to signal to the rest of the organization and potential corporate partners, the strate-gic importance and benefits of a cause-marketing program. This includes being prepared to provide resources, make cause marketing a priority, and participate in meetings and stewardship of corporate cause partners.

Having that support right from the start is critical for a cause-marketing rela-tionship to work. The first step in implementing the Canadian Parks Partnership and Parks Canada's cause-marketing program was senior leadership buy-in. A presentation was made to the senior official and a formal agreement with guide-lines and policies and procedures developed.[17]

Another cause marketer states the importance of senior buy-in. "We have a very good relationship with our cause partner and we committed to it right from the start. I gather that is not the case at the other organizations. Their leadership was lukewarm right from the beginning and they weren't sure if the alignment was right. It has affected the way their relationship has developed."

Encourage an Entrepreneurial and Marketing-Focused Culture

Nonprofit organizations must have a mind-set that is open to creating marketing partnerships with businesses. It makes sense that organizational cultures that en-courage reasonable risk, new opportunities, and welcome challenges are more likely to be open to and successful with cause relationships.

Support and understanding of the importance of this new way of working with corporations must extend beyond the development and marketing team. It must be an accepted way of operating throughout the organizations. Staff and boards must view cause collaborations in a positive and beneficial light, and be ready to address any commercialization concerns early in the process. This can be a chal-lenge for some organizations, whose staff members do not appreciate the bene-fits or feel they are "above" this form of support.

Dedicate Staff and Resources to Execute

Once the nonprofit organization determines its interest in developing cause programs, staff time and resources must be dedicated to building a plan, finding partners, and developing and maintaining collaborative marketing arrangements. To ensure success takes time, resources, and trained staff who are committed to leading and managing the program on behalf of the organization. As cause-marketing programs grow, so do the number of nonprofit organizations moving into this funding field. Corporations are seeking nonprofit partners who have marketing knowledge and capabilities, access to legal advice, a sophisticated understanding of how programs work, and can be response-driven. They want partners who can sit across the table, participate, and cooperate in a spirit of mutual respect and trust. In the early days of cause marketing, programs were developed as add-ons to fund development or marketing staff's responsibilities. Today this is still the case in many institutions. But standalone cause-marketing positions are being created by some national nonprofits and larger local organizations. A key new requirement for these positions: a marketing and sales background with the ability to sell and "ask," and an understanding of how nonprofits are structured, their organizational objectives, and how they function and how decisions are made. Many sophisticated nonprofits have cause marketers who come from the for-profit sector. Share Our Strength, a cause-marketing leader has staff members who came from Disney, McKinsey, and AOL.[18]

Ensure Solid Planning

Like real estate where location is everything, in cause marketing, planning is the key. Planning is needed to put all the pieces in place to ensure successful implementation and execution. Cause-marketing programs need disciplined thought, action, and execution.

Develop Solid Processes and Procedures

Processes and procedures to manage and guide cause-marketing relationships are critical for success and to ensure nonprofits manage risk. Every nonprofit organization considering a cause-marketing program should have good governance tied to innovation. This means an approval process that includes who will be involved and how it will work, defined standards including a guidelines checklist to assess benefits, and a risk management assessment system specific to the organization; for example, an environmental group will have to consider a company's environmental record. All these are required to provide timely and efficient decision making. Because programs include not only rewards but also potential risks and costs, it is important to establish parameters and adequate guidelines and procedures for staff that are developing corporate cause relationships (Exhibit 7.2).

EXHIBIT 7.2   BUILDING COLLABORATIONS: GUIDELINE CHECKLIST

Guideline	Points
1. Is there strategic alignment? Does it help fulfill organization's mission and goals; align with mandate, values, and programs?	
2. Do you have the capacity to undertake the program?	
3. Does it meet the minimum dollar amount for contribution? Or is revenue greater than costs? Or at least (if for profile) neutral?	
4. Does it build membership, donors, and volunteers?	
5. Will it market messages to target audience?	
6. Will it heighten awareness of organization?	
7. Does it generate incremental revenue?	
8. Will it target new markets—get message out to new audiences relevant to organization?	
9. Does it compete with existing corporate partners?	
10. Does it fit geographic scope of operations (local, regional, national)?	
11. Is the company, product, service noncontroversial, and does it have a good reputation?	
12. Is the program short term, one-off, or longer term, deeper relationship? (Score according to need.)	
13. What are the risks? Risk assessment undertaken will vary according to each sector. In health care this could mean review by medical professionals, in the environmental field, review by scientists.	
14. Is there partner compatibility—open communications, mutual respect, and trust?	
15. Does the partner demonstrate a commitment to corporate social responsibility?	
16. Other considerations particular to your sector, community.	
TOTAL	

Points system: High: 3, Medium: 2, Low: 1

Cause marketing can potentially provide great benefits for nonprofit organizations but potential risks as well. Nonprofit managers must approach this issue with great care and caution. A corporate marketing collaboration can potentially damage a nonprofit organization's hard-earned reputation for integrity. A good name is a nonprofit's chief asset. If this is depreciated in the course of doing business with a corporation, the ability of the nonprofit to address its charitable mission can be seriously harmed. For most organizations less than 10% of their overall support comes from the corporate sector. Individual supporters are charitable organizations' greatest source of financial support and they are trusting that nonprofits are going to be impeccable in maintaining their integrity and reputation.

Staff members negotiating cause programs must know the limits so that they can speak on behalf of their organization. The approval framework can guide them in seeking opportunities and then ensuring an effective and efficient internal review and approval process. These processes ensure that senior management and board members if necessary understand any program that might be developed. Once negotiated, agreements or letters of understanding and tools for managing the partnership, including joint planning, timetables, and roles and responsibilities, must be in place. Finally, constant, open communications is central for success.

Know and Understand Industry Guiding Principles, Regulations, and Tax Implications

Finally, cause marketing has not been without its controversy. It is important for the nonprofit to know or have access to someone who can help with the

APPROVAL PROCESS—HEART AND STROKE FOUNDATION OF CANADA

The Heart and Stroke Foundation of Canada has developed a process to review possible cause-marketing relationships. A preliminary opportunity assessment of a relationship is done that looks at a range of criteria and can involve third-party research. When a cause-marketing alliance is proposed, it is taken to the national corporate alliance network where agreement to proceed is sought. The national network has representatives from each province. An evaluation of the proposed alliance is measured against strategic fit to ensure that it aligns with priorities of the foundation, that the company is financially stable, and that the timelines are reasonable. After the evaluation, a determination of the proposal is made, and it is a red, green, or yellow. The organization looks for sufficient agreement that the relationship will be good for everyone. Getting the money and awareness is one thing; losing a reputation is another. Over one-third of Canadians donate to the Heart and Stroke Foundation, and protecting the name and reputation of the organization is vital. If there are issues, it is taken to the next level of all the provincial Executive Directors. Challenges or issues beyond that group are finally taken to the board nationally. Although this has never happened, there is a clear process of evaluation in place that ensures risk assessment, national buy-in, and maximum benefit for the organization.[19]

GUIDELINES AND APPROVAL PROCESS— THE NATURE CONSERVANCY, USA

The Nature Conservancy began developing corporate relationships in the early 1990s by building cause-marketing programs. At that time the focus was on royalty-based sales programs where a portion of the proceeds was donated to support the organization. As the organization has grown and the brand has become more valuable, they have developed new guidelines and process for reviewing and approving these relationships. Like the development of the cause-marketing field, they now include what they call gift-based cause-marketing programs (where there is an exceptional promotion of the gift through paid advertising) in their review process.

The process begins with a review of alignment with an approved list of types of companies that make sense for their brand. The second step is to analyze if they are getting an appropriate return on the brand. They have put a minimum amount in place that can be measured in direct dollars or in marketing/publicity dollar value, which is pegged at a higher value level. The arrangement cannot imply endorsement and must meet the Better Business Bureau's Wise Giving Guidelines (see following). An overview of the arrangement with a recommendation for or against is presented to the CEO, who has final approval. If approved, it goes to the final stage of the process—a formal written agreement.[20]

regulatory and legal guidelines and requirements to participate in cause-marketing arrangements. Public credibility is essential if charities are to be effective in raising funds and if their work is to be recognized as valuable and contributing to the public good. As many nonprofit cause-marketing leaders stressed, it's important to talk with potential partners about these requirements. Don't forget to outline your own guidelines and internal processes. As companies get more sophisticated in cause marketing, they will want to work with nonprofits that know and understand this side of cause-marketing arrangements. Here are the key areas of consideration for nonprofits to follow best practises for cause marketing today.

- **Tax Implications, UBIT:** If a nonprofit is actively selling something that is not part of their mission, the potential exists for them to be considered for an **U**nrelated **B**usiness **I**ncome **T**ax. Provided the nonprofit knowingly chooses this route, this isn't an issue. But don't fall into it by accident. Check with your treasurer or accountant if you are undertaking a cause-marketing program that might raise doubts.

- **1999, Attorneys General Report:** The final report (discussed in Chapter 3) reviewed what they saw as a growing trend that "raised significant

legal and policy concerns." It outlined six key principles and legal requirements to protect "the public interest and to assist both the commercial and
nonprofit entities engaged in product advertising in meeting their legal
obligations."[21]

- Comply with laws that prohibit false advertising, deceptive trade practices, and consumer fraud.

- Avoid misrepresentations of whether the nonprofit has actually endorsed
  a product.

- Avoid making claims of superiority of the product, unless the nonprofit
  has substantiated such claims.

- Disclose that the corporate sponsor has paid for the use of the nonprofit
  name or logo.

- Prohibit misleading messages that lead consumers to believe their purchase
  will affect the corporate sponsor's charitable donation to the nonprofit.

- Avoid exclusive product sponsorships or, if used, disclose the relationship
  in advertisements.[22]

- **State and Provincial Regulations:** Research regulations around commercial coventure. Currently over 40 states in the United States have charitable
  solicitation laws including relating to commercial coventures and "charitable
  sales promotions." In Canada, only the province of Alberta has formal legis-
  lation. In both countries, many nonprofits have their own fundraising ethical standards and guidelines or follow the AFP established guidelines.

- **National Health Council Guiding Principles for Voluntary Health
  Agencies in Corporate Relationships:** The National Health Council is
  a dynamic forum for policy development—the place where all segments of
  the health-care community meet for reasoned discussion and persuasive advocacy. The council has developed a set of guiding principles for health
  agencies participating in cause marketing and other corporate relationships.
  These guidelines are useful for any nonprofit seeking cause-marketing
  relationships. The full guidelines can be viewed at **www.nationalhealth
  council.org/aboutus/corp_relations.htm.**

- **Better Business Bureau's Wise Giving Alliance: Standards for Charity Accountability:** The BBB Wise Giving Alliance standards were developed to assist donors in making sound giving decisions and to foster public
  confidence in charitable organizations. The overarching principle of the standards is full disclosure to donors and potential donors at the time of solicitation and thereafter. Standards relating to a charity's benefiting from the sale
  of products or services are outlined in the guidelines. Promotions should disclose at the point of solicitation:

- The actual or anticipated portion of the purchase price that will benefit the charity (e.g., 5 cents will be contributed to abc charity for every xyz company product sold)

- The duration of the campaign (e.g., the month of October)

- Any maximum or guaranteed minimum contribution amount (e.g., up to a maximum of $200,000)[23]

ONE LAST THING ABOUT CAUSES . . .

Cause Support: Not Always With an Established Nonprofit Organization

Not every cause-related program involves a specific nonprofit organization. There are two ways cause programs can be implemented. First, the company will partner with a nonprofit organization that can best represent the cause. The second option is through indirect support where the company will take on cause action themselves through a charity they establish or by providing support to a number of nonprofits involved in the cause. Dove "Real Beauty" is an example of a charity taking on a cause. Established to raise awareness of the link between beauty and body-related self-esteem, Dove established marketing around this cause and set up a Self-Esteem Fund in the United States. The fund sponsors "uniquely ME!"—a partnership program with Girl Scouts of the USA that helps build self-confidence in girls ages 8 to 14.[24]

The direct approach can bring significant benefits in terms of credibility, infrastructure, and connections. On the other hand, working with a nonprofit partner can add complexity to a program. The indirect approach has the business taking on the cause itself through establishing a charity arm that can undertake implementation of the action or by distributing the resources to a number of charities representing the cause. This approach can work if there is no obvious nonprofit partner or there are a number of organizations that could be supported.

Liz Claiborne and Relationship Violence is an example of a nondirect approach. Since 1991, Liz Claiborne Inc. has encouraged women and men to speak out on the issue of relationship violence through its award-winning public awareness and educational campaign. By 2004 in its 13th year, the program—known by its tagline, "Love Is Not Abuse"[25]—had reached millions of Americans with targeted antiabuse messages and had been a catalyst for men and women, organizations, and communities to speak out against violence.

Annually the program incorporated a range of awareness elements and Liz Claiborne products created for the program. Revenue generated from the sale of the products, ranging from T-shirts to books, went to a range of charities chosen dependent on the theme and focus of the program each year. Donations were made to nonprofit organizations from domestic violence agencies in communities across the United States and early in the program to Reading Is Fundamental and The Harold Washington Library Center when a book was one of the products sold in support of the initiative.

CONCLUSION: THE FIRST STEP IS CREATING A CAUSE-MARKETING ORIENTATION

The first step in building a cause-marketing program is focused on the **Cause**, creating a cause-marketing orientation. For businesses, cause marketing is first and foremost about the cause, then the nonprofit organization. So what does a nonprofit need to do to become a cause of choice?

First, they must start by proactively developing an internal cause-marketing orientation that aligns a cause program with organizational goals and needs. The nonprofit must define who it is and what it does and present this information in an authentic and succinct fashion. Analyzing and cataloging assets that could be brought to a cause-marketing arrangement is the next step. These assets must be viewed from the corporate perspective—how can they be used to benefit the nonprofit and the potential corporate partner; what does the nonprofit have to offer to a corporate cause relationship? Determine the focus for the program remembering that big simple idea needs are easiest to understand and therefore sell. With this information in hand, a nonprofit can begin the process of creating a list of potential corporations that could align with their goals, mission, and assets.

Finally, nonprofits serious about building cause-marketing programs must have an internal structure that is committed and ready to collaborate. To participate in cause relationships, nonprofits must have senior leadership buy-in, an enterprising culture, adequate resources, and processes and procedures in place to move any potential program through the system efficiently and in a timely fashion.

The next chapter looks at building the cause-marketing program through **collaboration, combining assets, and creating value**.

ENDNOTES

1. Interview, Kevin Martinez, Home Depot, March 30, 2005.
2. Ibid.
3. www.childrenshungeralliance.com (June 23, 2005, summer, 2005 cause-marketing promotion).
4. Interview, Kurt Aschermann, November 22, 2004.
5. Interview, Cynthia Currence, American Cancer Society, January 25, 2005.
6. www.cibcrunforthecure.com/html/en/ab_sponsors.asp.
7. Interview, Kathy Rogers, American Heart Association, January 24, 2005.
8. Interview, First Book, January 26, 2005.

9. Interview, Kyle Zimmer, First Book, January 24, 2005.

10. From Cause Marketing Forum session, January 11, 2005.

11. Interview, Kristian Darigan, Cone Inc., December 13, 2004.

12. Ibid.

13. Carol Cone, Mark Feldman, and Alison DaSilva, "Cause and Effects," *Harvard Business Review* (July 2003): 3.

14. Interview, Vicki Gordon, InterContinental Hotels Group, April 5, 2005.

15. From www.worldwildlifefund.org (Edelman, March 2003).

16. Interview, Kevin Martinez, Home Depot, March 30, 2005.

17. Presentation made in early 1990 and the program was launched later that year.

18. Interview, Howard Byck, January 26, 2005.

19. Interview, Laurelea Conrad, December 1, 2004.

20. Interview, Josh Knights, February 14, 2005.

21. Ibid.

22. Press release, Office of New York State Attorney General, Eliot Spitzer, April 6, 1999.

23. www.give.org.

24. www.dove.com/real_beauty.

25. www.loveisnotabuse.com.

CHAPTER 8

Building the Cause-Marketing Program: Collaboration, Combining Assets, Creating Value

BUILD THE CAUSE-MARKETING PROGRAM

A marketing program is built on the four *P*'s: product, promotion, price, and place. A cause-marketing program's four *P*'s are partner, purpose, passion, and profits. This begins by proactively seeking a strategic collaborative fit where there is partner alignment. The purpose of the cause-marketing arrangement must then be built so that it sees the combining of assets (with a passionate commitment to the cause) and creation of value (profits) for both partners. Tying it all together is joint planning and an agreement that outlines the goals, roles, and responsibilities; decision-making process; and structure for the cause-marketing program.

COLLABORATION: STRATEGIC PARTNER ALIGNMENT

The second component of a cause-marketing framework is collaboration. If you are being proactive or are approached by a company, having the right strategic partner is critical to the success of a cause-marketing program. A good collaborative alignment will see each partner actively seeking to advance each other's agenda and sharing responsibilities, contributions, and risks. It will also ensure that the relationship is a mutually beneficial relationship and based on trust, respect, openness, and transparency. The steps to building a collaboration are

- Research fit: Your brand + assets + corporate needs = partnership potential.
- Make the connection: Proactively seek a strategic collaborative alignment that achieves mutual benefit.

- Prepare presentation material: Simple document focused on "what's in it for them."

- Explore, and agree: Find the right fit for both partners.

Research, Information Is King!

Proactively building a cause-marketing program starts with your list of potential cause partners. Now further research is necessary to confirm strategic fit. This includes learning about the business and their potential goals and needs, what assets and resources your organization could bring to assist them in achieving these goals, and how the relationship would benefit your organization. Finally, cultural and values compatibility needs to be considered. Successful cause-marketing alliances depend on the partners' ability to achieve mutually beneficial goals and work together in an open, respectful relationship.

The list of possible partners needs to be researched fully, including ones where you already have a relationship. Remember, you're looking for marketing and business objective fit, not alignment with their corporate giving objectives. Research can be undertaken by reviewing corporate Web sites, annual reports, and community relations reports; keeping track of articles through newspapers and journals; and making informal queries through your organization's volunteers and business networks. Information obtained will not only help determine fit, but will also assist in preparing for a marketing approach. Research must do the following.

Analyze the company and create a profile: What, who, where, when, why, how? What is their business? What is their competitive position in the marketplace? Who are their competitors? Where do they operate? Who are their consumers? What is the demographic of their consumers? Who might be future consumers? How do they advertise to the consumer? What media coverage do they currently get? How many employees do they have? What is the employee demographic? Who are their suppliers? How do they drive business? What is their current community involvement? "We sit and think what is the demographic for this company, where are their growth areas, what are their historic themes. We really do our homework,"[1] says Kyle Zimmer, president and cofounder of First Book, the national literacy organization. "Then we review elements of our organization and its programs and analyze how they would best serve the mutual goals of a cause-marketing initiative." First Book calls this "asset mapping."

Review their business goals, needs, and challenges. Create a list of potential goals, priorities, and needs of the business. What are they worried about? Is their business growing? What are their current priorities? Do they have new products? This list will help you start to hone in on potential areas of importance to the company.

Think about their needs and challenges. Seasoned cause marketer Kurt Ascher-mann of the Boys and Girls Clubs of America has created what he calls the "hi-erarchy of felt needs." "When we're working on a relationship, we look at every single audience that we're dealing with on the corporate side and every indi-vidual that will be impacted. We then figure out what would spin the propeller on his or her need, what would get them excited, what would help them. We cre-ate these hierarchies of felt needs to describe the two or three things that would affect everybody."[2]

Ask yourself, do they need to increase customer loyalty, attract and retain loyal employees, raise their profile, or increase sales? A local car dealer needs to en-courage people to test drive their cars; a local hardware store wants to increase sales of paint in their store; a manufacturer has a priority to increase diversity in the workforce; a national financial institution needs to connect to a cause that res-onates with their largely female staff. What do your potential partners need, what are their business goals, their challenges?

Look for a match between their needs and your assets, programs, and resources. Which of their needs or goals could benefit from an alignment with your organization? What assets, programs, and resources of the nonprofit could mesh with specific business goals and needs? A simple way to analyze fit is through a matrix that ranks corporate goals to nonprofit assets. Listing nonprofit assets on the vertical and corporate goals on the horizontal in a simple ranking of 1 (low) to 3 (high) can help pinpoint potential alignments and focuses for a cause program. (See Chap-ter 10, First Book case study for example.)

Outline how a cause-marketing relationship with the company will help you achieve your mission and goals. The collaboration must be win-win, enabling both partners to achieve goals that could not have been met without working together and un-dertaking the cause program. Shared goals and objectives could include reach-ing a specific target audience, driving attendance and participation in an event, or collaborating on educational messaging. There must be common ground and interests for an alliance to work. As Cynthia Currence, National Vice President, Strategic Corporate Marketing Alliances, says, "We are looking at relationships that can further our objectives. We have mission priorities and we look for relationships that will extend our message and help to create the ambiance for behavior change. Two-thirds of cancer is correlated to choices people make everyday. Many of those are consumer choices, so why not work with people who are experts in influencing consumer behaviour."[3]

Research compatibility and company's reputation. Another central tenet for a strong partnership is compatibility. Although individuals from a business and a nonprofit organization may work well together, if the overall cultures don't mesh, the strength of the cause-marketing program can suffer. Shared values, mutual respect and trust, excellent communication, and commitment are all essential to a good cultural fit. There must be a commitment to transparency and accountability. Talk to people who know the company, read about them in the newspaper, and review their annual reports and corporate social responsibility statements. Sometimes values and culture can't be fully determined until a face-to-face meeting occurs.

A nonprofit organization's name and reputation is its most valuable asset and usually the most critical element in a potential cause-marketing program. An alliance between a nonprofit organization and a corporate partner builds an associative link between the two. But the link can and must be one that does not jeopardize either organization's core values and mission. More in-depth research is an important means of determining the company's reputation. Making a wise choice depends on asking questions such as: Are their products compatible with your values? How is the corporation viewed? Does it have a track record of good corporate management, governance, and social responsibility? What are the company's policy and track record regarding environmental and human rights issues? What are the employee hiring and benefits programs like? A nonprofit marketing collaboration cannot be an antidote to a damaged or poor reputation. It is a way of making a strong brand or company stronger.

Nonprofits must also recognize that companies will do the same with them. Cause programs are built to support causes, not charities, and potential partners will want to work with the strongest partner representing their special issue. Nonprofits must be prepared to answer questions about how the public views them and to position themselves as strong, credible partners.

Finally, what risks might this collaboration involve? Be honest with yourself. Potential risks shouldn't necessarily eliminate a potential partner, but it is important to think about this right up front. Articulate them and make sure they are carefully considered. In the end, rewards must outweigh risks in any cause-marketing arrangement.

An Important Discussion—Same Meaning: Different Words

Different organizations describe their corporate cause relationships using different language. Is there any right one, more commonly used, or relevant for today? Here are three different perspectives from three cause-marketing experts.

Partnership was the first and most commonly used way of describing cause programs. The word was used to express the combined synergies and benefits and to paint a picture of a close relationship. Kyle Zimmer of First Book still refers to the word *partnership*. "I am of course cautious if talking about legal relationships, or using the word in legal documents, but most of the time I don't worry about it because the people we are doing business with understand that we are partners in reaching our joint goal of reaching kids in need," she states.[4]

Cynthia Currence's experience with the American Cancer Society has led her to prefer collaboration or alliance as the way always to describe her cause-marketing arrangements. The organization never uses the word *partnership*. IRS auditors look at the word *partnership* in agreements or marketing materials as a red flag. In legal language, partnership means that both partners are active in a commercial activity. This can mean a nonprofit's activity is subject to Unrelated Business Income Tax. "You can easily avoid raising flags by not using partnership or joint venture in your presentations or contracts," states Currence. "ACS is very careful to call its relationships "alliances" and "collaborations.""[5]

Alignment is another word becoming more commonly heard to describe the cause-marketing relationship. Canadian cause marketer Laurelea Conrad would rather use the word *alignment* than *partnership* or *collaboration*. "In my view they are not of the same ilk. We come together synergistically. The charity offers a proposition to the corporation or brand that strategically meets their business goals and at the same time aligns with the charity's priorities. The charity cannot afford to share liability and the organizations are equal which the term partnership would imply. It is safer and simpler for both parties at the start to be clear about the exact nature of the relationship to avoid misunderstanding later on."[6]

Make the Connection

Connecting with potential partners and exploring possibilities is the next step in creating a collaborative cause program. With your research in hand and a list prepared, it's time to make the connection. Connections can be made through several different means.

- *Those closest to you:* Finding a cause-marketing partner starts with looking at those you already know. Following the 60-30-10 rule, these are your best prospects for building cause-marketing programs. The corporate relationships that already exist are the most likely prospects for deeper cause-marketing programs. You already have an understanding of each other's goals, culture, needs, and where there could be a collaborative fit. Many cause-marketing partnerships are extensions of existing relationships or developed as a result of established connections. An added benefit is that presenting and discussing cause-marketing collaborations will help you refine your messages and presentation to potential new partners. Remember as well, your existing partners could introduce you to other possible corporate supporters such as their suppliers, distributors. Ask for their advice and suggestions. You'll find many will be pleased to help.

- *National organizations with local affiliates:* Another part of the 60-30-10 rule applies for national organizations with local affiliates. Many local affiliates have their own relationships with local corporations that could be built into cause-marketing partners. Companies located in certain cities might already have established relationships with the local organizations. Use their connections and expertise to assist in making the connection. Have them participate in organizing and preparing for the meeting, and have them join you in the presentation and discussions. Not only will they add great value, but the essential buy-in process will have started. The American Cancer Society is one organization where local affiliates are key sources of connections. "Many of our conversations wouldn't happen without local relationships."[7] states Cynthia Currence of the Society. The Society uses a team approach that always involves a local and national person in the meetings.

- *Personal connections—board, volunteers:* Cause marketing can open up opportunities to work with new corporate partners. Board and community members help connect you to the targeted corporations identified in your research. A company might be targeted specifically because a board member has a strong connection. A phone call from them asking for a meeting with your organization will smooth the way and give you a chance to present your organization. Volunteers already engaged in your organization can also be great advocates for the nonprofit. It was CIBC staffers who were already involved and participating in the Canadian Breast Cancer Foundation "Run for the Cure" who were driving forces in establishing that long-term cause relationship. "Many of our cause-corporate alliances came from employees who brought us forward internally,"[8] explains Mark Hierlihy, National Director, Development, Canadian Breast Cancer Foundation.

- *Advertising agencies, third-party connectors:* Many companies work with advertising agencies, and they can be important conduits into the corporate world. Often they will be aware of their clients' needs and if there is a fit. As cause marketing becomes more mainstream, more and more agencies are building competencies in this area and adding it to the mix of services they provide. Once the purviews of niche firms, some of the more prominent nonprofits are now receiving a high percentage of their leads this way.

  Many nonprofit organizations work closely with agencies and have them do prospecting for the organization. Having a relationship with a nonprofit can help an agency land a client they might not otherwise have secured. The agency will be paid by the company to coordinate and execute the cause-marketing program.

  Working with advertising agencies as go-betweens can be helpful but also create a layer of complexity. Agencies will be protective of their clients and can put their interests and those of their clients ahead of the nonprofit organization. In the end, it's the company that pays their bills. Know this, and work to build the relationship with the corporate partner through direct meetings and regular contact. Establish this connection as soon as possible is the advice of leaders in the cause-marketing realm.

- *Cold calls:* Sometimes the only option for nonprofit organizations is a cold call. Although this is a difficult approach, it can work, especially if you have done your homework and are confident of a fit and the potential to provide benefit to the company. The biggest challenge will be finding the right person. Also persistence is a key when making cold calls. Don't expect anyone to call you back. Find a way to keep calling until you reach the contact directly.

- *If they contact you:* Companies are proactively building cause-marketing programs themselves, and some organizations will be contacted directly. Research is needed to make sure of fit, and any proposal that is presented by a company should follow internal processes for review before moving forward. Follow the seven *C*'s cause-marketing framework to build, execute, and achieve nonprofit goals and outcomes.

Different Levels of Connection Will Result in Different Programs

Cause marketing can be created at many levels within a company from the brand manager to the president and CEO. The level of connection and the responsibilities of the person will determine the size, scope, and nature of the cause initiative. If a program is built through a brand manager responsible for a specific product, it will likely be a promotional or sales-oriented and a one-off initiative. Deeper, longer-term commitments tied to the company brand or corporate social responsibility programs traditionally are made with senior members of the management team. They have the authority and capacity to build cause campaigns that are broader than a specific product and involve substantial messages and behavior impacts.

Connect in Person and Begin to Build the Relationship

Once a connection is made, a request for a face-to-face meeting is an essential part of building a cause-marketing collaboration. Before going into a meeting, be prepared. "I don't want a meeting where I have to spend the whole time explaining what we do and what our needs are" is a comment I heard over and over again from corporate cause marketers.

KINTERA, CONNECTING BUSINESS AND NONPROFITS FOR MUTUAL BENEFIT

Kintera is a for-profit business providing technology solutions to the nonprofit sector. One of their overarching goals is helping nonprofits make the best use of technology and getting it in their hands as quickly as possible. The company's philosophy and approach is very simple: through a value-added service their cause-marketing department helps to bring corporations and nonprofit organizations together to assist with the company's marketing goals while helping to further a cause's mission and ability to succeed through technology solutions.

Early in 2001, Kintera was assisting a national health charity develop fundraising sites for their network of over 1,000 chapters. While the nonprofit was completely sold on the benefit of the technology, one of challenges was rolling out technology across the 1,000 individual chapters, many of which had a different understanding and ability to implement the technology. The cost to implement quickly was formidable, several hundred thousand dollars. As a result, the charity had a three-year rollout plan to get all the chapters up and running.

Kintera had an alliance with a major credit card company that was interested in the nonprofit sector. In 2005, over $250 billion was donated to nonprofits in the United States, and 97% was done through cash or check. The company saw the nonprofit sector as a burgeoning market and the opportunity to have Kintera act as the go-between to put together a cause-marketing alliance that would be win-win-win.

The credit card company agreed and paid through their new and emerging markets departments to cover the initial setup fees for the charity. This enabled them to go from setting up 12 chapters to 350 chapters in the first six months and to having full activation in the next six months. On the donation page (called point of sale by the corporate partner) the default is set to this particular credit card company. It is in the first drop-down box and beside this is a very subtle message saying, "This site is made possible by a gift from the credit card company."

Simple and yet it is highly effective for all concerned. One of the charity's major annual events raises over $50 million annually. Now people can make their donations online—through their credit card. So with the help of Kintera and some marketing dollars from the corporate partner, the charity has full activation of their Web sites from coast to coast, the credit card company met their business goals—18 months in advance of target—and Kintera achieved its goal of helping nonprofits with technology solutions—win-win-win.[9]

Prepare a Tailored Presentation: "What's In It for Them"

Take the information you have learned from your research and translate this into a tailored presentation that shows them you know and understand their company, its needs, and its challenges. Also take the time to find out more about the people who will be at the meeting.

Remember, this is an exchange of value, not just philanthropy. So the focus of the meeting has to be on what you can bring to a relationship, what synergy and benefit can be created by working together. That doesn't mean you can't share your story and mission—that's an important part of building the passion. What it does mean is the meeting is not about your needs. It's about looking for a mutually beneficial relationship where assets can be combined to create value for both parties.

How formal should a presentation be? Your material needs to be succinct and professionally presented. A Powerpoint or desktop flipchart gives focus to a meeting and is a great leave-behind document. Use lots of visuals; make the presentation entertaining and inspiring. Go in with specific ideas—that's very important! It shows you've done your homework and understand what matters to them. Know their two or three priorities—things that would help them achieve their goals and objectives. A company whose interests are directly related to sales means presenting your image and impact and specific mechanism on how this might help with the company. If branding the organization with the cause, an event or specific program that could give them high profile might be the focus of the presentation and discussion.

"When we go in for a meeting, we say 'we believe you are focused on kids in this age range.' We want to show that we think about how our assets overlap and how we can tell a story to that demographic. We then bring the passion in, by talking about how we can change the world by having them involved," says Kyle Zimmer of First Book. "Not one time during the meeting do we say 'you really should want to do this because it is the right thing to do,' because there are thousands of right things to do. We want to talk to them about why First Book is the right thing to do for their business goals as well as the cause."[10]

The Arthritis Foundation calls these meetings their "capabilities presentation." "We outline what we could do including media, public relations, and other possible collaborative efforts and then we listen," says Mary Norman, Vice President, Strategic Marketing Alliances. "We do a lot of research to look where there might be a fit and how we can make it work for the partner."[11]

Examples of past programs you've been involved in or other cause-marketing programs that have worked can speak volumes, build your credibility, and make a concept real. Remember the two key rules: simple and executable. **Number one**, keep it simple. They need to be able to see how easy it is to understand and execute and how it will work for them. **Number two**, cause-marketing veterans stress the importance of presenting a turnkey operation; show how the execution will happen. If you're being proactive in your approaches, you need to have a program well laid out that shows you have thought through all the details and how they fit into the plan. The execution piece has to be as easy as possible because often they don't have resources. Simple and solid are important features for a cause-marketing program presentation.

Although the presentations will explain the program, some flexibility will be needed to customize and tailor to their specific needs. No matter how much research you do, there will always be factors of importance to them that you can't foresee or know. That's why half the meeting should be listening and asking questions. What are your immediate priorities? Would a program that involved your employees be a goal? Is a national, regional, or local area important for execution? What is your definition of success? Why were you willing to meet with us? How do you measure results? Once you've learned this information, you can start to narrow down possibilities and make more formal suggestions at the next meeting.

A desired outcome of the meeting will be to determine potential for collaboration and compatibility. After the meeting, a debrief session should explore a few questions that will help determine if the conversation will be continued and opportunities explored.

- *Potential for collaboration:* Is there interest in a cause-marketing collaboration? Does it make sense? Is the time right? Is there a fit between their needs and priorities and yours and alignment between assets and resources? What was their response to which ideas? What were key learnings?

- *Compatibility:* You could have the potential for collaboration, but you have to ask the question— Is there compatibility between culture and values? Does it feel right? Is there interest and passion in your mission and brand position? Would there be enough similarity in problem solving? Work style? Ethics? Communications style?

- *Timing:* Don't think that a cause-marketing program will be built in a few short months; any cultivation will take at least 8 months. "The number one piece of advice I could give," states Matthew Goldstein, formerly of the Food Bank for New York City, "you've got to get them turned on early. Any cultivation takes between 8 and 12 months or even longer. When you do your research on partners check their review time and budget period. They need lead time to fit a program into their cycle."[12]

- *No doesn't mean no, it means no not now or no not this program:* Persistence is the hallmark of a good cause marketer. It can often take time to find the right fit. Getting to know a partner and where their interests lie means that while one cause proposition might not work, another could.

Explore Different Ideas and Concepts

If interest is expressed in a possible cause-marketing collaboration, it can take time to explore how to make the program work and to fine-tune it to their needs. Another meeting could be needed to allow for a full exploration of possibilities. Ideas will be tested, further suggestions investigated, and what could work narrowed down. Nonprofits have to be diligent in following up on ideas or information that might be needed; be timely in your response, and be persistent in keeping the conversation and wheels moving forward. This is also important in building trust and convincing the potential partner you have the drive and capacity to deliver on commitments.

Propose, Remembering That Most Relationships Start Small and Use the Big Simple Idea

It's important to remember that newly established cause-marketing collaboration will likely start off small and build as respect and trust is earned—on both sides. Baby steps can led to big things. One seasoned nonprofit cause-marketing professional tells the story of working on tight timelines on a small program. The pressure was high, the execution challenging, but the group pulled it off, and the results were a great success. Today, that relationship has turned into one of their largest cause alliances.

HALLMARK CARDS (CANADA), CANADIAN PARKS PARTNERSHIP, PARKS CANADA

The first meeting indicated a clear interest in building a cause-marketing program. There was an overlap between goals that could result in a mutually beneficial relationship, and the cultural fit was strong. The question was what would a cause-marketing program look like? How it would it work? After 18 months of meetings, discussions, and lots of persistence on our side, an agreement was reached that saw the creation of a series of holiday cards featuring national parks and national historic sites. The cards were sold through a newly launched corporate card program and were the first step in a larger, more in-depth program that saw the creation of a whole product line including note cards, journals, travel diaries, and cards sold in their stores across Canada.

Agree but Check Against Guidelines, Run Through Approval Process and Risk Assessment

Final proposals developed must be taken back and run through the approval process of the nonprofit organization. This is where having the process in place will facilitate decision making. Although this was covered in Chapter 7, and suggested criteria were outlined, the importance of a clear approval process can't be overstated.

"Having a clearly outlined process has really helped us along the way," says Kathy Rogers, VP Cause Initiatives and Integrated Marketing, American Heart Association. "It may seem common sense to us, but we need a framework for approval and buy-in."[13]

Approval processes should be straightforward and allow for quick decision making. Most of the nonprofits I spoke with had a similar approach where the proposed cause alliance was written up outlining all the details. Every nonprofit approval line was a bit different, ranging from a board committee to the executive leadership of the organization. The committee has agreed on parameters of what they will do and commit to cause relationship. Don't make it too complex or difficult to make decisions quickly.

Internal review and assessment will be critical in making the program work. This includes making sure that the program can be fully activated, especially important for a national nonprofit with local chapters or affiliates; it meets all the outlined guidelines for cause-marketing alliances; there is internal buy-in at all necessary levels of the organization; and a risk assessment is completed. The corporate partner will likely have a similar process that ensures top-level buy-in.

The depth of analysis will depend on the size and scope of the proposed program and the nature of the nonprofit and potential corporate partner. For example, a local food bank working with a local restaurant might have a decision-making process that involves the executive director and head of fund development talking and approving the relationship. Final agreement sees both partners achieving mutual benefits in an atmosphere of respect, open communications, and trust. A broader, deeper program with a national nonprofit that involves local affiliates would need to involve approval at several levels within the organization.

COMBINE ASSETS AND AIM FOR MAXIMUM BENEFIT

Any cause-marketing partnership is an important two-way value exchange that relies on each partner to succeed. Ultimately, cause-marketing partners come together for mutual benefit by building on each other's strengths and combining assets to create a win-win partnership. By working together they produce an outcome far greater than anything that each organization could have achieved independently. Each partner contributes different capabilities and resources and by working together with frankness and trust they add a second level of value.

Once a cause-marketing program is determined, partners should

- Analyze individual assets: Are they complementary, supplementary?
- Determine how to combine: Aim to leverage for maximum benefit.

Put out the entire assets and resources that each partner can bring to the alliance and determine which can complement and/or supplement the relationship. Non-profits have their intangible assets of name, logo, and reputation that are a fundamental part of a cause collaboration. But they also have programs, events, and resources that can add value to the relationship. Corporate assets can include employee volunteers, marketing and media contacts, leveraging of resources, or professional skills or know how. Look where it makes sense to combine assets to maximize the benefits of the collaboration.

For example, the initial collaboration between Post Cereal, Canadian Parks Partnership, and Parks Canada included a contest for five trips for four to national parks across Canada. The organizations worked with the local superintendents, parks staff, and friends groups at each of the chosen national parks to provide unique behind-the-scenes tours, which added value to the promotion and a unique experience for the winners and ensured buy-in from local parks staff, who had an opportunity to bring their expertise and enthusiasm to make the trip unique and educational.

Employee Volunteers: An Important Asset for Both Sides!

An important asset in a cause-marketing alliance is a company's employees. Look at all the opportunities you can to engage and excite them in the relationship. Encouraging employee volunteers can be drivers in cause-marketing programs, and nonprofits can benefit enormously from this support. Cause partners can be critical sources of human muscle and brainpower for cause programs. London Children's Museum's cobranded program, 3M Science in Your World Gallery, would not have been possible without the financial commitment of 3M. But equally significant was the contribution of the company's science staff in developing messaging, experiments, and activities that made the gallery come alive. The benefit to the company: creating pride, building loyalty, and most importantly giving employees a sense that they are part of something bigger than just making and selling products and services.

Celebrities and Cause-Marketing Campaigns

Another asset that can be brought to enhance a cause-marketing relationship is a celebrity. Many corporate partners will bring their own connections or work with their partner to help secure a celebrity for the campaign. For example, First Book and Universal Studios Dr. Seuss' "Cat in the Hat Challenge" involved celebrities from the movie; Lee Jeans' "One Day, One Cause" features a celebrity spokesperson coordinated by the company.

Celebrities can add great value, increase media coverage and public interest, but also create a level of complexity in the mix. It's hard to negotiate with a big celebrity; consider expert help or support from your corporate partner.

CREATING VALUE: DETERMINE FOR BOTH PARTNERS

Collaboration and combining assets are the means used to form a cause-marketing arrangement, but creating mutually beneficial value for both sides is the intended outcome. For corporations, creating shareholder value is paramount. The expectation is that cause-marketing programs will result in additional sales, new customers, expanded markets, and marketplace or company positioning. Although there are often hard marketing objectives, cause programs also are undertaken for soft marketing reasons such as expressing corporate values that can strengthen human resource management and corporate culture while enhancing the community reputation.

Nonprofits should view the relationship the same way. Their name, reputation, and the cause for which they stand is being associated with a corporation and their brand to generate sales and improve their business partner's image. They have to make certain they negotiate terms that represent the full and fair value their partners will receive from the cause relationship, based on the value they bring.

Front-end-loading the relationship by joint planning is critical. Determine what the alliance will achieve, who is responsible for what, and how it will be evaluated. Joint planning will outline the value being created for each partner up front; this means before launching the program, do the following.

- Define value: Outline the expectations, goals, roles, responsibilities, and benefits to each partner through a joint planning process.

- Finalize value: Create a legal agreement that puts in writing the details of the program, including roles and responsibilities, decision making, approvals, and structure.

- Evaluate value: Determine how success will be measured.

Define Value That Each Partner Will Receive

What are the expectations and benefits that will accrue to each partner? This is the time when you start to drill down and outline the goals, objectives, and expectations and benefits that will be delivered by each of the collaborative alliance partners. Concrete goals and objectives must be developed that are clear to all partners and can be realistically attained.

A key learning for nonprofits: underpromise and overdeliver. This is the time to be realistic about what you can provide on items like level of execution, support, and turnaround for approvals. Too often in the nonprofit sector, we think we can make a little go a long way. The reality is too often different. Consider your resources and staff capacity before committing to undertake specific initiatives in the cause program. Nonprofits need to take a hard and realistic look at the impact of the cause collaboration on the organization. For example, if you're going to advertise the 1-800 line, are the folks in that area properly resourced to handle extra calls? Make sure you can meet commitments without overwhelming your organization at any point throughout the implementation and, equally important, without disappointing your partner by not delivering on promises. Manage expectations, be honest, and then work like the dickens to do what you said you would do and then some!

Pricing: How Much Are You Worth?

The next consideration is how much should a cause collaboration generate for the nonprofit? What is the value to a company to be aligned and associated with your organization? How much is a trusted brand worth? Many companies regard it as their most valuable asset. But nonprofits are just beginning to fully appreciate their value and know how to put a dollar value on its worth. That's largely because it can be a difficult and costly thing to do.

As we've discussed, cause marketing is about a value exchange, not a donation, which is traditionally based on the budget of the project. The idea of valuing a nonprofit brand alignment is still quite new to the charitable community. However, some organizations have started to establish a monetary figure for their brand with a view of helping them grow the value further. A number of agencies have developed specific formulas to analyze and determine value of an event, program, or overall brand itself. Brand valuation for nonprofits considers factors such as the public's level of trust that the donation will be used effectively, the public's perception of the organization's financial stability, the public's personal experience with the cause, the organization's level of contact with the donor, and the ease of transaction for the donor.

So how do you value your organization, especially if it isn't practical for your organization to spend the dollars to do a formal valuation? Some organizations establish a minimum level that they require for association. One well-known national organization looks for "a minimum first year guarantee of $250,000." Another environmental group looks for a minimum of cash, in this case $50,000 or

HABITAT FOR HUMANITY

Habitat for Humanity hired the Interbrand consultancy, based in New York, to put a financial value on its brand. The 2002 valuation came in at $1.8 billion—an enormous figure that the organization has used to leverage corporate support. Before learning its value, Habitat was raising approximately $26 million in cash and gifts in kind from corporations. In 2003, armed with this information, they were able to raise $39 million from corporations and teamed up with Lowe's and Whirlpool for a multimillion-dollar cross-sector cause-marketing relationship.[14]

double that amount of in-kind support, for example, $100,000 worth of in-kind promotional support. The reason for establishing a minimum guarantee is to keep an appropriate premium on the organization's name and logo and to recognize the work that is needed in these more involved cause arrangements. Often, nonprofits will build in a "growth scenario" in the pricing structure of a cause-marketing collaboration. They will start with a minimum and the return to the nonprofit grows if the cause program is successful—a built-in bonus structure that creates incentives for success.

Minimums can be difficult for some companies to understand. The Canadian Breast Cancer Foundation (CBCF) is one organization that has recently put a minimum on cause-marketing relationships. The reaction from one company to this requirement was, "Aren't you happy to take our money as a charity?" "Our response," explained Mark Hierlihy, National Director of Development, CBCF, "was clear. I responded if you want to give us a gift as a company of any amount we will be grateful, very grateful. But what you're talking about is not a gift; it's a cause-marketing relationship. You're asking to use our brand to forward your company's image and that's marketing, not just philanthropy. That was painful for her to understand."[15] But it's an important distinction and one nonprofits need to consider to ensure that their brand value is preserved.

Putting a value on a nonprofit's brand, especially ones that are smaller, new to the field, or aren't as well known, takes research, and even then determining a price is half science and half art. Several experienced cause marketers said, "Frankly, it's often about what the market will bear." Finding the sweet spot starts with analyzing four key factors.

1. *Organization:* What kind of an organization do you have? What sector are you in (e.g., health care, social services, arts, environment)? What's the organization's scope (e.g., national, regional, local)? What is your

profile in the community? These will all be factors that will influence the prices your organization will receive.

2. ***Benefits and costs:*** What is the focus of the cause-marketing collaboration (e.g., product sales, event, program)? What are your corporate partners getting in return? Are there any costs involved for the nonprofit (e.g., event costs)? The direct costs are the science part of the equation. The value of the assets and benefits are where art comes in.

3. ***Environment:*** These factors relate directly to the variables of your environment. What are the economic conditions in your community? What is the competition? Do companies have lots of options as to who they could partner with? What are other nonprofits earning?

4. ***Strategy:*** If a nonprofit's strategy is the awareness a cause-marketing program can provide, the dollars you request from a corporate partner may be lower, because you want to get the most companies possible involved. If it is revenue, you'll price higher to protect the value of the brand. If a nonprofit doesn't determine focus and strategy, it could be easy to sell out to every company that comes along and nine times out of 10, when you get done with your promotion, you haven't raised as much money as you would have if you put a stake in the ground. It's important to be focused.

Contribution: More Than Just Dollars

All cause-marketing collaborations involve more than just a financial contribution to the nonprofit. In fact, it is not uncommon that this value is significantly more than the dollars involved. One of the biggest challenges for nonprofits is putting a financial worth on these contributions. But it is important to do. This not only can help sell the collaboration internally, but it will also put a true value on what the corporate partner brings to the relationship. Consider all aspects of what a corporate partner provides:

- Cash contribution: Total amount of dollars contributed to alliance
- In-kind contribution: Total amount of in-kind contribution the organization would have had to purchase without the contribution; and/or a percentage of amount of in-kind support that would be nice, but not needed.
- Corporate advertising contribution: Value for advertising dedicated solely to the partnership and/or advertising where the partnership is an add-on
- Employee contribution—volunteers, employee fundraising, and employee giving

Often, the biggest benefit of cause-marketing relationships is the profile they provide and, because profile is such a big benefit of cause marketing, some nonprofits are requesting right up front a set amount of money be spent on advertising the cause program. UNICEF, for example, seeks not only a minimum financial guarantee, but also minimum advertising dollars spent around the collaboration to promote it. The Arthritis Foundation does the same, ensuring a certain level of advertising and promotional support will provide much valued profile building for the organization—and of course the cause alliance.

Create a Written Agreement

A written agreement is a central element of a cause-marketing arrangement. It puts all discussions and decisions in black and white and is the time for misunderstandings to be reconciled and clear processes and structure outlined. Depending on the complexity, it can be as simple as a letter or memorandum of understanding or as formal as an in-depth legal document created by a lawyer. Always consider getting the agreement, regardless of the depth, reviewed by a lawyer. Many will provide pro bono support to charitable organizations. Regardless of whether this is a local cause alliance between a local health charity and an independent retailer or a big national arrangement, key elements of an agreement should cover the following.

- Description of goals, objectives, purpose: Rationale for cause-marketing arrangement
- Responsibilities: Expectations of responsibilities of each partner
- Term of the agreement: Length of agreement
- Milestones: What happens and when
- Payment: How much, when, and minimum guarantees
- Decision making and approval process: Outline how decisions will be made, lines of communications and how review and approval of all materials will take place
- Use of logo: How trademarks can be used and approval process
- Disagreements: A clause that will explain any steps that will be taken in case of a disagreement or unforeseen result with the program
- Termination: How and why the agreement will be terminated
- Notice: Who will be the key contacts of both sides
- General: Anything that has not been covered, including confidential and proprietary information of both the organization and the company, hold harmless, etc.

Words to Avoid in Agreement

- *Partnership:* This term implies equal liability and should *not* be used.
- *Joint Ventures:* This word implies a legal partnership and should *not* be used.

Evaluate What You Want to Achieve

What does success look like for each partner? Evaluating what you want the cause alliance to achieve up front helps in the analysis at the back end, after the cause program has been executed. The three important elements to evaluate are outputs, inputs, and outcomes.

- **Outputs:** What are the tangible, measurable results (that can have a number attached to it) that the arrangement is targeted to achieve? This can include dollars raised through program/event/promotion, media impressions received, number of people reached through the program (e.g., in-store, at events), number of employees engaged in the cause activity, and assistance with achieving mission (e.g., increase number of women having mammograms).

- **Inputs:** What are the tangible items that are contributed to make the cause-marketing program take place? This will include in-kind contributions such as the additional marketing value to the nonprofit of in-store promotional information, employee volunteer contributions, or in the case of the non-profit's inputs, introductions to community influencers, for example.

- **Outcomes:** What are the intangible benefits, which can be hard to measure, but are intended program benefits/outcomes/impact from a cause-marketing program? This could include such things as capacity building of nonprofit organization as a result of cause program; access to new and broader publics; new relationships built with a company, employees, suppliers, or stakeholders; broader awareness of organization and mission; increased credibility of nonprofit because of cause relationships; and leveraged dollars.

CONCLUSION

A cause-marketing program is built on the four *P*'s of partner, purpose, passion, and profits. Begin by proactively seeking a strategic **collaborative fit** where there is partner alignment. Building a collaboration takes time, research, and perseverance. A nonprofit needs to research potential partners to determine fit. Once found, they must connect, explore, propose, and finally agree on a collaborative cause-marketing arrangement.

The purpose of the cause-marketing arrangement must then be built so that it sees the **combining of assets** (with a passionate commitment to the cause) to leverage for maximum benefit.

Although collaboration and combining assets are the means used to form a cause-marketing arrangement, **creating mutually beneficial value** for both sides is the intended outcome. Front-end-load the relationship by clearly defining goals, expectations, and benefits for each partner and what success looks like. Finally, create an agreement that puts in writing the details of the program, including roles, responsibilities, decision making, approvals, and structure.

The next chapter looks beyond the final elements of the cause-marketing framework and into cause partner satisfaction and retention through execution and wide-reaching communication, and finally achieving cause-marketing goals and objectives that result in positive community and corporate outcomes.

Endnotes

1. Interview, Kyle Zimmer, First Book, November 4, 2004.
2. Interview, Kurt Aschermann, Boys and Girls Clubs of America, November 22, 2004.
3. Interview, Cynthia Currence, American Cancer Society, January 25, 2005.
4. Interview, Kyle Zimmer, November 4, 2004.
5. Interview, Cynthia Currence, January 24, 2004.
6. Interview, Laurelea Conrad, December 1, 2004.
7. Ibid.
8. Interview, Mark Hierlihy, Canadian Breast Cancer Foundation, July 22, 2005.
9. Interview, Kelly McMakin, Kintera, July 1, 2005.
10. Interview, Kyle Zimmer, First Book, November 4, 2004.
11. Interview, Mary Norman, Arthritis Foundation, January 25, 2005.
12. Interview, Matthew Goldstein, Food Bank for New York City, July 29, 2005.
13. Interview, Kathy Rogers, American Heart Association, January 24, 2005.
14. John Quelch and James Austin, "Mining Gold in Not-for-Profit Brands," *Harvard Business Review* (June 2004): 24.
15. Interview, Mark Hierlihy, Canadian Breast Cancer Foundation, July 22, 2005.

CHAPTER 9

Implementing the Cause-Marketing Program: Execution and Corporate and Community Outcomes

EXECUTION AND OUTCOMES

This final chapter in "Getting It Right" looks at the last components of the cause-marketing framework. The first part focuses on ensuring cause-marketing partner satisfaction and retention. This starts with strong **execution** and delivery on commitments. Communications is a major goal of any cause program and key to partner satisfaction; proactively **communicate** the cause initiative through every possible means.

The last piece of the cause-marketing implementation framework is achieving the cause-marketing goals. Create a win-win-win program where there are positive **community and corporate outcomes** for the nonprofit, community, and corporation. Celebrate, evaluate, and build on what has been achieved.

IMPLEMENTING THE CAUSE PROGRAM

Building a cause-marketing collaboration takes lots of hard work, persistence, and determination. But for both partners it can't stop there. The success and long-term sustainability and growth of the collaborative cause-marketing alliance is determined by satisfying each partner's goals and objectives and building a relationship of mutual trust, respect, and openness. In cause marketing, nonprofits can't be passive recipients; they need to be active business partners to ensure that the relationship can be ongoing and flourish, not just a quick fix without lasting benefits.

EXECUTE: RELATIONSHIP MANAGEMENT AND DELIVERY

Cause-marketing relationships are more than just "deals"; they are collaborative alliances that take time and resources to manage, execute, and deliver. Many cause relationships start small. As trust and respect is built through delivery of results and communicating regularly and openly, relationships can grow. The ultimate effectiveness of the cause-marketing program and long-term relationship relies on how well the partners work together and execute the cause program. The steps to ensuring a strong execution are

- Manage delivery: Develop the internal structure, systems, and procedures to ensure delivery and accountability throughout organization.

- Create a communications structure: This includes regular, open, honest communications.

- Deliver on commitments: Follow through and deliver on all levels. Accountability is critical to building respect and a longer-term relationship.

Relationship Management Needs an Internal Structure

The first step in executing and managing the cause-marketing relationship is the development of an internal structure along with accompanying management processes and procedures. Strong relationships must have focused attention, adequate resources to achieve results, and an understanding of one another's expectations.

"We customize communications and execution strategies for each of our partners," explains Anne-Marie Grey, Chief, International and Corporate Alliances for UNICEF. "Cause marketing isn't a question of getting a cheque once a product is sold. We're working with that partner every step of the way. Often we'll educate them as to how to leverage our programs with the cause marketing program."[1]

Many nonprofits divide the "sales" and "execution" into two functions and have different staff manage each. The initial connections and constructing of the collaboration, the sales side, is most often done by one person, the relationship builder, who is skilled in this area. The "sales" work includes building the collaboration, structuring the program, and finalizing the value and agreement. Depending on the size and scope of the cause-marketing alliance, it will be done at a staff level or more senior level. Higher-level cause relationships almost always engage a senior manager of a nonprofit organization. If a deeper, longer-term cause arrangement is being built, it is ideal to have a senior leader to senior leader relationship.

Execution of the program is the next step. The execution needs to be managed on two levels. The first is tactical, ensuring delivery on commitments outlined in the agreement. The second is strategic, focusing on maintaining the relationship and looking for opportunities to leverage the program as it is being executed.

Structure to Manage Execution: Relationship Manager

To make the relationship operational, a designated staff should be assigned to manage the cause-marketing program execution. Many leading nonprofit cause-marketing organizations have adopted an advertising agency's strategic account management approach to overseeing their relationships. Strategic relationship management is a systematic process for managing key interactions and relationships. The relationship manager who oversees the collaborative relationship is responsible and accountable for execution and ongoing and long-term growth of the relationship. They are the guardian of the relationship, orchestrating the deployment of organizationwide resources to provide comprehensive support and fulfillment to the cause partner. In national organizations, this person usually coordinates and is the contact with the local organizations.

In small organizations, execution is often handled by the same person who built and negotiated the agreement. Whether it is the same person who negotiated the relationship or is a completely new person, execution requires different skills and competencies than those that built the relationship. Relationship managers need to have a respond-at-all-costs mentality, be very results driven, and be detail oriented.

A relationship management structure should not eliminate the people involved in building the relationship. They'll want to stay connected, perhaps meeting occasionally with the relationship manager and/or the corporate partners to ensure that the execution is living up to what was committed. But 80% of the day-to-day activities relating to the collaboration rest with the relationship manager.

Internal Approval Processes and Procedures

Internal processes and procedures must be established to manage the relationship and obtain the necessary approvals required for cause alliances. Processes and procedures should be done right up front when the organization is preparing for cause-marketing collaborations. What needs to be approved and delivered on will be outlined in the agreement, including sign-off of logo use, promotional material, or anything that features the organization's name and/or brand.

There should be a clear line of authority so the relationship manager can move approvals quickly through the system. It is their responsibility to follow process and handle the necessary approvals. They must engage the affected internal staff. This means regular communication with everyone in the organization touched by the collaboration. What are the necessary approvals? What is the time frame? If there is a problem, how will it be solved? As the "go-to" person, they will need to carefully develop a list of approvals or follow-throughs and timelines and responsibilities.

Use the agreement as the point of reference to develop this tool. By going through it in detail, the relationship manager can create a list of needed approvals and commitments the organization has made and time frames. For example, if the communications department needs to review and sign off the logo or brand presentation, they'll need to know what needs to be done and turnaround expectations. Circulate this information. Make sure everyone has the time they need to do their part of the job right.

Beyond the legal commitments, consider how the rest of the organization might be impacted. It is important to make sure that any of the other arms of an organization touched by the cause program are ready to handle any activities that might result after its launch. For example, if the 1–800 line is advertised as part of the promotion, the partner relationship manager should make sure the phone team has all the necessary information about the cause program and knows when to expect calls. Make a list of all possible impacts and make sure they are clearly communicated internally.

Cause Marketing 101 for Staff

One national literacy organization that was established over 35 years ago generates a significant percentage of its corporate support from cause-marketing arrangements. To have everyone understand the value of these relationships, a one-page "Cause Marketing 101" was created to explain why it's important and why help is often needed from other departments.

Benefits of a Multilevel Management Approach

Building and executing a cause-marketing relationship at several levels within a nonprofit organization has several important benefits. First, a structure that extends beyond one person is critical because staff turnover can occur. Second, it takes different talents and skills to coordinate the details of a cause-marketing relationship. You need someone who is detail oriented, has good internal relationship skills, and is driven by being results orients. It takes time, effort, and attention to detail to deliver on commitments. Finally, you want the organization to own the relationship, not just the person or team that built it. By involving others in the execution, it helps to embed the relationship in the broader organization.

Managing Multiple Alliances

For nonprofits with multiple cause relationships, managing a complex portfolio takes thought and careful management of time and resources. Many strategic partner managers will be responsible for numerous relationships, the number dependent on the complexity of the cause collaborations. Each relationship will be unique and will be different in terms of size and scope. Because of limited time and resources, priorities must be set as to the significance and importance of each relationship and resources dedicated accordingly.

National Organizations Working with Local Affiliates

All marketing is local in impact and circumstances, even when through a national vehicle. Local implementation can be a critical piece of fulfilling a national cause-marketing alliance. Some cause relationships won't require it specifically, but keeping in touch with the local affiliates and making sure they know about the relationship can build an understanding at the local level of cause marketing's importance and value. If the local affiliates are central to execution, clear and regular communications will be critical.

The Arthritis Foundation has established "CAT," the Chapter Alliance Team. This group meets quarterly (in person or by phone) to discuss potential cause relationships, programs that need their support for execution and any issues. "We are one big organization and we need to work to help each other,"[2] explains Mary Norman of the Foundation.

A major consideration is ensuring that there are benefits and rewards for local associations. Sometimes the returns are obvious and there is a direct payback for their involvement. Sometimes that is not the case. First Book has taken an incentive approach to involving their local affiliates. They have introduced financial inducements for their local groups and have found that this has really made a difference. The group identifies criteria for success and structures the rewards system based on going beyond set minimums.

Stay Connected by Communicating Regularly

Once an internal structure is built and processes and procedures finalized, partners must work to implement the program. Communication is a key to sustaining any meaningful alliance and building a relationship of mutual trust and respect and to ensuring success. It is also helps to generate ideas and generally keep informed about issues or challenges with the cause arrangement.

Every cause-marketing relationship should have a management plan that includes the best forms of communications and how often partners will meet face-to-face to review progress and performance. In the case of the CIBC and Canadian Breast Cancer Foundation, the execution team on both sides meet every second week for about six months before the event to make sure plans are running smoothly, that things are on track, and that they are meeting each other's expectations. The National Director of Development and CIBC's vice president responsible for the relationship meet monthly to iron out any strategic issues and make sure the relationship is strong.

Communications should be frequent, open, and honest. It should involve those responsible for establishing the collaborative alliance as well as the relationship manager.

As the cause-marketing initiatives unfold and partners meet regularly, many relationships with strong communications will move from colleagues to friends.

Communications should be a two-way flow of information and fully engage both partners. One of the benefits of regular communications is the opportunity to leverage resources and assets and make the program even stronger.

If You're Going to Miss a Deadline or an Issue Arises, Communicate!

It is important to try to prevent problems and to stay on target, but internal changes or challenges can impact either side's ability to honor commitments. For nonprofits it's important that if a deadline is going to be missed or an obligation unfulfilled, the issue is raised as early as possible so that damage is minimal and the opportunity to take action or revise the plan is maximized.

Handle Disagreements in Person

When disagreements do occur, they must be dealt with immediately and in person. Don't send an e-mail in frustration that you will later regret. If issues need to be addressed, pick up the phone or make an appointment to meet face-to-face. Before doing that, create a facts-issues-resolution sheet, a legal technique used to take disagreements away from being personalized and to focus on trying to find a solution. For example, in the case of a missed deadline: Facts: a deadline was agreed upon in the agreement; Issues: because the deadline was missed an advertising schedule was missed and an opportunity was lost to promote the product/program; Resolution: in the future move deadlines up several days to ensure that more time is available for internal approvals or work. Send an e-mail outlining the discussion and the final resolution.

Equal but Different: Cross-Sector Challenges

Although cause-marketing partnerships can be fruitful, making a collaboration work takes an appreciation and respect for the differences between the nonprofit and for-profit worlds and *a commitment to work as equal partners*. Although stressing the differences doesn't build a partnership, understanding and even discussing them can help make it work.

- **Resources:** Business partners will likely have more financial and human resources available to dedicate to a cause relationship. As one corporate cause marketer stated, "We'll have a dozen people involved in implementing a cause program and our nonprofit partner will have only one or two people working directly on it. You can imagine each one of our people sending e-mails asking questions. It can be overwhelming to respond to all the implementation needs and yet it is essential to stay on target and meet timelines for delivery of a cause-marketing arrangement." Resentment is another spinoff of resource differences. When you have two partners working together, working equally hard, it's not always easy to accept your corporate partner potentially has so many more resources available. Business has to understand the sensitivities of the nonprofit organization. On the other hand, nonprofits must appreciate the commercial needs of business to survive in a highly competitive environment.

- **Language:** Each sector has its own language and jargon. Appreciate that your partner might not know this language and take the time to explain. For example, nonprofit organizations will be looking at outcomes and outputs. Corporations will be interested in return on investment, and target markets.

- **Culture:** Business is in the business of selling products and making money; nonprofits are in the business of delivering services and providing community support. By this very nature the cultures of the organizations will be different. Business needs quick decision making and is driven by "time is money." Nonprofits can be slower moving and more consensus oriented. This is changing as more and more nonprofits take an entrepreneurial approach to running their organizations and need to generate the resources for success. Respect, understanding, and willingness to meet each other's needs is critical to success.

- **Equal, but different:** Cross-sector partners must respect each other and work as different but equal partners—this is critical for success. Nonprofits must not look at businesses as "part of the problem" to societal challenges or just as cash cows. For-profit partners must not look at nonprofits as the weak link or poor cousin, but must break down traditional stereotypes and collaborate for mutual benefit.

- **Bottom lines:** Success is measured in different ways by each partner. It's important to appreciate these differences and understand that goals for the collaboration will be different for each. The relationship must be mutually beneficial for it to work, and both must be committed to helping each other achieve their results.

- *Ownership:* Whose program is this anyway? Territoriality can pop up in cause-marketing relationships. One thing that is really important is making sure that a cause program initiated and driven by a charity doesn't lose that connection to the charity. The Canadian Breast Cancer Foundation recently reintroduced their name into the title of their annual signature fundraising event, Run for the Cure. The event is now cobranded as Canadian Breast Cancer Foundation, CIBC Run for the Cure. It is important that the charity, where the money will go and the research is done on finding a cure, doesn't get lost. Both sides agreed this was an important change.

Delivering on Commitments Builds Trust in a Relationship

Whatever a corporate partner's early relationship might have been with the nonprofit organization, their experience of implementation and delivering on commitments will determine the future relationship. Implementation is when the corporate partner finds out what can really be delivered as an organization and whether the reality lives up to the expectations and promises. Effective partners expect a lot of each other, but not so much that there are unrealistic expectations. Managing expectations is an important part of success. Promise what you can deliver on; don't overcommit. If results and delivery on commitments is not forthcoming, then value is not being created. If either side doesn't deliver, it puts success at risk. Nothing undermines trust more than a string of broken promises, so don't be tempted to say things you think your partner may want to hear, knowing your chances of delivering on them is low.

Nonprofits earn respect by delivering on expectations, and by delivering they earn the opportunity to continue or even expand a cause-marketing collaboration. Many relationships start with one activity and as the trust builds, new ideas come forward to try.

Overdeliver, and You Build for the Future

"Underpromise and overdeliver" is the message to all nonprofits involved in cause-marketing collaborations. Manage expectations on what the organization can realistically deliver and then go the extra mile to deliver beyond the commitments. This ensures that the company will have a great experience with the organization and will more likely result in an extension and expansion of the cause relationship.

KaBOOM!'s founder Darrell Hammond explains that a large part of their success is based on the underpromise, overdeliver formula and their willingness to patiently grow a relationship. When an insurance company approached the organization several years ago and asked them to coordinate a playground build with their employees, he was reticent. Why? The build was only six weeks from the time they first spoke. The company had committed to contributing $1 million to the organization if they had a good experience. With that incentive, the organization put their heart and soul into making it happen. The company was so pleased with the result, they doubled their initial commitment to $2 million, and over the next five years, the organization received an additional $2 million in support.

Suggestions on How to Overdeliver

Thinking creatively, nonprofits can add value to a relationship by having an employee day at the company; this could include bringing in expert speakers to talk about the cause, sharing information, generally engaging them, and giving them a sense of ownership of the cause. Another way to connect with employees is to engage their families. Company after company stressed the importance of employee pride with their cause-marketing relationships. "There is nothing our employees appreciate more than bragging to their children about the good things their company is doing," stated one senior-level executive at a utility company.

Introduce one set of supporters to another. The Susan G. Komen Foundation provides opportunities to promote business-to-business connections for their partners. The Foundation annually hosts a summit for their entire group of corporate supporters—a chance for them to talk to each other and explore possible business opportunities while sharing their passion for the breast cancer cause.

COMMUNICATE: INTERNALLY AND EXTERNALLY

Cause marketing is undertaken to publicly communicate the values of a company. That's an important corporate goal and one that must be part of cause partner satisfaction and retention. As well, communicating a company's support when done by a credible third party, such as a nonprofit organization, lends great value to the way their support is viewed in the community. As discussed earlier, the 2004 Cone Corporate Citizenship Report findings show the value of the nonprofit's communication tools. Companies have a challenge if they communicate it themselves. Only 23% wanted to hear from the company about their community support. The greatest credibility on information was obtained from third-party sources.[3] So what is the best way to get the word out?

- Build your communications messages: First, make sure you have clear, consistent messages and incorporate them in all the promotional material supporting the cause program.

- Communicate internally: Good communications starts from the inside out. Cause relationships need exposure and buy-in from internal stakeholders—your best advocates and enthusiasts in the community.

- Communicate externally: Use the cause-marketing collaboration to communicate with key stakeholders. Get your message out and that of your corporate partner.

Have a Consistent Message

Communicating starts with building some specific messages and then sticking to them. What you say as an organization internally top to bottom and side to side and externally to people outside the organization, including community stakeholders, suppliers, retailers, and customers, anyone that is touched by the cause-marketing program, must be consistent and clear.

Communications must come from the top-level leadership of the nonprofit organization. Staff needs to see that there is a clear commitment to the cause-marketing alliance. And communications can't stop at announcing the program. Let people know what's happening as the program unfolds and as results are achieved.

But beyond consistent, clear, and regular communication, what is being said must completely align with the program's actions and execution. When you say one thing and do another, whether it is with a staff member or an external partner, that feeling is the result.

Start the Communications Within Your Organization, Communicate Regularly, and Include Results

Don't neglect the rank and file. Especially for nonprofits, cause-marketing collaborations can be a completely different way of achieving goals and objectives. Many nonprofits professionally will view these arrangements as "selling out," changing the way the organization has operated in the past, and might be viewed with cynicism and concern. Even in large nonprofits where cause marketing may have been part of the fundraising and marketing structure, doubts can exist. Change is often seen as a threat, and people can quickly latch onto setbacks or problems as proof that it isn't going to work. Make sure staff members understand the program and how it will work to stop the buildup of negative feelings.

Engaging your staff by giving them an opportunity to participate in the cause-marketing arrangement can go a long way to explaining what you're doing and having them experience the benefits firsthand, even if they are not sure they should be comfortable with such arrangements. There are lots of ways of making this happen, and they don't have to be complicated to implement. For example, when the Canadian Parks Partnership and Parks Canada developed a cause-marketing relationship with Hi-Tec around hiking products, including boots, staff had an opportunity to receive a product discount. Sales opportunities were set up in key locations, and staff was invited to meet the president, do some shopping, and directly benefit from the relationship.

First Book had fun with their employees as they unfolded their Universal Studios "Dr. Seuss' Cat in the Hat" challenge. Every time a goal was met, it triggered a staff member doing something fun for everyone in the national office. The program had targeted 27 markets participating in the program, when they reached 10, one staff member promised to bake cookies for everyone. At 15 markets they ordered pizza for lunch, at 25 the CFO made lunch for the staff, and when they reached their goal, Executive Director Kyle Zimmer, a devoted pantsuit wearer, promised to put on a skirt and wear pantyhose.

Whatever you do with staff doesn't have to be complicated or expensive. The team at Hospice Calgary took a field trip to visit the show home of their cause partner, McKinley Masters Home Builders, to see firsthand how the program was working. It was simple and gave everyone a sense of pride in the program.

See the Benefits When Your Corporate Partner Does the Same

As marketing experts advocate, brands are built from the inside out, and that starts with talking to their employees. In so many cause programs, employees see the ads, events, and glitzy celebrities. But what's most important to make programs really work is having employees understand and be supportive. Encourage your corporate partners to announce cause programs internally first and engage the employees in helping make it work.

The Nike/Lance Armstrong Foundation "Live Strong" yellow bracelet phenomenon is an example of how starting from the inside and moving out builds a successful program. When Nike committed to selling five million bracelets to support the Lance Armstrong Foundation in the spring of 2004, the task seemed daunting, if not impossible. The solution: the VP responsible for the program started by getting Nike staff excited and passionate about the project. Nike President Phil Knight sent a message to employees encouraging them to participate. "When we focus our collective passion," he stated, "our potential knows no limits."[4] Staff stepped forward, pledged purchases, and the movement that was the cause-marketing sensation of 2004 was begun. Find a powerful way to communicate the emotional content of a cause-marketing initiative with staff, and big things can happen.

Make Sure Your Organization's Message Is Part of the Cause Program and Use It to Extend Fundraising

One of the biggest benefits of a corporate cause relationship for a nonprofit organization is a connection to their stakeholders from employees to suppliers to retailers to consumers. This is an important opportunity to reach this broad and often new audience with messages about your organization and the cause, issue awareness, and behavioral actions and changes. Keep the messages simple and tight—remember the 10-second elevator message. Feature your Web site, 1-800 line, and address and encourage them to contact you directly. Not only will getting your message out help achieve your mission, but it's also an opportunity to build your database of new potential supporters. Take full advantage and make sure you communicate at every turn.

Now Move Your Communication Outward

Part of the partner satisfaction and retention process is publicizing the cause-marketing program and publicly recognizing the partner's contribution and commitment. Nonprofits need to proactively communicate and promote a cause-marketing relationship.

As was discussed earlier, communication from a third party is the most credible way to promote a company's commitment in the community. Cause marketing is very much about publicly demonstrating a corporation's community involvement and its corporate values. Nonprofits have their own communication vehicles that can be used, such as Web sites and newsletters. Launch events to recognize the program can create visibility; media photo ops can be staged to generate interest and coverage of the program, and nonprofit media partnerships can help promote the collaboration.

Media Partnerships: An Important Cause Partner

Many cause-marketing relationships include media partners who work to help extend the message and reach. Although their commitment will not likely include a dollar contribution, their in-kind support allows nonprofits to get their message out to a wider audience.

CAUSE-MARKETING GOALS ACHIEVED: COMMUNITY AND CORPORATE OUTCOMES

As corporations seek innovative ways to compete and differentiate themselves in an increasingly complex global marketplace and nonprofits aim to meet rising social needs, cause marketing is a way to meet both business and mission objectives. Cause marketing is about creating win-win alliances and working for mutual benefit. A carefully executed and implemented program will meet both partners' needs and achieve goals that could not have been achieved working alone. A third piece of a cause-marketing program is the end audience—from employees, to retailers, to suppliers, to consumers. It is important that they are part of the positive outcome and that their needs and goals are satisfied.

The final step in the cause-marketing framework is citizenship and community—seeing your mission accomplished and benefits delivered to the community, your organization, and the corporate partner. Now is the time to evaluate, build for the future, and celebrate achievements, the final stages in the cause-marketing framework process.

- Evaluate program: Review and evaluate the program against goals and objectives for key learning.
- Build for the future: The collaboration multiplier.
- Celebrate program: Celebrate successes.

Evaluation Is a Key Learning Tool

Ultimately, a cause-marketing arrangement must create value for both partners if it is to continue. As cause-related marketing founder Jerry Welsh says about evaluation, it's hard to do. "After all, you've got to remember, we're not working in a scientific laboratory, we're working in a public marketplace."[5] Although cause marketing's full return on investment may be hard to quantify, it is important to analyze results to monitor the effectiveness of the program in reaching goals and to measure its true value. Regardless of the motives, performance measures do enhance program management and future planning.

By having laid out expected outputs, inputs, and outcomes, both partners can see the benefits and learn from the experience. Now, compare what was targeted to what was actually achieved (see Exhibit 9.1). What was expected to be a great success might not have worked. Why? What elements turned out to be even more successful? Does the collaboration need to be revised to make it work better for each partner?

EXHIBIT 9.1   EVALUATION OF RESULTS: COMPARISON
TARGET TO ACTUAL

	Outputs	Inputs	Outcomes
Targeted	Measurable results: • dollars raised • media impressions • people reached • employees engaged • mission benefits, e.g., increase in mammograms	Contributed to program: • financial • in-kind • advertising • employee volunteers	Intangible benefits of alliance: • capacity building • new and expanded relationships • new market/ target reached
Actual			

As has been stressed, cause marketing is more than the revenue and in-kind support that is generated. Measuring mission outcomes not just dollars is critical. Gathering additional food, encouraging women to get mammograms, and increasing the number of children playing are all intended outcomes of cause-marketing programs. The messaging and deeper understanding of the cause, the impact on behavior, although difficult to measure, has to be considered. Even if it is anecdotal evidence, people saying they heard about the program, were moved to make an additional donation, or changed the way they behaved is information that must be recorded.

On the other side, measurable results are equally important for corporate partners. If the program is a proven success, the opportunities to expand and build on what has been achieved are greater. Remember cause-marketing collaborations are more than philanthropy. There is an expectation of results that will provide a competitive advantage to the company. Seasoned cause marketer Rich Maoire, formerly Director, Corporate Marketing, Reading Is Fundamental, is a strong believer in demonstrating results. "Measurable results that gauge impact and reach of the program really help to sell it internally. If you want a corporate partner to sign up for year two you need to show solid results from year one."[6] He recommends putting together a formal report, including information from the corporate side. "Press them on it, to get what you need. Then add your internal information. Call up people and get anecdotal information as well. Talk to 100 people and put the results in a bar graph so you can show someone besides you that this was a great idea."[7]

A report on the collaboration should include the numbers and tangible information, but don't forget to add photos, examples of the advertisements, and comments from staff, employees, or customers engaged in the program. The account doesn't have to be a *War and Peace*-size document, but it does need to capture the essence of the program and its results. This is a great keepsake and record in addition to an important information tool.

Cost-Benefit Analysis

After you've looked at final results, a cost-benefit analysis must be done on cause collaborations. This doesn't have to be complicated, but the discussion needs to involve all those touched by the relationship. Opportunities could continue to arise with a partner, but if they don't advance the mission of the organization and provide tangible benefits, extending the alliance cannot be sustained. Nonprofits have to ask the tough questions and really determine in the end, was it worth it? Did the organization generate enough money to cover costs and then some? Did it achieve mission goals that could not have been done without the collaboration? In general, did the return justify the time and effort?

For many nonprofits, especially those just getting started, this is a critical piece of work that needs to be done. Evaluation helps filter enthusiasm for doing certain cause collaborations with the reality of limited resources. What was the most effective use of resources? Where should you spend your valuable time and efforts? Does the program need to change to be effective? The first Hallmark holiday card program of the Canadian Parks Partnership, Parks Canada, and Hallmark Canada didn't net the results expected, and when the time and effort was added into the equation, all sides knew changes had to be made if the program was going to truly work. The photographic collection of Parks Canada did not have the commercial appeal expected. As a result, the decision was made to purchase professional stock images and take a broader approach with note card sets, journals, and travel diaries that were considered to have stronger saleability than the holiday cards.

Use the "Collaboration Multiplier"

Developed with care, cause marketing can be an effective means of extending a nonprofit's fundraising program beyond just the financial cause-marketing contribution of the company. This takes follow-up and building of relationships with potential new supporters and looking for ways to extend your existing partner collaboration. This includes connecting with a whole new audience of individuals and increasing a nonprofit organization's credibility with other potential funders.

Connecting to Individuals: Often a Whole New Audience

As discussed earlier, cause marketing connects a nonprofit with a whole new audience of potential individual supporters including corporate employees and the company's customers. Look at ways you can build your database of names and stay connected. When Investors Group engaged their clients with a Comedy Tour supporting the food bank, the spin-off results after the program was over were an unexpected bonus. Almost all the food banks in the program noticed an increase in both cash and in-kind donations right after the event. Can a donation be encouraged as part of the cause-marketing program? Hangtags on products can provide information on how to donate. Web sites can be added to promotional information. Encourage this as a part of any cause marketing and the benefits will increase significantly.

Increasing Credibility: Leveraging Awareness with Other Funders

Cause marketing raises an organization's profile and lends credibility to the organization. It also can connect nonprofits to a whole new range of other potential corporate supporters from suppliers to retailers. Build these new relationships by involving these potential supporters in celebrating the success of a program.

Consider Your Partners as New Friends

The 2004 tsunami and the 2005 Hurricane Katrina are examples of how cause-marketing relationships can expand and move beyond just a cause collaboration into the philanthropic realm. UNICEF contacted every one of their corporate partners to ask for support and raised over $65 million from the corporate sector in the first two weeks after the tsunami.[8] The Home Depot and the Red Cross's relationship extended to support the emergency relief agency's work with Hurricane Katrina. Many cause-marketing relationships provide opportunities to generate traditional philanthropic gifts and should be part of the ongoing relationship building you need to do with your partner. Treat your cause-marketing partners like your best donors, and it will always pay dividends.

Renew and Expand the Alliance

Small beginnings can often lead to even more significant programs. "We like to think of our initial programs as dating, before we get serious and start going steady," says Carrie Suhr of KaBOOM! Most organizations' cause-marketing relationships start off small and build on success.

Many of the Susan G. Komen Foundation's cause relationships have grown as the organization captures the hearts of their corporate supporters. The Foundation proactively helps their partners to think about other ways they can support the cause and organization. Their KitchenAid relationship is a great example of this approach. The first component of the "Cook for the Cure" program started with a product sale. A portion of the proceeds from a pink mixer developed specifically for the program benefited the Komen Foundation. The next piece added a grassroots program that involved local consumers hosting dinners in their home and making a donation to Komen in lieu of a hostess gift. Later, professional chefs and restaurants were engaged in supporting Komen and the breast cancer cause. The Foundation looks hard to find opportunities to expand their relationships and engage broader audiences and touch different groups.

Continuous Learning and Joint Planning

Having a commitment to continuous learning is essential to generate benefits for both parties on an ongoing basis. By looking to make changes and adapting a cause-marketing program, each subsequent one can yield greater benefits and outcomes. Once an evaluation is complete, commit to joint planning for future success. Planning that is undertaken together in a collaborative fashion allows for strong ideas, leveraging of assets, and early buy-in and commitment to the next collaborative marketing arrangement.

Cycles of a Cause-Marketing Relationship

All nonprofits must recognize that cause collaborations, no matter how strong, have life cycles. Some cause-marketing collaborations by their very nature will be short term, very much focused on immediate impact and outcomes. A one-off promotion or product sales might not have the potential for renewal. Sometimes, the arrangements come to an end when leadership or staff changes. No matter how successful, the new team wants to put their own stamp on their community and marketing commitments.

Regardless of the strength of a cause alliance, nonprofits must prepare for the fact that the relationship will ebb and flow. At times there will be opportunities to collaborate. Other times there could be downtimes, and even if an opportunity isn't immediate, it's important to stay connected and continue to maintain and build the relationship for the next possible opportunity. Finally, there is the inevitability that at some point the relationship will come to an end. There is a natural cycle; even the longest-term alliances change. Nonprofits must be constantly looking for new partners and take their learning to new relationships. This will build the long-term health of the organization.

Define Success and Celebrate It!

Too often, in this busy and harried world, we don't take the time to stop and celebrate our successes—warts and all. No program will go off without some snags; that is to be expected and then managed to get it back on track. But don't forget to celebrate and appreciate what the organization and its partner have achieved. Remember, cause marketing is only just over 25 years old and only just becoming a mainstream way for nonprofits to work with corporate partners. We're all learning, and much of what is being done is still in the "pioneer" stage, undertaken by "early adopters."

Once the numbers are in, start the celebrations by letting staff and key stakeholders know about the final results of the program. How much was raised, how many people were touched by your organizations' messages, and other benefits of the cause program. A celebration with the internal team is a way of thanking them for all their help. Publicize the results with stakeholders, and let the media know the impact of the cause collaboration.

Finally, celebrate success with your partners. Host a luncheon (invite potential prospective cause partners to get them excited); do a reception. Whatever it is, it ideally should involve three things: getting together in person, breaking bread, and above all, saying thank you. Make it fun and informative.

Final Thoughts: Cause Marketing Is a Commitment . . . Not Just a Campaign

Strong cause-marketing alliances cannot be bought. They take time to develop, take root, and grow. Perhaps one of the most overlooked principles of cause marketing is patience and persistence. Don't give up, and always be looking at ways to improve. Even if your cause alliance is well structured, there may be practices and policies within your organization that need to shift to be in alignment with the underlying foundation of the program. Recognize the ebbs and flows and the importance of relationship building with your current corporate partners while always looking to build new alliances and cause-marketing collaborations. Finally, as with all marketing goals, your cause-marketing program requires commitment top to bottom and across your organization.

CONCLUSIONS

Cause marketing doesn't stop with the signing of the agreement. It takes a continual investment of time and energy to execute and manage. How the execution and delivery is handled will determine its effectiveness, how satisfied your partners are, and ultimately if the relationship can be sustained and grown.

Execution requires dedicated staff and resources, a commitment to good communications, and a dogged determination to deliver for results. Nonprofits need to build execution and communication plans for each cause relationship. Determine how the relationship will be managed internally. Many organizations have a relationship manager who is the guardian of the cause programs, orchestrating the deployment of organizationwide resources to provide comprehensive support and fulfillment to the cause partner. As the program is executed, communication between partners needs to be frequent, meaningful, and honest. Finally, accountability for realizing commitments is a critical part of the execution process. Delivering on results builds trust. Overdeliver and an organization builds for the future.

Cause marketing is an important way for companies to publicly communicate their community contribution and values and a key goal of any program. Nonprofits must play a lead role in publicizing the cause relationship and crediting their partner. Begin by creating messages that are consistent and sincere. Then make sure that communication occurs internally with nonprofit staff and externally through a nonprofit's own communications infrastructure such as newsletters and Web sites, and through events, media activities, and photo opportunities. Don't forget to use your existing media partnerships to help.

Finally, cause marketing is about achieving win-win-win goals: for the nonprofit, the community, and the corporation. Cause-marketing collaborations create outcomes and results that could never have been achieved by each partner working on their own.

The final stage in the cause-marketing framework process is to evaluate, build for the future, and celebrate achievements of the program. Evaluate the results of the program by looking at outputs (tangible numbers and results), inputs (what was contributed by both partners), and outcomes (intended program benefits and impact from a cause-marketing program). The nonprofit partner must be concerned with their corporate partner's results. This knowledge will help them serve their partner better in the future. Use all learning to build for the future.

Finally, celebrate, reward, and publicize the results. Regardless of the future of the cause-marketing alliance, because they are organic and ever changing, thanking everyone involved builds a commitment to cause marketing, which, when done right, can pay significant dividends for your nonprofit.

With the cause-marketing framework outlined, it is now time to look at four case studies to see how this framework is implemented in real-life situations. Using two national and two local nonprofits, the case studies will prove the benefits of following the process of "getting it right." These concrete examples document and illustrate the theory just presented and the benefits of a structured approach to the cause-marketing process.

ENDNOTES

1. Interview, Anne-Marie Grey, UNICEF, April 5, 2005.
2. Interview, Mary Norman, Arthritis Foundation, January 25, 2005.
3. Cone Corporate Citizenship Study, 2004.
4. Presentation, Cause Marketing Forum, June 16, 2005.
5. Interview, Jerry Welsh, Welsh Marketing, April 6, 2005.
6. Interview, Rich Maoire, January 14, 2005.
7. Ibid.
8. Interview, Anne-Marie Grey, UNICEF, April 5, 2005.

PART IV

Making It Happen: Best Practices Case Studies

This section of the book is about connecting the dots by taking the cause-marketing framework, the seven C's, and showing how the framework is translated into practice.

The seven C's framework draws on my own experience and interviews and discussions with over 25 nonprofits about their process for creating and executing cause-marketing programs. From these interviews I have chosen four nonprofits to feature as practical case studies, real-life examples of how the framework works and its effectiveness as a process for nonprofits to follow in building and implementing their own cause-marketing programs.

The first two examples are national nonprofits: American Heart Association and First Book. The American Heart Association is a long-established national organization and is the largest voluntary health organization fighting heart disease with a broad base of over 1,000 community chapters. First Book is a national organization with over 200 local chapters. Just over 10 years old, the organization has a mission to get first books in the hands of children from low-income families.

The second set of examples is two local nonprofits: Food Banks for New York City, a major local nonprofit based in a major city, and the Vancouver Island District of the British Columbia and Yukon Division of the Canadian Cancer Society, a grassroots nonprofit part of a well-known cause. Each case study provides different insights and learning and demonstrates the effectiveness of the Seven C's Cause-Marketing Framework.

THE SEVEN C'S CHECKLIST:

Create Cause-Marketing Orientation:

1. Cause: Are you prepared internally?
   - ✓ Aligned with organizational goals and needs
   - ✓ Defined assets and brand position and looked for associative links
   - ✓ Listed potential corporate alignment
   - ✓ Prepared internally ensuring:
     - • Senior management buy-in
     - • Entrepreneurial and marketing culture
     - • Dedicated staff
     - • Processes and procedures
     - • Knowledge of guidelines, regulations, and tax implications

Build Cause-Marketing Program:

2. Collaboration: Are you proactively seeking strategically aligned partners?
   - ✓ Researched fit to determine their needs and fit where:
     - • Your goals + brand position + their needs = potential collaboration
   - ✓ Made the connection and arranged a face-to-face meeting
   - ✓ Prepared a tailored presentation focused on "what's in it for them"
   - ✓ Explored, proposed, agreed
3. Combine Assets: Have you analyzed and aimed for maximum benefit?
   - ✓ Compared and combined for maximum benefits.
4. Create Value: Are the values defined that both partners will receive?
   - ✓ Jointly planned and defined goals, responsibilities, and benefits.
   - ✓ Agreed and prepared a formal agreement.
   - ✓ Determined outcomes and what success looks like.

Implement Cause-Marketing Program:

5. Execute: Are you ready to deliver on commitments?
   - ✓ Prepared internal structure to manage cause collaboration.
   - ✓ Communicated regularly with your partners.
   - ✓ Delivered on promises and ready to go the extra mile.
6. Communicate: Have you developed a communication strategy for internal and external audiences?

✓ Prepared key messages that are clear and consistent.

✓ Started communications from the inside and moved out.

✓ Made sure your organization's message is part of the cause program

Achieve Cause-Marketing Goals:

7. Corporate and community outcomes: Do you review, measure, and celebrate win–win–win results?

    ✓ Reviewed and evaluated program against goals and objectives for key learning

    ✓ Built for the future: The collaboration multiplier

    ✓ Celebrated successes

CHAPTER 10

National Organizations: American Heart Association and First Book

"Go Red for Women" Social Marketing Campaign

The American Heart Association (AHA) is the largest voluntary health organization fighting heart disease. Headquartered in Dallas, Texas, the American Heart Association has 2,000 division offices and over 22 million supporters and volunteers across the nation. The organization raises over $600 million annually to advance its mission "to reduce disability and death from cardiovascular diseases and stroke." Established in 1924, the American Heart Association is one of the most recognized and well-respected non-profit health organizations in the United States. The organization generated close to 5 billion media impressions in 2004 and has a 96% awareness of its name, 98% favorable consumer reaction to the AHA logo, and 90% of consumers saying they are more likely to buy a product displaying the AHA logo.[1]

With a goal to reduce coronary heart disease, stroke, and risk by 25% by 2010 the organization has introduced a number of science- and medical-based initiatives designed to meet the target. Recognizing awareness could play a critical role, the first of a series of national social cause-marketing campaigns, Go Red for Women, was launched in 2004. Go Red for Women is a call to action to empower women to take charge of their heart health. Heart disease is the number one cause of death for women in the United States, with more women than men dying from the disease every year. Currently, only 13% of women recognize heart disease as their greatest health threat, and it is estimated that over eight million American women are living with heart disease.[2] *Go Red for Women's national sponsors are Macy's and Pfizer.*

In 2005, the American Heart Association was honored with several awards for the work on Go Red for Women, including PRWeek 2005 Nonprofit Campaign of the Year award and the Cause Marketing Forum's Golden Halo Award for nonprofit of the year, for its long-standing record of working with the corporate sector to provide credible heart disease and stroke information for prevention and treatment.

Refining a Cause-Marketing Orientation

The American Heart Association has long been a pioneer and leader in corporate cause-marketing relationships. The national health organization's Heart Walk and Jump Rope for Heart signature events have attracted strong support from the corporate sector. Corporate cause relations have helped AHA implement programs, achieve important mission goals, and raise revenue and profile. The organization considers them to be a priority and has established key positions to manage and grow these relationships, including a vice president responsible for corporate relationships in their national headquarters in Dallas.

To be a leader in the cause-marketing field means constantly looking at trends, considering the organization's goals, and listening to the needs of participating corporations and the marketplace. Standing still isn't an option, and the AHA is always exploring how to grow and evolve their program.

Kathy Rogers, then titled Vice President, Corporate Relations, explains how the organization decided to develop their *Go Red for Women* initiative: "We had great success with our corporate partnerships and they were growing and expanding. But we had reached a plateau. Our corporate partners were telling us they were looking for more. They didn't want more benefits, what they wanted was to do more, have a higher level of involvement and messaging. We had to listen to what they were saying and it began our thinking about the AHA's approach and model. We knew we needed to do more, not just for our partners but for our organization to advance our objectives and mission. We had to figure out how to position ourselves so that companies could wrap around our cause and the issue of heart disease rather than a very specific program or event."[3]

Around the same time, the organization had launched a new strategic plan aimed at reducing heart disease and stroke by 25% by 2010. The American Heart Association is a strongly science-oriented and health-driven organization. When it established this goal the focus was on the health-care system, changing the way hospitals and doctors treated people. "Awareness, while not directly impacting heart disease reduction, could help us reach individuals with key messages that would help the organization to reach our target. We knew our corporate partners could help us advance this mission,"[4] states Kathy.

With this strategic direction in mind, in early 2003, the American Heart Association approached Boston-based Cone Inc. to help them reposition the organization as a cause and infuse passion into the AHA brand. The AHA was also working with several other agencies around becoming more passionate and to develop an advertising campaign. Cone was chosen to work with AHA to specifically identify cause platforms for the organization. Cone is an internationally recognized consultancy in the field of strategic Cause Branding® and has been at the forefront of creating and implementing innovative strategic cause programs for over 20 years. Well known for their market research on the field of cause marketing and Cause Branding®, Cone Inc. produced nine respected reports between 1993 and 2004. At the time they were approached, they had used their learning and expertise to help numerous companies build Cause Branding® initiatives, but had never worked with a nonprofit client.

"I respected the Cone thinking," said Kathy. "With their help we wanted to reposition the organization in a way that would afford us the opportunity to present a passionate message through cause platforms to consumers, while positioning ourselves for new and stronger corporate relationships. The ultimate goal was to generate more revenue, increase awareness of key heart issues and strengthen our position as the leading heart and stroke organization."[5]

Discovery Research

Cone began conducting internal research spending time interviewing staff, conducting brand briefings, and looking at all the organization's materials. "As part of our research we began to uncover where the organization had been for many years," explains Kristian Darigan, Vice President, Cone Inc. and lead on the project. "The organization is very forward thinking. They had a ten-year strategic plan, focusing on reducing heart disease and recognized the importance of passion. They had an earlier initiative, the Passion Project, which was to infuse passion into the brand. Our research also showed AHA was well respected and very clinical and scientific in their approach. What it didn't have was consumer relevance or the passion and emotion of some causes. But as we completed our research we recognized heart disease was something that could have an incredible emotional appeal."[6]

Concurrently, Cone undertook external research, including a media analysis, to see what issues and megatrends were emerging that could help reposition AHA. What they found honed their direction. First, it was clear that there were a lot of misconceptions about heart disease and who it impacted. Of particular interest was the lack of realization that heart disease was the number one killer of women. Second and third, the issue of childhood obesity and a growing lack of physical activity in the general public—both potential risk factors for heart disease—were growing in media attention.

As the discovery phase was being completed, concept and positioning direction started to become clear. There was a recognized need, health information disparity, and some very tangible assets that could be brought to bear.[7] The question became how to infuse passion in the brand and stand for something specific, not just heart disease and stroke. Cone recognized that the AHA needed to be more targeted, consumer focused, and aligned with current market trends.

Positioning and Packaging: From White Coat to Red Dress[8]

Together the Cone and AHA teams identified four focused platforms and audiences as potential cause-branding campaigns: women and heart disease (women); childhood obesity (children), physical inactivity (everyone), and stroke targeting African Americans, a group considered to be high risk.[9]

Based on limited resources of time, people, and dollars the organization decided to start with one campaign. The immediate priority: put all the forces behind women and heart disease, something the AHA and Cone team felt could be implemented and put into the marketplace within an ambitious six-month period. The campaign was developed with the goal of aligning alongside new corporate partners to help spread this important message to women and raise funds for the issue, while simultaneously building the AHA's consumer image. "From white coat to red dress" became the motto to infuse the brand with more relevance and passion and evolve the AHA's consumer position (see Exhibit 10.1).

EXHIBIT 10.1   THE ESSENCE OF THE MOVEMENT

Go Red For Women

The essence of the movement

- A national campaign to fight heart disease in women, launched in Feb. 2004;

- A passionate and emotional rallying cry for change and call-to-action;

- An opportunity for companies to take leadership roles to champion the issue.

The movement has begun

Go Red for Women®, American Heart Association®, the heart and torch logo and the red dress logo used in conjunction with the Go Red for Women name are registered trademarks of the American Heart Association, Inc., and used here with permission. Advertisement © 2004 AHA.

Campaign Elements and Assets: Go Red for Women

As the planning around the cause-marketing campaign unfolded, the team recognized it needed to have several key elements for success. First, credible science was central to attract the attention of the medical community; second, a media hook that could infuse emotion and excite people with an easy-to-understand message; next a consumer engagement piece was essential to generate involvement and enthusiasm; and finally there needed to be grassroots activation, something the AHA had in spades. The grassroots activation that would also allow for local corporate involvement, along with AHA's science credibility, were viewed as the AHA's two greatest assets.

The American Heart Association, with guidance from Cone Inc., organized its assets into four categories, analyzing and defining them from a corporate and consumer perspective. The four categories were:[10]

1. In marketplace: Focused on how the "Go Red" campaign information could be used in stores to reach a mass audience—women

2. In corporations: Focused on ways corporations could use the program to engage their employees and do on-site AHA programs

3. In government: Focused on AHA's advocacy efforts

4. In science: Focused on AHA's science strength and credibility and information that could be provided about the issue of women and heart disease, including treatment guidelines

Red became the color of the campaign, and the organization adopted the red dress as the symbol for women and heart disease, which was being used by other organizations as well. Specific activities and programs were developed to create media interest, impressions, consumer engagement, and to generate revenue, including Go Red luncheons, wear red day, and lighting up of iconic buildings in red during American Heart Month in February. Promotional material was produced, including red dress pins, media kits, posters, wallet cards, bookmarks, and a wear red workplace fundraising program. A Physician's Toolkit was created specifically for health professionals.

Women and Heart, a Growing Marketplace Trend

Women and heart disease had been identified as an issue by the organization in the mid-1990s, and the organization had developed a woman and heart program in 1997, called Take Wellness to Heart. The program, although a start in the right direction, did not have the impact that they were able to achieve with Go Red for Women. Equally important was timing. "It was launched before its time," says Kathy. "There was not a lot of awareness of the issue and the market was not ready for the program. I firmly believe that you to have make an issue a marketplace trend before you can have success," says Kathy. "That is one of my recommendations. Build up the issue in the marketplace and the rest will come."[11] By the time the AHA launched "Go Red for Women," the issue was picking up speed and gaining media attention, including a front cover story on women and heart disease in a 2003 *Time* magazine issue. The awareness gap was closing on an important women's issue.

Associative Links to Target a Broader Corporate Partner Base

Women and heart health were specific focuses that could be used to build corporate alliances. One of the major goals of the initiative was to build cause relationships with a broader base of corporations. Many of the organization's previous relationships had been with mission-related companies such as the pharmaceuticals industry and health/wellness companies. An earlier experience with Subway and its involvement in the Heart Walk event had shown the organization the benefits that could be provided through a retail partner, a nontraditional alliance for the AHA. The AHA was able to integrate with the Subway's new line of low-fat sandwiches, "7 under 6" (sandwiches and grams of fat). The relationship allowed the company to align with the AHA to promote its low-fat sandwiches while simultaneously advancing the AHA's heart health messages in stores and throughout its advertising. "This was a tipping point for our organization," says Ms. Rogers. "We saw the power that their advertising provided for our messages and helped to position us in a different way as well as with a different audience than our traditional corporate partners. We wanted to figure out how to get other consumer companies interested in working with us."[12]

Cone was fundamentally attuned to this focus. "Our research needed to help the AHA attract partners that fit with its mission and help AHA advance what it was they were trying to do in the marketplace,"[13] explained Cone's VP, Kristian Darigan. Cone wanted to help the AHA build mutually beneficial relationships that would have a social impact, share brand equity and leadership, create multitiered stakeholder relationships, and help each be a leader in an uncluttered, trending area.[14] To help focus the AHA's thinking and targets, Darigan developed an alignment pyramid of high, medium, and low (see Chapter 7). Cone developed a list of companies that could fit different aspects of the campaign—from national partners to media and theme partners.

Building Internal Support

As all the pieces for the cause campaign were being developed, another important element was being put in place. In a large national organization like the American Heart Association, internal due diligence is critical to implementing new programs. "The will was there to support the program but there are always so many implications when you make changes. We had to consider the potential effects on volunteers, staff, local and national structures and existing corporate supporters,"[15] explains AHA's Kathy Rogers.

As the cause and brand positioning were developed, changes to the corporate relations policies and procedures of the organizations were parallel-tracked by the AHA. Appropriate staff and volunteers were consulted, and the policy changes were developed that were taken to the American Heart Association Board of Directors for approval.

"It took time to move through the system. We knew we wanted to be more identified as a cause and be more relevant to consumers and companies, but the hard part of this was looking at what were the practical implications of these changes," states Kathy. "We had to look at policies as intricate as where our logo would be allowed and then play out possible scenarios. Here's what it might look like. Here's what is needed to change our policies to allow for a different approach. People were strategically aligned with the new direction, but it was important to have them clearly understand the impact of what we were doing and show them how that would look."[16]

The program was going to be different than anything the organization had done in the past. The logo for "Go Red for Women" was to be part of a consumer brand and featured in stores and on corporate promotional material. After almost a year of diligence and plain old hard work, all the policy pieces were approved by the board and put in place (see Exhibit 10.2).

Building the Cause-Marketing Program

The next step was finding the right strategic partners who could align with what the AHA wanted to achieve. The program was built to reposition the American Heart Association brand with a consumer-oriented focus and a goal of attracting a different kind of corporate support. The organization wanted to appeal not only to highly aligned companies like health brands, but also to companies that had extensive reach in the marketplace through in-store and external advertising campaigns that could help the AHA reach consumers.

EXHIBIT 10.2

nationally sponsored by

Go Red for Women®, American Heart Association®, the heart and torch logo and the red dress logo used in conjunction with the Go Red for Women name are registered trademarks of the American Heart Association, Inc., and used here with permission. Advertisment © 2004 AHA.

National Partners—Traditional and Nontraditional Alignment

Pfizer was a company that had worked with AHA before because of their cardiovascular portfolio. "We knew this cause initiative would be of interest

to them from previous conversation,"[17] explains Kathy Rogers. When the organization presented Go Red for Women to Pfizer, they saw the fit and understood how this could benefit both the AHA and the work they were
doing.

Macy's was the new kind of partner the organization wanted to cultivate.
The retailer had nationwide presence and a direct link with consumers, with
a particular emphasis on women—the specific target for the "Go Red" campaign. "We learned that they were looking for a cause to be associated with
that related to women. A phone conversation initiated the discussion and
after the first face-to-face meeting the relationship took off. We outlined our
goals and objectives and the timing was right for them to be aligned with a
program like "Go Red,"[18] said Kathy.

The goal of the program was to target the medical community and consumers, especially women, for the women and heart issue. "With these two
national partners the fit was ideal," says Rogers. "With the support of these
two partners we would be able to connect to the medical community, and
to consumers."[19]

"The remarkable thing, and a credit to both partners, was we went to
them before we actually launched the initiative. They came on board from
the intent of what we wanted to achieve without all the specific tactical elements defined," states Kathy. "They saw an opportunity to take a leadership
role on an important issue to women and they committed on the knowledge
of the concept, messages and the icon of the red dress. We really felt we
could create the buzz and have women stand up and take notice and we had
a strong, local grassroots component planned. These features were very important to both of them."[20]

Combining Assets and Creating Value
Whereas the two national partners committed based on the initial objectives,
as the campaign evolved, the American Heart Association looked for opportunities to dovetail their goals with their corporate partners' goals. For example, an important consideration for Pfizer was information for health-care
providers. The American Heart Association had developed treatment guidelines that it wanted to distribute to the medical profession (Physicians Toolkit).
The two organizations worked together with the AHA developing the content,
and Pfizer distributing it through the system.

"Macy's and Pfizer had strategic business objectives they wanted to
achieve," explains Kathy Rogers, "but both came in understanding there was
a bigger purpose. We looked at how we could use our assets and their assets to reach physicians, health care professionals, their employees and consumers in order to make an impact. We all realized that this was a value to
them, to AHA and to their employees, customers and consumers. We were
creating a win-win-win situation. That was the perspective we all had."[21]

Both national partners involved their employees in the execution of the
program and as active participants in providing messages to key target mar-

kets. Pfizer's employees actively handed out women and heart information to the physicians, and during National Wear Red Day they gave away red dress pins. Macy's CEO did a videotape talking about the program and the issue of women and heart disease for all their employees to roll out the program. Macy's employees were provided with red dress pins and information on women and heart disease. Local stores connected with local AHA offices, and they actively participated in Go Red for Women events in their community. "The Cone research has shown that employees are just as important for the company's involvement as consumers. They now have their own stories of employees who received the information on Go Red for Women, contacted their physicians, and subsequently found out they had high blood pressure or other risk factors. So they have started to see an impact from the employees' perspective,"[22] explains Kathy.

Macy's has also worked to make Go Red for Women really visible in some of their stores with window displays of red dresses and signs, and they continue to roll it out to all their individual local stores as the program has moved forward. The retailers created in-store consumer advertising pieces, participated in Go Red for Women luncheons, and were engaged in localized activities in different regions.

"A formal agreement was put in place, and both Macy's and Pfizer contributed significant financial and in-kind support to the program and made a three-year commitment to Go Red for Women and defined goals,"[23] states Kathy Rogers.

Implementing the Program

The American Heart Association established an account management system to implement the program with its national partners. There is a lead for each one of their major corporate partners, and a cross-functional team represents different areas of the organization including field representatives, a healthcare team member, and communications staff. Each team has established processes, plan together, and they have regular meetings to get updates, execute key commitments, and make sure the program is on track. The Macy's account also has a whole separate local team that interacts with each of Macy's regions.

The American Heart Association involves its local organizations and has developed a strong communications system that ensures the organization can deliver on national and local commitments. "One of our strengths is we can commit to what happens at the local level," says Rogers.[24] Kathy Rogers began working for the American Heart Association in their Detroit office and was hired for the national job in part because of her understanding and commitment to involving local organizations in their corporate initiatives.

Each partner has a customized communications strategy that includes face-to-face meetings, regular phone calls, and e-mails. It's a huge communications undertaking to make sure AHA staff has all the information they need and that it is then communicated to the two national partners. "We have to make sure we're doing our part to integrate our local offices with these partners, explaining the infrastructure and then making sure they can help Macy's and Pfizer do the same thing," says Rogers. "This has been an evolving process and it's really starting to click and work well. We customize what works best for each. This week for example our account team for Macy's was going out and doing a road show in each of the regional offices. We just developed this approach last year and we keep working to improve and learn the best way to work with our corporate partner's infrastructure. Pfizer's system is slightly different and they have a good process in place that communicates from the national to local level."[25]

Kathy Rogers was instrumental in building the initial partnerships and stays involved as the executive sponsor on the accounts. "I go to all the major meetings where we're talking about new strategy or developing new ideas or plans for the coming year. That is how I interact with our partners,"[26] she explains.

Executing a major new national initiative was a massive undertaking. The first year's short time frame, signing agreements with Macy's, for example, in November 2003 and launching the program in February 2004, didn't provide as much lead time as normally would have been in the case. "When you're working with a retailer, you have to understand their business and business cycle, learn their timelines, their environment, how they operate and their approval process,"[27] explains Kathy. Doing things far enough in advance and realizing how complex a program of this size and scope was were key learnings from the first year of the campaign. As the AHA moved into its third year in 2006, planning was well in hand, and many of the original challenges had been worked out.

Getting out the Message, a National Integrated Communications Campaign

The "Go Red" program was launched in February 2004 through a nationally integrated communications campaign. Education and awareness material was developed, and events were held, including luncheons, landmarks going red, and a fundraising National Wear Red Day. In 2004 Daryl Hannah served as the national spokesperson, and in 2005 Toni Braxton served in that role and helped "roll out the red carpet" at Radio City Music Hall before illuminating the Empire State Building red. Cities Go Red was a marketing component created for local AHA affiliates to secure corporate support and hold events and encourage local landmarks to "Go Red" (see Exhibit 10.3).

Each corporate partner also contributed to the launch through their own communications initiatives. All related major advertising material features the corporate partners and the AHA campaign logo. Corporate partner Macy's held a fashion show featuring designer red dresses at Macy's Herald Square (NYC), and Pfizer held a kickoff dinner for employees and stakeholders in 2004.

EXHIBIT 10.3   INTEGRATED ACROSS ALL CHANNELS

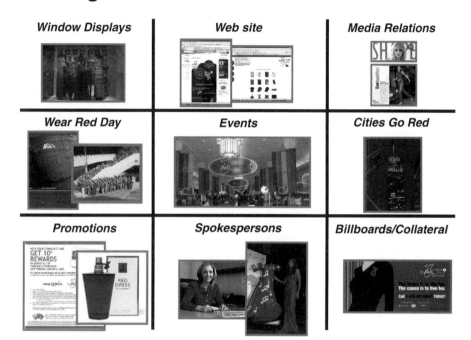

Integrated Across All Channels

Window Displays	Web site	Media Relations
Wear Red Day	Events	Cities Go Red
Promotions	Spokespersons	Billboards/Collateral

Cause Goals Achieved

From its launch in 2003 to 2005, over seven million collateral pieces have been distributed, more than 150 landmarks and buildings lit up with the color red during February, over seven million red dress pins were handed out, 80,000 copies of the AHA's guidelines for preventing heart disease among women have been distributed to health-care providers, and 40,000 health-care tool-kits were provided to physicians, providing them tools to treat their patients. In addition, over 9,000 companies have participated in National Wear Red Day, 13 million households have learned of the program through a direct-mail campaign, and over 2.3 billion impressions have been created.[28] With the "little red dress," the fashion must-have in 2006, a movement has been started. To celebrate this success with their partners, AHA holds a special thank-you reception in February for all the partners of the initiative.

The AHA is working on the next phase of their program, going from generating awareness to taking action. "We have evolving goals and objectives.

We couldn't be more pleased with the awareness, media impressions and growing number of women and health providers we are reaching with this message. Now what we want to do is move to action and have women personalize their connection with heart disease. We want women to know their cholesterol, blood pressure, BMI and also want to reach more health care providers with our new guidelines"[29] says Kathy. Although they have a long way to go on their women and heart initiative, they are working on launching the next cause campaigns. Kathy Rogers' position has expanded and changed in the Dallas headquarters. Appointed VP, Cause Initiatives and Integrated Marketing in 2004, she has responsibility for overseeing and managing lots of players involved in implementing all the cause initiatives and campaigns.

Final Thoughts and Advice

Building, growing, and staying on the forefront of a program takes leadership, vision, courage to change, and patient persistence to drive an initiative. It can only happen if you stay on course and see it through, bumps and all, to the end. "I feel so privileged to have been part of this important issue. Everything clicked, but it was a huge undertaking. So many people were instrumental in our success—it really did take the whole organization to make this happen. When I explain the program and tell the story of how it came to be, it can sound so easy," Kathy Rogers warns. "But it's never that easy! I heard people at a recent conference say I have to change agencies or we need the big simple idea. But that alone won't do it. You have to stay focused, work hard and drive it. Do your due diligence and find one idea you think could work and drive it as hard as you can to make it happen. You really have to stick with it."[30] Good advice for any cause marketer!

FIRST BOOK, RANDOM HOUSE, AND UNIVERSAL STUDIOS

"Dr. Seuss' The Cat in the Hat/First Book Challenge": Promotional Cause-Marketing Initiative

First Book is a national nonprofit organization with a single mission: to give children from low-income families the opportunity to read and own their first new books. Founded in 1992, the First Book model was developed to leverage the work of local organizations to reach children through existing community literacy programs based in Head Start centers, libraries, soup kitchens, church basements, housing projects, afterschool initiatives, and other settings. In this way, First Book plays a critical role in transforming the quality of preschool and afterschool programs nationwide. Since its inception in 1992,

First Book has provided more than 33 million new books to children in need in hundreds of communities nationwide.

At the local level, First Book leverages the strength of its core model of 250 volunteer Advisory Boards to spark social change. All books distributed by First Book are provided at no cost to the child or program. With the support of First Book, these programs are able—often for the first time—to develop a curriculum around the books they select, distribute these books to participating children, and enable these children to share the magic of their new books with siblings and other family members at home.

First Book was named a "Gold Star Charity" by Forbes *magazine and in 2004 and 2005 it received a Fast Company/Monitor Group Social Capitalist Award. In 2005, First Book was one of 10 finalists in the Amazon.com Nonprofit Innovation Award and was one of four grand prize winners of The Yale School of Management–The Goldman Sachs Foundation Partnership on Nonprofit Ventures.*

In November 2003, First Book and Universal Studios launched an innovative promotional cause-marketing initiative with the goals of getting out the First Book message, delivering more books to children, and helping promote Dr. Seuss' legacy and The Cat in the Hat *that would tie into the holiday release of Universal Pictures live action motion picture adaptation of the book.*

Building on a Cause-Marketing Orientation

Kyle Zimmer, President and CEO of First Book, is a savvy and experienced cause marketer. Over her years of involvement, she has seen the field evolve and grow as nonprofit organizations produce measurable and strategic results for their corporate partners. Now more than ever, it is recognized that cause campaigns have the potential to create value, achieve revenue and other bottom-line goals, showcase values, implement mission, and build brand awareness for both partners.

An Organization Built on Cause-Marketing Partnerships

First Book, an acknowledged leader in the field of social enterprise, has continually relied on cause-marketing campaigns. Since its inception cause marketing has been used to generate operating revenue and drive the implementation of the organization's programmatic activities. In 2004, over $3.5 million was raised from cause programs, representing over 90% of their total operating budget and $33 to $34 million in programmatic support.

Kyle, along with the other two founders of First Book, was a corporate lawyer. "You go with what you know and play to your strengths," she states. "I had little experience in the foundation world and the kinds of mechanisms that drive traditional philanthropy. What I did have was an understanding of the corporate sector and the strengths they could bring through mutually beneficial relationships. When we got started, we recognized the time was ripe for a change in paradigm that integrated the private sector into social sector issues to benefit everyone involved in new and powerful ways."[31]

The organization has been marketing focused from its founding, intent on raising its profile and building the organization through a private-sector approach. "Marketing has been a critical means of generating revenue," explains Kyle. "It's not just First Book out selling relationships. We design campaigns with a focus on achieving mission and it has helped us to become well-known, just by being creative and entrepreneurial."[32]

But Kyle and the First Book team were also motivated by the realization that the funding resources available for the social sector were already stretched, and they didn't want to pull resources away from other vital social efforts. And they felt they had a mission that was simple and tangible assets that could translate into the consumer marketplace easily. Abundance thinking, creativity, and enterprise are firmly established as the way the organization has evolved and grown. Their 10-second elevator message: "Giving children from low-income families the opportunity to read and own their first new books."

A Mission-Driven Heart with a Business Head

Right from the beginning of the organization, First Book has used cause marketing to generate revenue to implement their mission. First Book staff members bring every resource of the organization to bear on the goals of their cause-marketing initiatives while faithfully maintaining the stewardship of the mission and integrity of the organization. This is the combination that creates win-win-win.

The national organization has a transorganization structure that pulls teams from every facet of the organization into designing and then implementing cause partnerships. The group looks to hire staff members that are entrepreneurial and marketing oriented in their thinking. "I look for staff members who have been involved in college politics, set up college clubs or been involved community activities. I want to see sparks, little indications that they have that entrepreneurial element and way of thinking,"[33] says Kyle.

Kyle has seen many changes since she first started in cause marketing, almost 10 years ago. In her early years, programs commonly featured logo-based campaigns that gave a company the right to put a nonprofit organization's logo on a product for which the company provided a $10,000 donation to the organization.

"I would get my picture taken with a big Styrofoam cheque," she reminisces. "Occasionally we still do these types of deals but they are becoming rarer as the field has grown to a much higher degree of sophistication. We don't do single layer programs very often any more. We try to focus on multidimensional deals that are more in-depth. Today we come up with promotional and programmatic ideas and now when we sit down with the private sector so they understand what we're trying to do."[34]

The organization looks for alignments that go well together, and they have built important strategic alliances with Random House Children's Publishing. But creativity reigns, and the group is always looking for linkages that could create cause-marketing arrangements. Relationships with General Mills' Cheerios® cereal, Baskin-Robbins, and Lowe's Home Improvement Stores are a few examples of the wide range of companies First Book has partnered with to benefit children and literacy.

Always Consider—"What Can My Organization Give to the Effort?"

When putting together cause initiatives, the organization starts by analyzing the client's business objectives to determine how First Book can best complement and further the client's goals. First Book then reviews its own organizational assets to identify linkages that could be efficiently and uniquely put to use in a cause-marketing campaign. These elements include everything from the Advisory Board model and subsidiary groups themselves to content and messaging to online "real estate" and products such as large-volume book distributions and access to celebrities and children's illustrators and authors. The organization has a clear idea of their assets and programs and is experienced in looking for associative linkages.

Building the Cause-Marketing Program

Finding Partners

As an organization that has always proactively sought cause-marketing alliances, they target specific corporations and use connections from their existing partners to make contact. In the early years, they worked hard to build cause relationships. "No one knew who we were," explains Kyle. "We were a long way from being a household name."[35] Now because of their reputation and significant experience, they are regularly approached by companies themselves or agencies working on a company's behalf.

Either way, once a potential partner is in sight, research, research, research is the next phase in their cause-marketing process. "First Book makes themselves students of the project and of the industry," explains Zimmer. They look to see what matters to the company and then how their assets can dovetail to meet all partners' goals and objectives. First Book has developed a matrix that allows them to link their assets with corporate goals. The matrix featured (see Exhibit 10.4) lists potential partners' goals and establishes how priorities can mesh with First Book's programs and or assets. This information forms the basis for building a marketing or promotional package.

An Existing Relationship Opens the Door

Random House Children's Publishing, a tremendous supporter of First Book and the publisher for Dr. Seuss Enterprises, first introduced the group to Universal Studios in 2000. Traditionally, when major studios release a family movie they select a nonprofit partner and donate a portion of the proceeds from the premiere launch to the group. When Universal Pictures released in the fall of 2000 Dr. Seuss' *How The Grinch Stole Christmas*, First Book was named the national charitable partner. The movie's world premiere, which took place on November 8, 2000, at the Universal Amphitheater in Los Angeles, highlighted First Book.

EXHIBIT 10.4 FIRST BOOK SAMPLE MATRIX FORM
KYLE ZIMMER'S BUILDING A NATIONAL PARTNERSHIP: FIRST BOOK AND A FINANCIAL
INSTITUTION TOOL FOR ANALYZING CORPORATE NEEDS WITH FIRST BOOK ASSETS

Corporate Goals →	Employee Involvement	Community Relations	Online	Media	Events	Direct Customer Link	Demographics	TOTAL
↓ **Programs/Assets**								
National Book Bank	1	3	3	2	2	1	1	13
Speed Read	3	3	2	3	3	0	2	16
Rural Initiative	0	1	0	1	1	2	0	5
Campus Advisory Boards	0	2	3	1	3	1	0	10
Advisory Board Model	3	3	3	3	3	2	3	20
The Literacy Site	3	1	3	1	0	2	3	13

Low (1)–High (3)

Although this was a traditional sales-driven cause program, today's more sophisticated approach saw First Book and Universal Studios adding other elements. Universal Studios developed an innovative cause campaign to support the launch of the movie. A First Book event in New York City was hosted by the movie's director, Ron Howard. The event included the unveiling of a special First Book promotional video produced by Universal Studios featuring messages from many Hollywood stars, including Jim Carey and Renee Russo, and prominent politicians, such as Hillary Rodham Clinton and Edward Kennedy.

The campaign was also supported by Random House Children's Books, a long-time First Book partner, who donated half a million new books to First Book as part of the promotion. The U.S. Postal Service, a newly minted First Book partner, helped out by displaying a special First Book/Grinch informational poster in all 30,000 U.S. post offices. A number of local First Book affiliates also hosted parties to celebrate the launch of the movie.

One Success Can Lead to Another

The national publicity campaign resulted in significant publicity for First Book and Universal Studios, and they won a 2001 Reggie Award from the Promotion Marketing Association for Best Cause-Related Promotion for the campaign. Kyle Zimmer strongly believes the promotion was critical in establishing the credibility of First Book and in laying the groundwork for bigger, more strategic initiatives with Universal.

After the great success of the early cause-promotional program, Universal Studios approached First Book in the fall of 2003 to work together again. This time, as Kyle Zimmer said, "we wanted to establish a new model for the relationship,"[36] one that focused on adding a value component to being involved with a nonprofit organization.

Prior to the first meeting, First Book performed a very thorough evaluation of both sides of the partnership, studying the movie project and the industry. "We always do an analysis and ask what the currency is for this potential partner. What is it that matters to them? Knowing the movie industry, we knew eyeballs or individuals knowing about the movie would be critical and this would have to be part of the deliverable for them,"[37] explains Kyle.

Before the first meeting, the organization had brainstormed ideas and concepts to promote the alliance and achieve goals for both organizations. In the first meeting, they put forward the goals and the range of concepts they had developed. They also asked lots of questions and solicited feedback on their initial ideas and proposals. "We weren't looking only for positive comments or validation of our ideas. We wanted to put people at ease in giving negative feedback. We knew this was vital in finding the right idea," states Kyle. "We discussed and evaluated different models, considered human resources both at the studio and at our organization."[38] Several ideas were considered and refined before landing on the final plan.

The Big Simple Idea—with Turnkey Execution!

What the partners settled on was "Dr Seuss' The Cat in the Hat/First Book Challenge." The concept was developed by First Book and was designed around a promotion geared to the launch of *Dr. Seuss' The Cat in the Hat* motion picture release. First Book put together a challenge box that consisted of a bright blue hat box containing a stovepipe hat from the *Cat in the Hat* book. The hat was stuffed with foam so it popped out when the lid was removed. Also included was a copy of the classic *Cat in the Hat* book and a challenge letter signed by Kyle at First Book and their partners at Random House and Universal Studios.

These challenge kits went to the news anchors in 25 markets across the United States. The letter urged the news anchor to put on the hat sometime during a designated week in November (the film was scheduled for release that month), The payoff: if the hat was worn by the news anchor, First Book and Random House committed to giving 5,000 books to children in that community in the name of the news station. All 25 markets participated, and a donation of 5,000 books was made in each community recognizing the specific channel.

The program was launched with Oprah Winfrey agreeing to be the first to wear the hat, which resulted in 50,000 books being donated to children in the Chicago area. This helped get all local anchors on board and resulted in the program concluding with the entire *Today Show* on-air team wearing the hats for yet another 50,000 books donated in New York City.

The execution was to be playful, fun, and above all, very simple, something that was very important from the perspective of all the partners. "I laugh at the gymnastics we put ourselves through to get to that simple idea,"[39] says Kyle. But it needed to be simple to understand, execute, and deliver to be a success and to create the kind of visibility the group was looking to achieve.

Combining Assets: You Get More When You Give More

All the partners contributed assets to the promotion. First Book developed the concept, created the basic design for the challenge kits, used their local groups to make the connections in the local markets, handled the request for the book donation from Random House, and coordinated the implementation and logistics.

For its part, Universal Studios provided the design work for the hat boxes and was generating plenty of attention about Dr. Seuss and *The Cat in the Hat* that made the program exciting for everyone to be a part of. The publicity strategy for the film allowed key personalities to participate in the program. The cast of the film were on the Oprah Winfrey Show making it simple and easy for Oprah to wear the hat—a turnkey cause promotion. Mike Myers' appearance on the *Today Show* helped get them all to wear the hat and support Dr. Seuss' legacy that encourages children to read. Random House contributed books, books, and more books—225,000 children's books to be exact: a major contribution to the success of the promotion and the cause of children's literacy.

Showcasing Social-Sector Worth and Building Value for All

Four goals were established that mirrored the benefits to each partner. First and foremost, give more books to children; second, create a large number of impressions through the iconic stovepipe hats to highlight the movie and increase the movie's and First Book's brand identities; third, reach a large number of markets; and finally, create a successful model of social-sector involvement in the launch of a movie. The collaborative promotion aimed to break the traditional model of one-sided arrangements and demonstrate how a social-sector organization could bring tangible value to a relationship.

Universal Studios contributed financially to First Book through the proceeds of the worldwide premiere opening of the movie. The contribution approach was the established norm for Universal Studios. At the same time, First Book had evolved in its sophistication regarding pricing. "We don't do some of the smaller ones we once did. Knowing what to ask for as a financial contribution is hard," says Kyle. "It is part art, part science and part gut feel. We try to be creative, but we figure out what it costs us and then build in the funding to advance our mission—more kids, more books."[40]

The organizations did not have a formal written contract for this cause-marketing promotion. "We didn't need one for this program. We had a long-standing relationship with all the parties involved and the program was not a complicated effort that required a formal agreement,"[41] outlined Kyle. Many of First Book's cause-marketing arrangements do have lengthy legal agreements, and First Book is very protective of its brand and identity.

Implementing the Cause-Marketing Program

Execution with National and Local Involvement

First Book forms a dedicated team to handle the execution of any cause program, and Dr. Seuss' *The Cat in the Hat* promotion was no exception. The team spanned the whole programmatic group from First Book, and a designated staff person was the main point of contact for the relationship and the lead for the group. The local affiliates for First Book coordinated the activities in their community, making contact with the local news anchors and then executing the distribution of the books triggered by the news stations' involvement.

As each market had the local news anchor successfully participate, the First Book team had developed internal incentives to celebrate success. The first 10 anchor appearances resulted in a staff member baking cookies for the whole First Book team, 15 markets triggered pizza for the staff lunch, 25 had Kyle serving lunch to the entire staff and donning a skirt and pantyhose, something that she hadn't done in years! The benchmark targets created an internal challenge and built a terrific spirit in the office that carried through the whole promotion.

Communicate, Constantly and Consistently

First Book works very hard at communication with all of the partners. They establish the best way to provide updates to each corporate partner on a case-by-case basis. "We never hesitate to communicate the latest developments so that new leverage points for the initiative can be identified on an ongoing basis and, of course, any issues are addressed at the earliest possible moment,"[42] explained Kyle.

First Book has established a culture that they describe, and diligently protect, as being: playful and creative, high-energy, very open, entrepreneurial, and overachieving. The commitment to the organization and its mission means that the staff routinely takes on far more than normal people and routinely overdelivers. This ability comes across loud and clear to all the corporations the organization works with. As Kyle says, "They know that we will stand on our heads to meet and exceed their expectations. When there is an issue— either internally or externally—we communicate immediately and address it straight on. We then provide a solution and jump back in the race."[43]

External Communication, TV in Major Markets, "It Doesn't Get Much Better"

Public communication is a major goal of any cause-marketing program. And this promotion achieved that and more. The focus for the cause program was on leveraging the reach of TV and highly watched news shows in key markets. The promotion was executed through TV—a major and high-impact communications tool. The creative and playful approach also gleaned lots of press coverage for the promotion.

Corporate and Community Goals Achieved

Although the program was implemented over a short time frame, the cause program was very strategic for both Universal Studios and First Book, and it cemented a commitment to work together again. Now both partners are looking at a bigger relationship, and a new collaborative standard has been established in the film industry. "We haven't identified the specific program yet, but we are definitely dancing," Kyle states enthusiastically. "We put forward a new model and showed it can have lots of snap and national strength that gave both of us nice visibility and ensured books were distributed in communities across the country."

Outputs—Impressions, Profile, Books, Support; Outcomes—Fun, a New Model and a Strong Relationship!

The Dr. Seuss' The Cat in the Hat/First Book challenge resulted in over 31.5 million impressions that were fun, playful, and family-oriented and achieved awareness results for Universal and First Book. The program resulted in First Book distributing over 225,000 books: a major mission goal. For the whole month and after, everyone talked about First Book. Explains Kyle, "Literacy is important, but in the social sector it's easy to forget that reading to kids is supposed to be fun. The program reminded people about laughing together and about being a bit of a ham for a good cause. When the anchors put on

The Cat in the Hat hat in front of a studio audience, no one looked dignified, but they knew that kids in their community would be getting books." As recognition of the success of the program for all partners and the community, Universal Studios and First Book won first place in the Cause Marketing Forum Halo Award, Education category, in 2004.

First Book followed up with a full report for the partners including the tangible results and some emotional letters from kids who had received their first book as a result of the program. "It's important for them to see the mission results as well," enthused Kyle.

Like good partners, First Book and Universal continue their relationship, which has also expanded to include Imagine Films, and Karen Kehela-Sherwood, cochair of Imagine Films has joined the organization's National Advisory Council. The two continue their conversation and look for the next strategic fit. Universal's world is film by film, and when the right opportunity comes along, First Book will "grab it and be going like the wind."

Words of Wisdom from a Pioneer

First Book has learned a lot about cause marketing in their almost 15 years of operation and offers five key factors to consider:

1. Build a value proposition that creates a relationship where everyone wins.
2. Ensure effective implementation.
3. Be creative with ideas for partnership.
4. Take a business approach to all aspects of your interactions: be buttoned-down and business-oriented.
5. Have results that are tangible, not just feel-good. Tell where the books are going and make it real. They need to feel the mission the way you do.[44]

Endnote: The Apple Doesn' t Fall Too Far from the Tree

First Book believes cause marketing can be done at any level and with almost any type of organization. What it takes is getting to know the goals and design of potential corporate partners. Do your research, be creative, and above all, don't be daunted by the prospect of doing this at the local level.

First Book's local Advisory Boards (there are over 250 local affiliates) have learned about the benefits and discipline of cause marketing and actively engage in the practice at the local level. For example, the Roaring Rapids Pizza Company donated 40% of profits on a designated night to First Book in Eugene/Springfield, Oregon. The Advisory Board sent e-mail announcements to all local school districts and mailed bright yellow postcards to friends and neighbors to increase customer traffic. Sororities from the nearby university agreed to purchase takeout pizza that night. A slice for literacy: pizza for a cause.[45]

ENDNOTES

1. Go Red For Women, American Heart Association Presentation, January 2005.
2. Ibid.
3. Interview, Kathy Rogers, American Heart Association, August 19, 2005.
4. Interview, Kathy Rogers, American Heart Association, January 24, 2005.
5. Ibid.
6. Interview, Kristian Darigan, Cone Inc., December 13, 2004.
7. Cone Presentation, "21st Century Cause Branding: Go Red for Women," 2004.
8. Cone Case Study, America Heart Association, "Go Red for Women."
9. Interview, Kathy Rogers, August 19, 2005.
10. Interview, Kristian Darigan, Cone Inc., December 13, 2004.
11. Interview, Kathy Rogers, January 24, 2005.
12. Ibid.
13. Interview, Kristian Darigan, Cone Inc., December 13, 2004.
14. Cone Presentation, "21st Century Cause Branding: Go Red for Women," 2004.
15. Interview, Kathy Rogers, August 19, 2005.
16. Ibid.
17. Ibid.
18. Ibid.
19. Ibid.
20. Ibid.
21. Ibid.
22. Ibid.
23. Interview, Kathy Rogers, August 19, 2005.
24. Interview, Kathy Rogers, January 24, 2005.
25. Interview, Kathy Rogers, August 19, 2005.
26. Ibid.
27. Interview, Kathy Rogers, January 24, 2005.
28. Ibid.
29. Interview, Kathy Rogers, August 19, 2005.
30. Interview, Kathy Rogers, August 19, 2005.
31. Interview, Kyle Zimmer, January 27, 2005.
32. Ibid.
33. Ibid.
34. Ibid.
35. Ibid.
36. Ibid.
37. Ibid.
38. Ibid.
39. Ibid.
40. Interview, Kyle Zimmer, January 27, 2005.
41. Written response to questions, Kyle Zimmer, August 4, 2005.
42. Ibid.
43. Ibid.
44. Interview, Kyle Zimmer, November 4, 2004.
45. Best practices: Advisory Board Success Stories, First Book publication, Spring 2003.

CHAPTER **11**

Local Organizations: Food Bank (New York City) and Canadian Cancer Society (Vancouver Island Region, British Columbia and Yukon District)

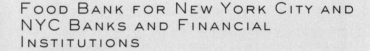

FOOD BANK FOR NEW YORK CITY AND NYC BANKS AND FINANCIAL INSTITUTIONS

NYC Bank-to-Bank Partnership:
Cobrand Cause-Marketing Program Initiative

The Food Bank for New York City, a member of America's Second Harvest, The Nation's Food Bank Network, and the only food bank in the city, was founded in 1983 to coordinate the procurement and distribution of food donations from manufacturers, wholesalers, retailers, and government agencies to organizations providing free food to the city's hungry. By the summer of 2005, over 676 million pounds of food was distributed to more than 1,200 nonprofit community food programs—including soup kitchens, food pantries, shelters, low-income day care centers, Kids Cafes, and senior, youth and rehabilitation centers—throughout the five boroughs of New York City.

The Food Bank supplies the food to help prepare over 240,000 free meals a day for New Yorkers who otherwise would go hungry or not eat enough, including families with children, the elderly, teenagers, the homeless, the homebound, low-income workers, and people living with HIV/AIDS. The Food Bank also acts as a resource center for member agencies, legislators, the media, and the public. It regularly conducts research about hunger in New York City and plays an active role in public policy issues at the city, state, and national levels. In addition to providing food, the Food Bank offers agencies ongoing support, services, and education.

In 2001, the board of directors launched an initiative to build the brand of the organization and create an external cause-marketing focus. In 2002, the Food Bank for New York City launched its first cause-marketing campaign: Bank-to-Bank, aimed at building bridges and forming an alliance between the powerful New York City banking sector and the Food Bank. The goal: to simultaneously build the brands, communicate values and further the missions of both sectors. In 2003, the Food Bank for New York City Bank-to-Bank Partnership (Bank-to-Bank) was awarded best "Public Awareness/Awareness Campaign" in the United States by America's Second Harvest, Hunger Hope Awards.

Creating a Cause-Marketing Orientation

When the board of the directors of the then-named Food for Survival decided to launch an external marketing initiative, it did so with the idea of growth: growth of the organization and growth of the cause-marketing trend.

For almost 20 years the organization had been a major contributor to distributing food to the city's hungry. "We had a great operation, a great cause, and great running of the day to day operations of what a food bank does," explains Lucy Cabrera, PhD and President and CEO for the Food Bank for New York City. "But this is New York City," she adds, "and it is a highly competitive environment for non-profit organizations. Being good at what you do wasn't enough to attract the business involvement we felt would help us grow, build our profile and generate additional funds and support for our cause."[1]

In 2001, the Food Banks' board of directors established an external relations department with the mandate to build and extend the organization's brand equity to keep a step ahead of the competitive landscape and to raise their profile and generate additional revenue and food streams to achieve the organization's mission and mandate. The department was tasked with creating a strong marketing focus, building the brand, and creating cause-marketing campaigns. The goal: to build extensive media coverage, attract corporate partners, which in turn were intended to extend the organization's message and profile, eventually translating into additional community support (see Exhibit 11.1).

Building the Brand Position

The board's first step was to hire an external relations expert to drive the changes needed to realize their goals. They sought someone who could re-brand the organization, understand who the audience was in New York City, and then use the brand to create value. At that point, the organization's only external focus was a traditional philanthropy program geared to foundation grant writing and securing individual support. Gregory Boroff, an experienced and innovative fund development and marketing professional, was hired to lead the initiative in the newly formed position of vice president, External Relations.

EXHIBIT 11.1   USING THE BRAND TO CREATE VALUE

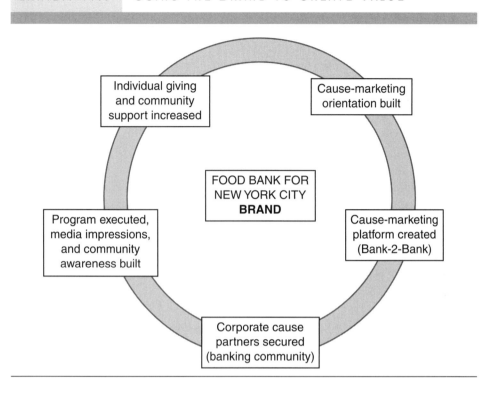

To get started, the organization was renamed and rebranded. The name went from Food for Survival to the Food Bank for New York City. The color orange, the color of hunger in the United States, was adopted, and food for survival was added as a tagline to the name. The new logo featured the crown in the Statue of Liberty, tying it to a landmark symbol of the city.

The name change was important to clearly describe what the organization did. As Gregory Boroff explained, people would always ask, "What is Food for Survival?" The answer was, well it's a food bank providing food for survival. There was always a second step needed to clarify the organization's name and raison d'être. It only made sense to change the name to unmistakably define what the organization did and who it served.

But rebranding means so much more than just changing the name and logo, and the organization went about looking at how all external material was presented. A Web site was developed, media kits created, and the annual report went from being just numbers to a major marketing tool that explained who the organization was, who they worked with, and how they did their job. All the external collateral material was put in place ready to start moving out into the community.

Assets Reviewed and Linkages Considered

At the same time, the organization did an assessment of what equity and assets it had. All nonprofit organizations have a certain amount of equity that is translatable into a dollar value, and the Food Bank was looking at their strengths and what might be used for external partnerships. At the time, the organization had a very small amount of equity. Their marketing and branding was new, and the organization did not have a strong identity in the community. An internal team, including Gregory Boroff as VP, External Relations and the newly hired Manager, Business Partnerships, Michael Hecht, looked at the audience in New York City, the organization's assets, and the rebranded Food Bank.

Operating in New York City, the financial capital of the United States, means that banks and financial institutions are a very attractive target for many nonprofits, including the Food Bank. Attractive not only for financial support but investment, retail banks also have strong consumer traffic and a large staff, two other attractive features for an organization. The question for the Food Bank was how to stand out among the crowd and position themselves to be equally attractive to the banking and financial sector?

"With our rebranded name as a Food Bank there was a natural fit. We're a bank, this is the banking capital—how about that!" explains Gregory. "We saw all the markers for a flagship cause-marketing campaign pointing to do something with the banking industry."[2]

Bank-to-Bank Partnership Cause-Marketing Platform Was Born

After much thought and deliberation, a cause-marketing platform was developed to be a catchy and obvious play on words. Bank-to-Bank Partnership was structured to be the cornerstone of the Food Bank's fall effort to generate and then distribute an additional one million pounds of food during the holiday season all the while raising awareness of the organization and generating a new source of financial support.

With the concept in hand, the Food Bank decided rather than immediately looking for support, the group would seek out input from the banking community. "This was, in hindsight, a great idea," explains Gregory. "We went out looking for feedback about the program. One of our key meetings was with the New York City Banking Commission, the governing body for banks in the city. They provided excellent input and unwavering support," states Gregory. "They really encouraged us and provided a list of contacts and banks for us to approach. Their support and connections were critical in opening doors to the banking community."[3]

As the Food Bank continued their meetings, they realized there were many differences in the way banks approached their operations: each one had different technologies, different ways of communicating with their customers, and different models of operation. "What was clear was we had to keep the core program really simple and uncomplicated. We could add a list of possible options that could be incorporated depending on the needs and interests of the individual banks, but the fundamentals had to be straightforward,"[4] explains Gregory.

The cause-marketing program was an example of how nontraditional alignments, a food bank and retail and financial banks, could fit and be associated for mutual benefit. Without the program, few banks in New York City had hunger or the Food Bank as areas for their philanthropic giving focus. The program opened the door to a whole new sector and more importantly reached out to their clients and employees, to generate food, funds, and awareness for the Food Bank at a critical time of the year.

The Food Bank's approach was both simple and familiar. The Bank-to-Bank Partnership was not going to solicit financial support from bank customers or employees on site; rather, the program aimed at reaching back into childhood and teenage memories of the food drives done in schools. Food Bank boxes would be placed in participating retail bank branches and bank corporate offices from November 1 to 30. With little human or capital resource impact, banks were going to be able to provide their customers and employees across New York City a convenient way to make a contribution of nonperishable canned items to the Food Bank, all the while publicly building the participating bank's reputation and brand as strong community supporters.

The program included support of a broad publicity campaign through media and marketing partnership, an important way to also generate awareness and recognition for the participating banks. Logistic details were worked out including securing UPS as a logistics partner. All these pieces were planned and put in place ready to launch the program.

Internal Capacity Built

While the organization was building its brand equity and a cause-marketing program platform, the external relations unit was expanded to include marketing and communications, philanthropy (individual giving and grant writing), and business partnerships. Business partnerships were originally housed under the philanthropy division. But their success and the recognition of the potential for corporate support resulted in it being split off in 2003 and established as a standalone division. The External Affairs department grew from an original staff of five in 2001 to 16 in 2005. Employees were hired who had strong marketing orientation and experience in the private sector as well as the nonprofit arena. Full support was provided by the leadership team to ensure success.

The Food Bank brand and associated cause-marketing campaigns were to be the central focal point for the unit, and the spokes coming from it were the three areas of the unit. All areas were interlinked and intertwined around the brand and the cause-marketing program to create a stronger external focus and fundraising capacity for the organization.

EXHIBIT 11.2   BANK-TO-BANK PARTNERSHIP

1 in 5

New Yorkers turns to a soup kitchen or food pantry
for food because they have no other choice.

**Help a Hungry New Yorker
by Making a Different Kind of Bank Deposit.**

Look for the
NYC BANK-TO-BANK PARTNERSHIP FOOD DRIVE
November 1-30, 2003
Drop off cans of food today at a participating location!

Go to www.foodbanknyc.org
to find a drop-off location near you and learn how you can support
Food Bank For New York City.

The Food Bank helps provide the food for over 200,000 meals served every day
by more than 1,000 soup kitchens, food pantries and other food assistance programs throughout the city.

FOOD BANK
FOR NEW YORK CITY

Bank 2 Bank
PARTNERSHIP

Fleet   JPMorganChase   Washington Mutual   Deutsche Bank

HVB Group   Morgan Stanley   UBS   Bloomberg L.P.   CRAIN'S   ups

DAILY NEWS   Time Out New York   WB11   am NewYork   American Park   MARK IV TRUCKING

Printing Sponsored by THE POSTER PRINTERS 718.377.7245   Sponsors as of 10/15/03

Building the Cause-Marketing Program

With the Bank-to-Bank platform and marketing orientation in place, the next step was to make connections with the banking community. The organization had a cause-marketing "product"—Bank-to-Bank; the potential "place" (distribution)—retail banks and commercial bank offices; promotion planned;

and a price established to participate in the program. Now the organization needed to secure partners, ensure both sectors' purposes would be achieved, create the passion, and confirm the profits (value) for both partners (see Exhibit 11.2).

Partners, an Obvious Target

The initial research meetings had already opened the door and made the first connections for the Bank-to-Bank Partnership. But because the program was a natural fit for banks, cold calls were also made to reach potential collaborators. The biggest challenge was finding the right person, talking directly to them, and then securing a face-to-face meeting. Once a meeting was arranged the Food Bank Business Development team wanted to show potential corporate partners that they were a "force to be reckoned with." "We wanted to erase the stereotype that the meeting would be with someone from the nonprofit sector coming in wearing jeans," said Michael Hecht, former Director of Business Partnerships. "There was a big push, if we were meeting with someone who was wearing a suit, we would wear suits. We had a very professional package with a full marketing plan and biographies of the people running the project." The presentation was very much geared to here is what's in it for you and how you can help us advance our mission at the same time.[5]

The response was strong right from the beginning. "There was a lot of early adoption by companies who really bought into the idea," stated Gregory. "It was action oriented and enabled customers and employees to engage in supporting the Food Bank. The goal was to create good will for the banks, to demonstrate their values, to raise our profile and to have a major food drive during a month-long period around the holiday season."[6]

Big Simple Idea, with Equally Simple Execution

"When you talk to any potential partner, they want the easiest possible program. They don't want to involve their human capital in designing sales, they want something out of the box—a turnkey solution," explains Gregory. "The Food Bank had the whole program fine-tuned before approaching potential partners. It was almost a no-brainer it was so easy to understand and to sell. It was important to have a detailed proposal that included a marketing and recognition plan. You can't just say, 'This is a great idea, let's just do it,' without having the supporting documentation to secure the confidence of a potential partner."[7]

The program is well developed and it has a clear structure and approach, but the Food Bank does leave room for customization for individual banks. Each partner has a different interest and different priorities for being involved. "Some are most interested in the number of media partners and the potential for significant marketing and media exposure. Others are genuinely excited about partnering with an organization like the Food Bank, which has such an interesting story to tell," explains Gregory. "We have to find the reason they'll get excited or they aren't going to partner with us. There is a different

motivation and directive for each bank partner and we work with them to deliver on their needs. We always talk about return on investment as well as how
they can help advance our mission."[8]

Combining Assets and Creating Value: Purpose, Passion, and Profits

Each partner brings important assets to the relationship to ensure the program's success. The Food Bank is responsible for the full execution of the program, including providing each bank with Food Boxes for drop off of items
and the arranging for the food to be picked up and delivered to their warehouses. The banks provide the venue and help support the program with in-
bank signage created by the Food Bank. Some of the banks have taken it a
step further and featured the program in their own advertising vehicles. Fleet
Bank, for example, provided the Food Bank with a billboard in Times Square
and tied their name and brand into it. The billboard was something the organization could never have afforded without the Bank-to-Bank relationship.

Employee Volunteer Opportunities

Another important feature that was added to the Bank-to-Bank program was
an employee volunteer opportunity for partner banks. After the food drive is
over, participating partners are invited to send employee groups to the Food
Bank's 100,000-square-foot warehouse in the Bronx for their annual Volunteer-A-Thon. Corporate volunteers receive a tour of the facility and then work
to repack the thousands of pounds of food collected through the Partnership.

Crossing the T' s and Dotting the I' s

An agreement is put in place with each bank partner that outlines the key
components of the campaign and the relationship. It puts in writing how the
logos of each organization will be used, who is responsible for what, and defines the lines of communication. "It's a standard agreement that is looked
at by both sides and has to be in place to ensure smooth operation and clear
understanding of roles and responsibilities,"[9] states Gregory.

Pricing—Always a Challenge

The Food Bank has established two pricing levels—one for the retail banks
and the other for the investment and corporate offices side. The pricing is
based on the costs and the value provided. Coordinating a program with a
retail bank involves more work than the corporate offices. The price point was
established in the initial year of the program and is at a level that enables
many banks to be involved.

Implementing the Cause-Marketing Program

Like all the other successful cause-marketing programs, determination, drive,
and old-fashioned hard work are what it takes to make a program a success.
Lots of people have great ideas, but having the drive to see the program
from idea to execution is what separates those who succeed from those who
only have a great idea.

Program Management

The Director, Business Partnerships, has the responsibility of finding and se-curing banking partners, including finalizing the legal agreements. Through the execution period the Director stays involved on the strategic issues and relationship side. A campaign manager handles the day-to-day logistics and ongoing implementation at each of the banks. The Bank-to-Bank program has attracted important logistic support. Since the beginning UPS has pro-vided free pickup of food from each bank location, and their involvement has grown as the program has grown. Bank contacts from the community relations and marketing side are identified, and they are responsible for on-site logis-tics for the bank and ensuring approvals of marketing material for the pro-gram. Every Monday morning during the month-long campaign, the Food Bank team has a partnership meeting. This is an opportunity to share information, make sure the campaign is on track, and work out any potential issues.

Communications—High-Profile Success

Communication of the program is a high priority for the Food Bank, and the marketing and communications division of the External Relations Branch has played the lead role in building a fully integrated and broad marketing and media relations campaign.

The campaign is featured on their Web site, and information is sent to all their supporters. A full range of corporate media partners plays a critical role in promoting the program and publicly featuring the cause partners' support. The Food Bank secured, for example during its 2004 campaign, radio, print, and TV partners: 1010 WINS radio station (month-long PSAs), amNew York (stories and print ads), Time Out New York (stories and print ads), New York Moves (print ads), and WB11 (month-long PSAs).

They also look to piggyback on their bank partner's advertising vehicles. "Don't be afraid to ask your corporate partners if they have ad space, such as air space, magazine or newspaper ads, if they will promote the program. Washington Mutual provided this type of support in the 2004 campaign, as has Fleet Bank," is a piece of advice that Gregory Boroff says has really helped all partners succeed.

Cause-Marketing Goals Achieved

Bank-to-Bank has helped the Food Bank achieve three important goals not possible without this cause-marketing signature campaign: new exposure, new sources of food, and a new revenue stream. The organization now estimates it is generating almost $400,000 hard cash for their fundraising efforts and well over $1 million in marketing and media coverage.

Working Out the Kinks

Bank-to-Bank has seen the number of banks involved each year go up and down. The first year, the organization was able to attract a strong critical mass. The first year's success resulted in an explosion of interest in participating in the program the second year. "The growth was fantastic," explains Gregory, "but we really had to look at it from a practical point of view. We had lots of small banks that didn't generate enough support to really make it worth our while. The next year we established some minimum requirements as to who could be involved. We had to look at it from a cost-benefit perspective and put our efforts where we were getting the greatest return."[10]

Finding the happy medium between what you can do and give and how much you can get is a balancing act. The Food Bank discovered there was a diminishing law of returns, and they have tweaked the program enough to know their partner limit. Entering its fourth year in 2005, the organization feels they have found the right balance for the campaign.

Results

Success is measured in tangible outputs and intangible outcomes. Outputs for 2004 were

- Corporate employee involvement: Over 350 corporate employees participated in the Volunteer-a-Thon, packed 250,000 pounds of food, and helped save enough money for the Food Bank to provide 19,530 meals for needy New Yorkers.

- Food collected: 756,000 pounds of food was collected and over 590,000 meals provided during the winter months. A key mission win for the organization.

- Visibility for partners: 30,000 corporate employees were made aware of the program through internal promotions; an estimated 12.5 million New Yorkers were made aware of the program as a result of media placement, advertisements, and public service announcements.[11]

- Financial support: Bank-to-Bank is a whole new financial revenue stream for the organization with a sector that would not have traditionally supported the Food Bank.

The Bank-to-Bank Partnership has achieved the goals established for it. The outcomes: The Food Bank has built additional new corporate relationships, received greater food donations for the important work of the Food Bank, and built credibility for the organization with the corporate sector, all possible only because of the program. But equally important, it has helped the Food Bank develop an integrated marketing and fundraising program that is extending its brand and building broader and stronger support.

Even as the department has grown in number (from five to 16), the results have been strong financially for the Food Bank. "The program had generated additional financial support and broad awareness of the Food Bank. We pride ourselves on our ratio of revenue raised going to programs. Before we launched the External Affairs area, the Food Bank was providing 94 cents of every $1 directly to Food Bank programs. We have been able to maintain that proportion even with the extra staff, all the while providing significant additional support."

Celebrating Success

Celebrating is a critical part of the follow-up and recognition for the program. A full summary of the year's campaign is provided to all participating partners, and a Bank-to-Bank luncheon is held every January. "We use it to showcase the results of the program and we do a compilation reel with a media partner that includes all the media coverage, interviews, and PSAs from the campaign. All of our partners are invited and we also invite prospective partners to get them excited about the program," explains Gregory.[12]

Next Step, Grow Bank-to-Bank and Add New Cause-Marketing Platforms

Concerned with continually improving and growing the program, the Food Bank is now thinking about how to develop the fundraising component beyond the corporate financial contribution. "We are talking to our corporate partners because we want to look to see how the program can be leveraged to the next level," says Gregory. "For example, this year, one bank in addition to being a partner, is developing an employee cookbook they will sell during the holiday season, tied into the program, with the proceeds coming to the Food Bank."[13]

Bank-to-Bank was seen as the first foray into building potential cause-marketing programs with the corporate sector. The organization's success with the campaign has led to the creation of the "Cans Film Festival" held every May to coincide with the Cannes Film Festival in France. The city is a major film center—another natural fit in the evolution of their cause-marketing programs. The organization is also looking at other seasons and how a cause program could fit. Summer is a particularly hard time; with all the public schools out, there isn't a free meal program. The Food Bank is currently considering what industry could be a fit for a childhood hunger program that could be the focus of a summer campaign.

Final Thoughts and Advice

What would the number one piece of advice be? Planning, planning, and more planning. Be organized and when seeking corporate partners remember any cultivation takes 8 to 12 months, and it's important to try to sign on partners early enough to maximize the results of the program—for both sides. The Food Bank is now sending out their proposal for the November program in early January and has seen a better response rate. As well, the extra lead time has given the Food Bank the opportunity to find "spillover" opportunities for those banks that didn't come on board for the Bank-to-Bank initiative. "If you rush your cultivation and you're just trying to get them on for that campaign, you don't have time to look at the bigger picture. We've generated additional revenue from banks that couldn't be involved with the campaign, but wanted to help in some way,"[14] states Gregory.

Finally, staff comes and goes, but cause-marketing campaigns that are created and fortified within the organization will survive personnel changes.

The Food Bank, like many nonprofits, struggles with institutional memory. Over the past few years, they have implemented a documentation process so if there is someone new, there is a "campaign in a box" that outlines the program and means that it could perform at the same level. Relationships and knowledge must be beyond one person, and a signature campaign like this one is an example of how that can happen.

VANCOUVER ISLAND REGION, BRITISH COLUMBIA/YUKON CHAPTER, CANADIAN CANCER SOCIETY AND CAUSE PARTNER THRIFTY FOODS:

Daffodil Cause-Marketing Product Sales

The Canadian Cancer Society (CCS) is a national, community-based organization of volunteers whose mission is the eradication of cancer and the enhancement of the quality of life of people living with cancer. The Canadian Cancer Society was formed in 1938 with the mandate to spread important information about the early warning signs of cancer to the Canadian public. The organization focuses on five areas of support:

1. *Research—CCS is the largest charitable funder of cancer research in Canada.*

2. *Advocacy—CCS mobilizes Canadians to create social and political change to help control cancer and reduce risk.*

3. *Prevention—CCS encourages Canadian to chose healthy lifestyles and environments.*

4. *Information—CCS provides reliable information.*

5. *Support—CCS offers individual or group support programs for caregivers, family, and friends.*

The Canadian Cancer Society has a national office and 10 provincial and territorial offices. Volunteers and staff also work at the local grassroots level to organize awareness and fundraising events, collect donations, support advocacy campaigns, provide programs and services such as emotional support to patients and their families, and many other activities that support the Canadian Cancer Society.

The daffodil is the Canadian Cancer Society's symbol of hope in the fight against cancer. The early spring flowers are sold every year from mid-March to early April and mark the beginning of the Society's annual door-to-door fundraising campaign. Today, the Canadian Cancer Society is the world's largest purchaser of daffodils, and the growers in British Columbia must arrange their plantings to meet the needs of the Society's spring demand for live blooms.[15]

The British Columbia and Yukon Division of the Canadian Cancer Society has creatively used the Daffodil Campaign to build local cause-marketing programs. The product initiative is a great example of how with the right idea, positioning, creativity, and hard work, cause marketing can be successfully implemented at any level.

Creating a Cause-Marketing Orientation

Cause marketing is not limited to large organizations or those located in major urban centers; it can be implemented at any level using the cause-marketing principles and framework as a guide. The seven C's: cause readiness; collaborative fit; combining assets; creating value; executing the program; communicating values; and achieving corporate and community goals are the foundation of any successful cause-marketing program. This case study demonstrates the effectiveness local cause-marketing campaigns can have for revenue generation, profile building, and achieving of mission and mandate for community-based nonprofit organizations.

Strong Brand, Clear Goals, Compelling Need

The Canadian Cancer Society is well known for its annual Daffodil Month Campaign in April, and support for the annual fund-raiser is strong. Not only will one in three Canadians be diagnosed with cancer in his or her lifetime, but cancer also remains the leading cause of premature death (death earlier than the average life expectancy). The Canadian Cancer Society enjoys widespread public support and instant brand recognition. Sixty-two percent of people polled (unprompted) named the Canadian Cancer Society as the number one cancer-fighting organization.[16]

The Daffodil Campaign has become an institution for the Canadian Cancer Society and has evolved into the focus for kicking off Cancer Awareness Month in April. The campaign sets the stage for the April door-to-door campaign by raising the organization's profile and generating revenue from the daffodil sales. Daffodil Days takes place on different days in different communities throughout Canada.

The Beginning of the Big Simple Idea

Daffodil Days began in Toronto, Ontario, in the 1950s. A group of Canadian Cancer Society volunteers organized a fundraising tea and decided to decorate the tables with daffodils. The bright, cheerful flowers created an atmosphere that seemed to radiate hope and faith that cancer could be beaten. Interest in purchasing daffodil flowers led to the Society selling the spring flower in Toronto in the mid-1950s as a fund-raiser and awareness initiative. The daffodils were an instant success, raising more than $1,200 the first year. The idea was soon adopted by other provinces across Canada as well as the American Cancer Society.[17] Continuing the tradition today, each year in late

March and early April, Canadian Cancer Society volunteers sell the bright yellow daffodils across the country to help raise awareness and money in support of the fight against cancer.

Internal Structure for Daffodil Campaign

The Canadian Cancer Society takes a decentralized approach to its fundraising programs, and the Daffodil Campaign is no exception. How each daffodil campaign is developed and implemented varies from provincial and territorial division to division.

The British Columbia and Yukon Region Division of the Canadian Cancer Society, headquartered in Vancouver, is divided into seven regions. Local programs and fundraising activities are coordinated through the divisional office, but each region takes responsibility for organizing and implementing the daffodil campaign in their communities. With this decentralized approach, individual regions can build campaigns that best suit their community and needs and allow for flexibility and creativity in implementation.

Corporate and Cause-Marketing Involvement, a Local Tradition

Corporate involvement in the daffodil campaign is not new. In most communities across the country, daffodil sales include a corporate component that largely focuses on sales through employee groups. Using the daffodil campaign for a cause-marketing-focused approach was initiated right from the beginning of the program.

In 1956 an early volunteer arranged for restaurants in Toronto to give part of their receipts to the Society on the opening day of the door-to-door campaign. Canadian Cancer Society volunteers were on hand at local restaurants to give patrons a daffodil as a token of appreciation when they paid for their meals.

The Greater Vancouver region of the British Columbia and Yukon Division pioneered a cause-marketing initiative in the mid-1990s when their then Daffodil Campaign Corporate Sales Coordinator, Karen Bronstein,[18] developed a cause-marketing promotion using the daffodils as the focus. "I had an idea to have companies in the Vancouver area purchase daffodils to give away as a customer appreciation tool," explains Karen. "I thought this was a simple way to engage the corporate sector, provide a benefit to them while helping the Canadian Cancer Society."[19]

Karen began by preparing internally: building a list of potential companies in the Vancouver area, developing a simple, clear message, and preparing marketing material to make the case. "I approached all types of companies, but focused on retail business or companies that had a large customer base and I went straight to the top—right to the owners or presidents of the companies," she explains. "The interest was there and there were a number of retailers that picked up on the campaign. For example, Plum Clothing in British Columbia had half a dozen retail outlets that bought the flowers and handed them out to customers."[20]

Karen's big break came through a connection in the airline industry. Canada 3000, a national airline company (now defunct), agreed to purchase daffodils for every one of its passengers on Easter Sunday. But more significant was their interest and willingness to make it a broad awareness campaign for the Canadian Cancer Society. Hand tags were placed on every daffodil, and meal tray liners provided information about cancer and the work of the organization.

"It was a great initiative that generated significant revenue but also awareness for the organization," explains Karen. "The airline coordinated a media blitz for the initiative including a photo op for the media of stewardesses boarding planes with armloads full of daffodils."[21]

Karen's entrepreneurial and marketing orientation combined with drive was a key factor in the cause-marketing program's success. "I had a vision of what could be done and tried selling the flowers not just from the charity's perspective but from what was in it for the corporation as well,"[22] she explains.

Building a Cause-Marketing Program

The Canadian Cancer Society (CCS) has a tradition of proactively building local cause-marketing campaigns using the daffodil program as a focus. Like the CCS, many nonprofits are becoming more proactive in seeking corporate cause partners. But the positive effect and impact of cause marketing for the corporate sector means that many organizations are regularly approached by companies with formulated cause programs. The same principles apply for building and implementing the program.

The Vancouver Island Region of the Canadian Cancer Society was approached by Thrifty Foods in 2004 with a cause-marketing program tied to the daffodil campaign in mind.

An Existing Relationship Expands into Cause Marketing

"We had the cause focus and internal readiness with the daffodil campaign and we already had a long term relationship with Thrifty Foods,"[23] states Karina Chow, previously Revenue Development Coordinator for Vancouver Island Region, Canadian Cancer Society, when the cause initiative was launched. Thrifty Foods had been a supporter of the organization's annual Cops for Cancer Tour de Rock since 1999. This fundraising event, a 1,000-kilometer (625-mile) police ride across Vancouver Island on Canada's west coast, raises funds specifically for childhood cancer research and programs for children with cancer.

Thrifty Foods chain owns 18 stores throughout Vancouver Island, Saltspring Island, and on the lower mainland of British Columbia at Tsawwassen, just south of Vancouver. Thrifty Foods also includes more than just grocery stores, with a state-of-the-art commissary known as Thrifty Kitchens and a 91,000-square foot wholesale warehouse that supplies products to each Thrifty Foods location and to more than 60 other independent grocers in British Columbia. All of this combined gives Thrifty Foods an over 40% market share on Vancouver Island. Thrifty Foods is the largest private-sector employer on the island with over 3,500 employees.[24]

"Thrifty Foods is very community minded and they do a lot of their marketing around being a caring oriented company," explains Karina. "They tend to chose a charity monthly and do some kind of cause initiative with them to support their fundraising programs. Because they have had such a good relationship with us, we both felt comfortable with the idea of building a cause-marketing arrangement tied to our daffodil campaign."[25]

Combining Assets and Creating Value for a Win-Win Program

Thrifty Foods proposed a simple approach. From March 10 to 30, the food chain would donate a $1 from each bunch of daffodils sold in their stores to the Canadian Cancer Society. Customers could also "top-up" their bill and make a donation to support local cancer services with their grocery purchase. Thrifty Foods also committed to match dollar for dollar every contribution made at the till.

"This was a wonderful new initiative for us," stated Karina. "Historically the daffodil program had been largely volunteer driven and over the past couple of years a number of long-term volunteer chairs had left the program. At the time Thrifty Foods approached us about a cause-marketing initiative tied to daffodil sales, our program was just limping along. With their proposal, we suggested providing volunteers in each of the Thrifty Foods stores during the weekends. The volunteers would focus on providing information about Canadian Cancer Society programs in the local community and promoting daffodil sales."[26] Thrifty Foods provided the daffodils, promotional support, and facilitated donations at the till. The Society contributed volunteers, information, the daffodil focus, and of course, the goodwill associated with supporting a cancer organization.

Value, So Much More than Dollars

The cause-marketing arrangement provided the Cancer Society a simple and risk-free way to sell flowers while generating revenue and getting out information about the Society's work and programs.

"It was great for us," enthused Karina. "We're not florists and that is part of Thrifty Foods key business. They have the expertise, the flower shops right in the stores and the people who know the flower business. They were already purchasing daffodil flowers from the same grower that was our main supplier. What it meant for us was we had no upfront costs, they provided the venue for sales and advertising and we had no worries about how to sell leftovers. It was completely risk free for us and we were guaranteed the $1 from each bunch sold."[27]

As well, the stores' flower shops provided the additional value of flower food and flower wrapping, something the Society was not in a position to do. Thrifty Foods committed to providing coffee and cookies or cake at each store that could be handed out by the volunteers to store customers. This is was a great way to connect with people and to engage them in a conversation about the Society's work and programs.

The two organizations decided to sell the flowers for $2.50 a bunch. This meant that Thrifty Foods would recoup their costs for the flowers, and the price was consistent with what the Society was already charging, thereby avoiding undercutting Society volunteers selling outside the Thrifty Foods arrangement.

The Society's long-term relationship meant the two organizations did not formalize their relationship with a legal agreement. Instead, they relied on verbal discussion and agreement and a follow-up e-mail outlining roles, responsibilities, commitments, and timelines.

Implementing the Cause-Marketing Program

Karina Chow of the Vancouver Island Region worked closely with Thrifty Foods on the development and implementation of the cause-marketing initiative. "In a small organization like ours, you do it all. One of the challenges of working for a large, well-known national charity is the assumption that we have lots of human resources available. The reality is quite different and I had to manage expectations in terms of execution. I wanted to make sure I could deliver on all our commitments"[28] she says.

Karina was responsible for coordinating the volunteers with each of the local Cancer units up and down Vancouver Island. The Vancouver Island region of Canadian Cancer Society has 10 units, and nine of them were able to pair up with the 18 Thrifty Foods' stores.

"Everyone was really excited about the program and we had strong volunteer support. The impact of the volunteers varied, but they were well received in the stores. I even volunteered at one location and set a goal of selling two cases or 250 bunches. I really worked it for the four hours I was there," tells Karina. "I handed out brochures and talked to people about what we do in the community. I had the posters for our upcoming door-to-door campaign and provided information on our community programs."[29]

Strong Mix of Communication Vehicles

Thrifty Foods and the Vancouver Island Region, Canadian Cancer Society (CCS), jointly sent out a press release. The news releases highlighted different programs that the Society offered, a great messaging opportunity for the organization. For example, the press releases explained the number of programs and then focused specifically on one of the programs. Press releases were issued each week during the campaign to provide an ongoing media push and to get the message out about a program. "The CCS offers over 20 programs across Vancouver Island, Salt Spring Island and Tsawwassen including the Volunteer Driver Program. Trained and supportive volunteers drive patients to their treatment every weekday and last year drove over 250,000 kilometers. We are told by patients, families and their friends that many cancer patients wouldn't be able to get to their appointment without the volunteer driver program," states Alice Pasoluko, Volunteer Driver Chair. "We are indebted to the dedicated volunteer drivers—without them it would never happen." In addition to the daffodil promotion you can take steps to reduce your cancer risk by joining our April Door to Door campaign as a canvasser. By doing so you'll be raising money to fund vital cancer research and keeping fit, which can help reduce your risk.[30]

Thrifty Foods also tied in radio promotions and in some stores did radio remotes that included profiling the daffodil promotion for the CCS. Store flyers featured the daffodil campaign, and in-store signage reinforced the cancer program messages and the donation to the Society (see Exhibit 11.4).

"We don't purchase advertising so it was a great way to get out our name and logo particularly before our door-to-door campaign," explained Karina. "It's hard to measure the impact it had for us but I believe any publicity helps."[31]

Goals Achieved

The program was run in 2004 and 2005. A program for the 2006 Daffodil Campaign is in the early discussion stage. "I really enjoyed having this relationship with Thrifty Foods," explains Karina. "The great thing was this was a program that supported all our work, not just one initiative like children and cancer. It gave us an opportunity to talk to Thrifty Foods about everything we do. As well, it was a completely risk-free way for us to generate important dollars for our organization and to reach their customers with our messages."[32]

Following each campaign, a postreview was undertaken to see what worked and what didn't work. As well, the organization provided thank-yous and recognition for each of the stores. "This is very important and since we have multiple relationships with Thrifty Foods we always try and ensure that we consistently recognize each thing they have done for us,"[33] states Karina.

Results of the Program

The cause initiative was a great success in the first year. In 2004, $20,000 was raised through daffodil sales, and $8,000 was raised through individual donations made at the till and the company's match. "This was $28,000 that we didn't have as an organization before, plus the benefits of awareness and message dissemination meant the program was a great success for us," explains Karina. "Thrifty Foods had a slight increase in the number of daffodil sales over the previous year period."[34]

In 2005, the decision was made not to involve volunteers in the campaign, and the result was lower sales and contribution to the work of the Canadian Cancer Society on Vancouver Island. Only $8,000 was generated for the organization. Karina was on maternity leave during the 2005 campaign and as a result was not directly involved in its development and implementation.

EXHIBIT 11.4 PROMOTIONAL CAMPAIGN DEVELOPED BY THRIFTY FOODS

Key Learning—Volunteers On-site Can Make a Difference

Passion is a big part of any cause-marketing initiative, and there is no better way to exemplify that than through a nonprofit organization's volunteers.
The first year the Thrifty Foods/Canadian Cancer Society daffodil raised significantly more than the second year. "There were several factors, but the
biggest in my mind was we didn't have volunteers on-site to help promote
the Cancer Society programs and the daffodils themselves,"[35] states Karina.

A Model for the Future

Karina and the team at the Canadian Cancer Society, British Columbia and
Yukon District, are sold on the benefits of cause marketing for their organization. "We see using this model for other similar programs and were just
in the earlier stages of considering what that could look like," states Karina,
now Manager, Community Fundraising for the British Columbia and Yukon
District of the Canadian Cancer Society. "This is a simple model and one that
any organization could do. The beauty of the program is partnering with a
company and benefiting from their expertise, marketing, brand, people and
willingness to use their resources to help the organization."[36]

National Brand Symbol, National Cause Campaigns

The daffodil is such a part of the Canadian Cancer Society that when the organization went through a rebranding exercise in 2000, it was incorporated
into the logo. "Before that we had the caduceus, a sword with a snake around
it as our symbol attached to our word mark," explains Karina Chow, Divisional
Manager, Community Fundraising, British Columbia and Yukon Division, Canadian Cancer Society. "But what our research showed was that it implied we
were a medically based organization not the community-based volunteer organization we are. With that change in our brand, it reconfirmed that the daffodil campaign will likely always be part of our fundraising mix because it is
so tied to who we are."[37]

The Canadian Cancer Society has a national cause-marketing program that
includes a number of initiatives tied to the daffodil and Daffodil Month. For
example, Petro-Canada, one of Canada's largest oil and gas companies, has
been a proud corporate partner of the Canadian Cancer Society since 1983.
For the last five years, Petro-Canada has encouraged its customers to donate
their PETRO-POINTS to the Society in support of its Cancer Information Service. Since the inception of this program, Petro-Canada customers have donated over 120 million PETRO-POINTS to the Canadian Cancer Society.

In April 2005, Petro-Canada renewed its support of the donation program
with a marketing and promotional campaign that encouraged Canadians, in
celebration of Daffodil Month, to donate their points to the Canadian Cancer
Society. The renewed program highlighted a change in the way customers
can donate their PETRO-POINTS. Petro-Canada customers will now be able to
donate their points in increments of 1,000 and make a difference in the fight
against cancer.[38]

ENDNOTES

1. Interview, Food Bank for New York City, July 29, 2005 and September 19, 2005.
2. Ibid.
3. Ibid.
4. Ibid.
5. Ibid.
6. Ibid.
7. Ibid.
8. Ibid.
9. Ibid.
10. Interview, Sept. 19, 2005.
11. Food Bank for New York City Proposal for 2005 Bank-to-Bank Partnership.
12. Interview, July 29, 2005.
13. Ibid.
14. Ibid.
15. http://www.cancer.ca/ccs/internet/standard/0,3182,3172_15826__langId-en,00.html.
16. http://www.cancer.ca/ccs/internet/standard/0,2704,3172_368020_16350_langId-en, 00.html.
17. Ibid.
18. Karen is featured in the cause-marketing best practices section with the Hospice Calgary, McKinley Masters Home facilitated giving example.
19. Interview, Karen Bronstein, August 30, 2005.
20. Ibid.
21. Ibid.
22. Ibid.
23. Interview, Karina Chow, September 6, 2005.
24. http://www.thriftyfoods.com/ourcompany/hstry.html.
25. Interview, Karina Chow, September 6, 2005.
26. Ibid.
27. Ibid.
28. Ibid.
29. Ibid.
30. Press release, Canadian Cancer Society and Thrifty Foods, March, 2004.
31. Interview, Karina Chow, September 6, 2005.
32. Ibid.
33. Ibid.
34. Ibid.
35. Ibid.
36. Ibid.
37. Interview, Karina Chow, September 6, 2005.
38. http://www.cancer.ca/ccs/internet/standard/0,3182,3172_451851_396310607_langId-en,00.html.

CHAPTER 12

Cause-Marketing Principles and Cautions: Seven Golden Rules, Seven Deadly Sins

Done right, cause-marketing programs can provide significant benefits for both partners. Unfortunately, not all cause-marketing programs have gone off without a hitch. Cause-marketing success is far from guaranteed, and not all nonprofit organizations or companies for that matter are sold on cause marketing and the associated benefits. Although cause marketing is growing both in terms of dollars spent and number of programs being executed, there are potential pitfalls and limitations. What is the value to nonprofit organizations versus the marketing benefits and goodwill generated for companies? Do cause-marketing efforts reflect a broader social responsibility program? Are cause-marketing programs an inexpensive way to develop corporate marketing programs? Can cause programs really make a difference?

These are questions often asked by nonprofit staff, board, and supporters. The answers lie in each individual cause-marketing relationship and how it's negotiated, implemented, and built. As nonprofit organizations gain experience and recognize their value to the corporate sector, they can maximize the benefits to their cause. The field is relatively new, and both sides are finding their way.

What are the cautions and concerns that nonprofits and their corporate partners must be aware of and be ready to answer as they move forward with cause-marketing initiatives? What are the core principles that need to drive cause-marketing programs?

PRINCIPLES: THE SEVEN GOLDEN RULES OF CAUSE MARKETING

Today's leaders in the nonprofit and corporate sector are challenged to develop meaningful, transparent, and sincere cause-marketing programs. To ensure success, seven principles should guide all cause marketers:

1. Put first things first, think and stay true to mission, goals, and values.
2. Be focused, marketing oriented, and proactive.
3. Choose carefully to ensure positive brand and DNA alignment.
4. Combine assets and strengths to create mutually beneficial programs that meet the goals of both partners and key stakeholders.
5. Build a relationship of equals that is based on mutual respect, trust, and open communications.
6. Cross the *T*'s and dot the *I*'s with structure, framework, and legal requirements in place.
7. Be disciplined in planning, action, execution, and evaluation.

Principle #1: Put First Things First and Be True to Mission and Values

One of the greatest risks of a cause-marketing program is the temptation to wander from one's mission and values to take advantage of an opportunity. It can be a challenge for nonprofit organizations to say no. A cause-marketing program must be aligned with the nonprofit's mission and values and allow them to achieve their main purpose.

"When we go in the door, we start talking mission first," explains Cynthia Currence, National Vice President, Strategic Corporate Marketing Alliances for the American Cancer Society. "If they are excited about meeting their goals, and we're excited about achieving our mission objectives, then we can consider an alliance."[1] A cause-marketing arrangement must fit mission and values and aid in advancing the organization's programs and goals.

Kathy Rogers of the American Heart Association is another strong believer in the importance of being mission driven. "You have to be true to who you really are," she states. "An organization can make it fun, relevant and more appealing to consumers, but you must stick with your core values of who you are. Credibility, being trusted, being the scientific experts on heart disease and prevention is our core. There are companies we can't work with because of it, but we focus on who we can work with. Most of our dollars come from $25 donations and we have to always think about those donors and keep to a high standard."[2]

Principle #2: Be Focused, Marketing Oriented, and Proactive

What was initially driven by business has now become a major strategy for leading nonprofit organizations. Focused on building longer, deeper corporate relationships that help leverage the benefits of cause marketing for the nonprofit organization, many are creating their own cause-marketing platforms and campaigns to provide focus with the big, simple idea and a turnkey operation. More and more nonprofits are seeing the benefits and growth of cause marketing and are proactively building a marketing orientation and positioning their brand to become a charity of choice. This more marketing-focused orientation makes nonprofits more attractive not only to potential corporate partners, but also to the community as a whole. The growing sophistication of the sector and competition means nonprofits can't just be worthy; they have to be worthwhile and relevant to the community. Those that can communicate this will be further ahead, regardless of whether cause marketing becomes a major focus for a charity.

Principle #3: Chose Carefully to Ensure Positive Brand and DNA Alignment

Choosing partners carefully is critical to the success of a cause relationship and to maximizing benefits of a cause program. A good alignment needs to have a shared affinity, make sense to stakeholders, and provide benefits to both cause partners. Not all alignments will be obvious, but an associative link is critical to making the initiative work. Either way, the right fit is important. As one cause marketer stated, "If it doesn't feel right, it probably isn't right—for either partner."

An example of a strong brand alignment is KaBOOM! and Stride Rite's 2005 announced cause-marketing initiative. "We're excited about the relationship," says Carrie Suhr, VP at KaBOOM!. "It's a perfect example of a children's brand that KaBOOM! wants to represent on the cause side: healthy, adventurous, active kids with opportunity to play."[3]

Stride Rite, a leading premium children's footwear brand, and KaBOOM! announced a partnership in early 2005 designed to raise awareness and public support for play and playgrounds. The relationship features the development of playgrounds and a donation from a specially designed Jungle Gym shoe collection that will raise funds through $1 donated for every pair sold.

Principle #4: Combine Assets and Strengths to Create a Mutually Beneficial Program

Cause marketing combines the assets and strengths of each partner to create a mutually beneficial program. Any cause-marketing partnership is an important two-way value exchange that relies on each partner to succeed. Ultimately, cause-marketing partners come together for mutual benefit by combining each other's strengths and assets to create a win-win partnership. By working together, they produce an outcome far greater than anything that either organization could have achieved independently. Each partner contributes different capabilities and resources, and by working together they add a second level of value that benefits both.

Principle #5: Build a Relationship of Equals That Is Based on Mutual Respect, Trust, and Open Communications

At the heart of strong relationships are equity, mutual respect, trust, and effective, open communications. One of the biggest challenges is establishing an effective working relationship among all parties. Many cause-marketing relationships are built based on long-term relationships where many of these tenets are already established. But a cause-marketing arrangement can add a new dynamic from the more philanthropic approach.

The cultural and capacity differences between nonprofits and businesses can pose challenges for a cause-marketing program. These differences require a commitment to understanding each other, to communicating honestly and openly with respect. But trust and respect are earned by actions, and it is important for a nonprofit to deliver on expectations.

Remember, cause-marketing relationship should be treated like all your most important donors—keep the lines of communications open, engage them in your work, invite them to your special events. You want to build a long-term relationship and have them feel part of your organization, connected to your mission, and an advocate for your work both in the company and in the community.

Principle #6: Cross the T's and Dot the I's: Structure, Framework, Legal Requirements in Place

An essential part of success comes from developing the structure and framework for the relationship. Internal support and buy-in on both sides is critical; developing joint plans, outlining decision-making processes and procedures, and formalizing the structure in an agreement ensures clarity around expectations and outcomes.

Nonprofits must be aware of legal and regulatory frameworks around cause-marketing relationships and ensure that they meet these requirements. Are you following the best practices for cause marketing today? The list of key considerations, is outlined in Chapter 7, Creating a Cause-Marketing Orientation. Review, consider, and always get guidance to ensure that your organization understands

the requirements in advance, not after a relationship has been built. I'
is ever audited on a cause-marketing program and the audit come
that organization has a major public relations and credibility issue
years to overcome.

Have someone on the team that knows all the requirements and have a template that can ensure your organization answers or adheres to all requirements,
so if you have to file through a regulatory process, it is simple. This is a critical
piece in the growing sophistication of cause marketing. Corporations want to
work with nonprofits that know this side of cause marketing; it's less of a risk for
them and tangibly demonstrates the readiness of an organization to be a cause
partner. Always talk to your potential partner about these requirements; it can
be difficult, but is a vital part of success.

Principle #7: Be Disciplined in Planning, Action, Execution, and Evaluation

Cause marketing requires a nonprofit organization to be marketing oriented and
outwardly focused, looking at how best to present their organization and cause
to an external audience. With the growth in the field and increasing sophistication, nonprofits must be businesslike and strategic in their approach.

Think, plan, and do. Follow the seven C's of "Getting it Right," be disciplined
in your planning and internal organizing, be proactive, and execute on what you
promise. If you veer from your strategy, do so consciously. Celebrate achievements; evaluate and continually learn as the program moves forward.

As leading companies demonstrate the benefits, more will follow in their
wake. Nonprofits who proactively build their capacity in this area stand to gain
and enhance their ability to achieve their mission, engage a wide range of people
in supporting their mission, build brand and message awareness, raise revenue for
their work, and provide societal benefit.

CAUTIONS: SEVEN DEADLY SINS

1. Having a cause-marketing relationship that is too one sided, self-serving,
   and/or commercial.
2. Having advertising that is not sincere, honest, or gives the perception of
   nonprofit endorsement and not handling criticism with open and honest
   communication. Nonprofits must take care as to use of logo, wording,
   and approach.
3. Not managing expectations—on both sides. Be aware of and clearly explain
   what you can and can't deliver to your corporate partner. Ensure your own

internal team understands what is and isn't being achieved by a cause-marketing relationship.

4. Not protecting the integrity of the organization's brand and visual identity.

5. Not recognizing that nonprofits have valuable assets to contribute and receive compensation to reflect this value.

6. Not doing due diligence, risk assessment, and receiving institutionwide support.

7. Not working with a corporation that walks the talk. The program must be part of larger corporate citizenship.

Deadly Sin #1: Not Being Mutually Beneficial with a Program That Is Too One Sided, Too Self-Serving, or Too Commercial

Cause marketing is a mutually beneficial relationship that combines corporate self-interest with altruism. Every relationship has to provide value to both partners, not be a one-sided transaction. Corporate cause marketers have business objectives and targets they must achieve annually and must be concerned about their bottom line. Nonprofit organizations have to be equally concerned about achieving their goals. The programs must help achieve mission-based goals, generate revenue, and receive other benefits that bring value to the nonprofit organization. Both sides must look for a balanced program that provides value to each.

Although cause-marketing programs can provide commercial benefit, the messaging has to be more considered. Programs that are too driven by commercial messaging and that focus on benefiting the company more than the cause can lead to cynicism and mistrust. The relationship can't be used solely to sell a product using a nonprofit trademark, connections, and reputation and paying them for that use.

A secondary concern is making sure corporations don't see cause marketing as an inexpensive way to develop marketing and promotional programs. Cause-marketing programs have to have dollars behind them so that the partnership can be presented and the nonprofit cause and mission advanced. Nonprofits have to receive fair compensation and support so that they can affect change and move their cause forward.

Unlike traditional corporate promotions, nonprofits have significant value to add with the human interest side, passion, and reputation. Compensation has to reflect this and have a meaningful impact from the cause-marketing support.

When you're considering a cause relationship, can you answer yes to all of these: partners, purpose, passion, profits? If not, then the relationship may be too one sided, and in the end it won't work. Be prepared to say no.

AMERICAN MEDICAL ASSOCIATION AND SUNBEAM

In 1997, the American Medical Association and Sunbeam announced a co-branding program for a line of home health-care products. The five-year exclusive agreement with Sunbeam Corporation exchanged royalty payments for product sales using the AMA name and logo. Criticism came from newspapers, consumer health organizations, and the AMA's own membership. The AMA had not tested the products, leaving its credibility at risk. The AMA Board of Trustees had also not endorsed the cause-marketing arrangement and contract, and in the end they voted to withdraw from the deal. The partnership was terminated before it started. As a result, Sunbeam sued the AMA, which paid $9.9 million to settle in July 1998.

Deadly Sin #2: Not Being Sincere, Honest, and Transparent, or Avoiding Perception of Nonprofit Endorsement

Consumers are savvy, and they want to know what the program is, how it works, and the benefits to the charity. In a cause–marketing relationship, corporations and nonprofit organizations can create mutual benefits and have a meaningful societal impact. But cause programs must be transparent, credible, and fully accountable. Society's trust of a nonprofit organization's credibility is one of the key factors that make it attractive for corporate partners to work with them. Nonprofits cannot afford to tarnish their image either through poorly executed cause programs or by a lack of their own accountability and transparency.

As well, the vast majority (over 80%) of giving to nonprofit organizations comes from private individuals. They are trusting that the nonprofit will be true to their mission and values and have an impeccable integrity. Credibility and trust

AMERICAN CANCER SOCIETY

In December 1998, the attorneys general of 12 states settled with SmithKline Beecham Consumer Healthcare because of its cause-marketing program with the American Cancer Society. In 1996, the society licensed its name and logo to the company for its stop-smoking products in return for $1 million in royalties. The attorneys general charged that the advertising phrase, "Partners in helping you quit," could mislead, deceive, and confuse consumers. It appeared that the society endorsed the products, which it did not. However, perception can be reality, and many cause-marketing programs can be interpreted to be product or company endorsements.

THE ARTHRITIS FOUNDATION AND McNEIL CONSUMER PRODUCTS

In 1994, The Arthritis Foundation built an early cause-marketing program with the McNeil Consumer Products Company. The Arthritis Foundation licensed its name and logo for over-the-counter analgesics made by McNeil. In return, Mc-Neil guaranteed $1 million a year, plus royalties, if sales reached a certain level. The attorneys general sued the partners, alleging consumer fraud because the products were promoted as new when, in fact, their active ingredients had been available long before. As well, advertising implied that the charity had helped to create the product and there was an implied endorsement. Third, the advertising stated the charity would receive a donation per sale, when in fact the organization would have received a guaranteed payment anyway. Finally, the product suggested that it was doctor recommended, when in fact only the ingredients, not the product, were recommended. Eventually in October 1996, the attorneys general in 19 states settled with the Arthritis Foundation and McNeil Consumer Products Company.

are the pillars of nonprofit organizations' brand strength and essence and are usually what interests a company. Critics can be vocal and cynical, and nonprofit organizations and their corporate partners must create cause initiatives that are credible, substantive, and relevant to their stakeholders. Although consumers are actively supporting cause programs and believe in their worth, nonprofits must

THINK BEFORE YOU PINK CAMPAIGN

Breast cancer, one of the most popular causes of the 1990s and early 2000s, has a plethora of cause initiatives with companies seeking to "cash in" on the current concern. These have left consumers confused about the benefits to the cause and spun off to taint legitimate programs. In 2001, Breast Cancer Action launched a campaign to encourage people to "Think before you pink." Aimed squarely at the breast cancer cause-marketing campaigns, the organization urged consumers to ask some critical questions before opening their wallets for these marketing programs: How much money goes to the cause? What is it supporting? How is it being raised? And will it truly affect the fight against breast cancer? "Make sure you know what your money is actually supporting, and consider whether shopping will truly make a difference, the Web site states. What the breast cancer movement needs is political involvement and action to create real change—and we don't mean the kind you keep in your pocket."[4] "Think before you pink" (Exhibit 12.1) warns consumers to check out where the money is going to make sure it is a reputable company and that it is going to a sound nonprofit organization.

EXHIBIT 12.1   THINK BEFORE YOU PINK

Who's really cleaning up here?

It sounds noble: Buy this vacuum cleaner and Eureka will give a dollar to a breast cancer organization.

But wait. A dollar gift on a $200 purchase is less than one percent— and Eureka caps its annual contribution from the sales at $250,000.

Is the company spending more on its "Clean for the Cure" ads than it's donating to the cause?

It's not just Eureka. American Express donates a penny per transaction when you "Charge for the Cure." BMW kicks in a buck per mile when you test-drive its cars, which produce chemical compounds linked to breast cancer.

Avon lipstick, Yoplait yogurt—the list goes on and on. During Breast Cancer Awareness Month, pink-ribbon promotions are everywhere.

Breast Cancer Action urges you to "think before you pink." Will your purchase make a difference? Or is the company exploiting breast cancer to boost profits?

Preventing, curing, and guaranteeing quality treatment for breast cancer will require real change—and not the kind you carry in your pocket.

BREAST CANCER ACTION

55 New Montgomery St., Suite 323, San Francisco, CA 94105 • www.ThinkBeforeYouPink.org

* Ad courtesy of Breast Cancer Action www.thinkbeforeyoupink.org and www.beaction.org

bility and that of their corporate partners. If concerns are raised,
ess them immediately. Collaborate with your partners so that
rdinated and are in sync with one another.

se-marketing initiatives are not designed to be an endorsement
roduct and or company, perception is reality. Cause-marketing
be professionally presented and meet all the required regulatory
and other guidelines. In the end, ask yourself, could your cause program pass the
Mike Wallace *60 Minutes* test?

Deadly Sin #3: Not Managing Expectations—on Both Sides

Nonprofits must manage expectations—for both their corporate partners and
their own organization. Cause marketing can do a lot, but there are limits to
what can be offered as part of a relationship and what can be achieved because
of the relationship. Understanding and clearly communicating this is critical to
the ongoing success of any cause-marketing program.

First, manage expectations with your corporate partner. Knowing what you
can and can't offer to a potential partner is a part of planning and preparing for
cause-marketing programs. There could be a host of expectations that are either
not possible or practical given a nonprofit organization's assets, abilities, and limitations. Assets that can't be used, time frames that can't be met, or advertising
deliverables that aren't possible are examples of expectations that have to be managed. It can be hard to be up front with a partner when a nonprofit is anxious
to build a positive cause-marketing relationship. Don't be tempted to over-
promise; remember one of the golden rules of cause marketing—underpromise
and overdeliver.

The second set of expectations to be managed is internal. Too often there are
unrealistic ideas about the benefits, a lack of understanding around how a cause-
marketing program will work financially, and the value of a program beyond
cash to the nonprofit. If nonprofits are looking to merely raise revenue, there are
more direct ways. In fact, before becoming involved in cause marketing, nonprofits most often have the traditional fundraising sources in place. What are the
specific considerations that your nonprofit colleagues need to understand?

Financial Contributions versus Other Benefits

Corporate "cash cow" perception. Public perception is high in terms of the contribution corporations should be making to society. Studies on this phenomenon report that the public expects to see corporations contributing 30% of overall
charitable revenue.[5] The reality? Giving by corporations in the United States
was just over 5% of all giving in 2004.[6] Add in marketing dollars, and that will

increase, but it's still a huge gap and one that many nonprofit organizations have to manage, including with their own staff.

As one corporate fund-raiser made clear, "One of the biggest challenges is the expectation that corporations are cash cows. It's a fantasy that there are millions to be made from corporations. My question to staff is how many dollars do they think corporations have? I must continuously remind people that the discussion cannot be exclusively about what we can get but we must talk about what we are giving for what we are getting."

Leveraged support: Putting a value on the greatest contribution. Many cause marketers agree the greatest value of cause-marketing relationships is the leveraged support provided by a corporate partner. Understanding and putting a value on it can be a challenge, but one that is important if the true contribution of a cause-marketing initiative to a nonprofit organization is to be recognized. More and more nonprofits are accepting the intangible value as a significant means of raising their profile, enhancing their brand recognition, implementing programs, and getting out their message to a broad public. Cause marketing can be very cost effective and impactful, and leading nonprofits are assigning an in-kind contribution value and including it with funds raised.

It's common when looking at cause-marketing relationships for those unfamiliar with the field to look at only the cash contribution. But often its most important value is marketing and awareness. This is especially true when the awareness value to a nonprofit organization is compared with traditional marketing vehicles like brochures. Cause marketing stands head and shoulders over it. As Kurt Aschermann, senior vice president of Boys and Girls Clubs of America, states about the exposure that comes from cause-marketing relationships, "We could never in a million years pay for it ourselves."

Dollars Spent versus Donated

Along with perceptions of corporations as cash cows, how much is donated versus spent on advertising and where the financial contributions come from is a reality that nonprofits must understand about cause marketing.

Sometimes more from consumers and stakeholders than the company. Cause programs can involve direct donations from individual consumers that are sometimes greater than those from the company getting much of the direct goodwill benefit from the program. Many of the programs feature add-on donations from consumers and other stakeholders as a component of the cause activity. This includes dollars raised through cause-marketing events, program donations, and extra contributions added on at the cash register. However, corporate facilitation of greater giving is a huge benefit to nonprofit organizations. The advertising and organizational support enables nonprofit causes to achieve much more than if they implemented a program on their own.

Publicizing support: Sometime more spent on advertising than is contributed. The average cause-marketing corporate partner will spend more resources publicizing their support than they will contribute financially. Sometimes it can be greater than the actual contribution. For example, in the first national cause-marketing campaign, American Express supported the promotion with a $4 million advertising campaign to reach existing customers and encourage new ones. In comparison, $1.7 million was raised to support the restoration of the Statute of Liberty. Is this a problem? Not if nonprofit organizations recognize the awareness and promotional support as a valuable contribution.

Deadly Sin #4: Not Protecting the Organization's Brand and Visual Identity

Cause programs will have the nonprofit organization's brand and visual identity attached to the program. A critical element for nonprofit organizations is protecting the integrity of the brand, which includes the name, visual identity, and public trust in the organization. Carefully developed agreements must outline use and approval processes for nonprofit logos, messaging, and program implementation.

Deadly Sin #5: Not Doing Due Diligence, Risk Assessment, and Receiving Institutionwide Support

Nonprofits have gotten into trouble by not having institutionwide support or doing a risk assessment. The American Medical Association and Sunbeam alignment described earlier did not have the backing or knowledge of the AMA board. The lessons from this failure are many, the least of which was the importance of full board buy-in and commitment to the cause relationship. It was an expensive lesson that cost the organization $9.9 million of hard-earned charitable dollars; it impacted the organization's reputation significantly, alienated key stakeholders, and resulted in the loss of three of the organization's senior management staff, including the chief operating officer.

Even if a cause-marketing campaign takes a turn for the worse, having institutionwide support and doing a risk assessment can ease the pain and minimize damage. The Arthritis Foundation and McNeil Consumer Products Company had been approved by the Foundation's board and even taken to the organization's House of Delegates because of the potential risk the cause relationship presented. When the criticism erupted over the program and the attorney general threatened to sue, a settlement was reached with the courts, and the McNeil Consumer Products Company was required to tell the whole truth in future ads about its products, provide refunds on request, and pay almost $2 million for consumer education, arthritis research, and fees. Although the Foundation still suffered from the adverse publicity, the board's backing of the arrangement and potential risk and the strong commitment of the McNeil Consumer Products Company helped them weather the storm. Neither admitted to any wrongdoing, and the two went on to build further cause-marketing relationships.

Deadly Sin #6: Not Understanding the Value a Nonprofit Brings to a Relationship

Cause marketing is about building a mutually beneficial relationship where nonprofit assets are aligned with a corporation's for mutual benefit. Cause-marketing partnerships are a means of delivering corporate citizenship strategy around specific objectives while providing value to the community. The partnership needs to be treated as a business relationship, not just as a philanthropic venture in order to achieve focused results. This means nonprofits must act businesslike and be compensated accordingly. Receiving appropriate financial support—both in cash and in-kind—is critical. Many leading nonprofits are setting minimum levels of compensation for involvement.

Deadly Sin #7: Working with a Corporation That Doesn't Walk the Talk. The Program Must Be Part of Larger Corporate Citizenship

Cause marketing has to be more than just a promotional gimmick; it must be part of the social responsibility and corporate citizenship efforts of a company. Although there is a desire to see more companies undertake and talk about their cause efforts, quality of products, fair prices, benefits to employees, responsible implementation of laws and regulations, and human rights and conscientious manufacturing are considered even more important than a company's support of community issues. Cause marketing will help a corporation's image and sales; it won't solve underlying problems.[7] Cause marketing helps a strong company become stronger.

In the 2004 Cone Corporate Citizenship Study, whereas 80% of those surveyed believed communicating corporate support of social issues was an important part of corporate citizenship,[8] several key values were even more important:

- 98% said they looked to the quality of products and services provided.
- Fair pricing for products and services was listed as important for 97% of those surveyed.

UNICEF AND McDONALD'S

In 2002, the cause-marketing program between UNICEF and McDonald's "World Children's Day" created a controversy and a call to end the relationship by Commercial Alert and 57 public interest groups, health professionals, elected officials, and child advocates. McDonald's took profits from one day of its sales and donated them to children's charities around the world. UNICEF was but one recipient and in only two countries. Many felt the publicity got out of hand. McDonald's passed all of UNICEF's rigorous screening and UNICEF were beneficiaries of McDonald's support. In the United States, they distribute UNICEF trick and treat boxes, and the alliance has been a very good one. The controversy erupted just at the time childhood obesity was becoming a major issue, and McDonald's was under attack for its high fat and supersized, high-calorie meals targeted specifically at children.

- 93% viewed employee benefits, laws and regulations, and human rights and manufacturing as being an important part of corporate citizenship and responsibility.[9]

An example of this trend is Wal-Mart. Although they received the highest name recognition as a strong corporate citizen, they recently fell to 28th in the ranking by the Reputation Institute and were among five companies listed negatively for not rewarding employees fairly.[10]

CONCLUSION

Cause marketing is growing in number, dollars spent, and sophistication. Today virtually any cause can find a home in a cause-marketing arrangement. With this growth has come a need for nonprofits to know and understand both the cautions and principles of a successful cause-marketing program. This chapter looks at the seven deadly sins and counters this with the seven golden rules of highly effective cause marketers.

To be a highly effective cause marketer involves putting first things first and staying true to mission, goals, and values; being focused, marketing-oriented, and proactive; choosing partners carefully to ensure positive brand and DNA alignment; combining strengths and creating mutually beneficial programs that meet the goals of both partners and key stakeholders; building a relationship of equals that is based on mutual respect, trust, and open communications; crossing the *T*'s and dotting the *I*'s with structure, framework, and legal requirements in place; and being disciplined in planning, action, execution, and evaluation.

The seven deadly sins to avoid in any cause-marketing arrangement are having a cause-marketing relationship that is too one sided, self-serving, and/or commercial; having advertising that is not sincere, honest, or gives the perception of nonprofit endorsement and not handling criticism with open and honest communication; not managing expectations—on both sides; not protecting the integrity of the organization's brand and visual identity; not recognizing that nonprofits have valuable assets to contribute and must receive compensation to reflect this value; not doing due diligence, risk assessment, and receiving institutionwide support; and not working with a corporation that walks the talk. The program must be part of larger corporate citizenship.

Following these principles and being aware of the cautions will guide nonprofits to build successful cause-marketing programs that will be win-win-win for all.

Endnotes

1. Interview, Cynthia Currence, January 25, 2005.
2. Interview, Kathy Rogers, January 24, 2005.
3. Interview, February 2, 2005.
4. www.thinkbeforeyoupink.org.
5. Interview, Chris Pinney, Canadian Centre for Philanthropy, November 30, 2004.
6. Giving USA 2003, The Annual Report on Philanthropy for the Year 2002, /www.aafrc.org.
7. 2004 Cone Corporate Citizenship Study.
8. 2004 Cone Corporate Citizenship Study.
9. Ibid.
10. Ibid.

Final Thoughts

PARTNER FOR PURPOSE, PASSION, AND PROFITS

Cause marketing is a new way for business and nonprofit causes to think and work in a mutually beneficial relationship. It is a powerful innovation that finds the intersection between societal needs and corporate marketing and business goals. Cause marketing consciously marries the credibility and assets of nonprofit organizations and the public's desire to support them, with marketing goals to achieve business and societal benefit and satisfy stakeholder needs.

Defined, cause marketing is mutually beneficial collaboration that aligns a company, brand, marketing, and people to a charitable cause's brand and assets to create shareholder and social value, connect with constituents, and publicly communicate values. The four key elements and focus for this book are partners for purpose, passion, and profits.

Partners: Realigning Corporate–Nonprofit Relationships

First, cause marketing sees business and nonprofit organizations build a strategic, collaborative partnership that is interconnected and interdependent. The partners must be aligned with each other's mission and goals. The relationship must be based on mutual respect, open communications, and trust, and be transparent, authentic, and honest if it is to be successful. A good collaborative alignment sees each partner actively seeking to advance each other's agenda and sharing responsibilities, contributions, and risks.

Driver Is What Nonprofit Can Offer, Not Needs

What a nonprofit can bring to the relationship is what drives cause marketing. Nonprofits have many valuable assets that can be attractive, but they have to think in a different way and consider the needs of their potential corporate partners.

Marketing Oriented and Externally Focused

Cause marketing is about nonprofits being entrepreneurial, marketing oriented, with a strong brand position and an external focus. To participate in cause relationships, nonprofits must have internal culture, capacity, and structure in place. Businesses have concrete objectives, and nonprofits must recognize the need for a different and more entrepreneurial approach to gain this corporate support.

Purpose: Value add Plus Philanthropy; Marketing Plus Fundraising

Cause-marketing relationships are uniquely different from traditional corporate philanthropy or sponsorship. Cause marketing is the third way. It is a combination of philanthropy, support for a cause and its purpose, and marketing, the tangible business benefits from a charity alignment and the assets they bring to a relationship. For corporations, cause marketing is the new marketing and corporate citizenship tool focused on driving corporate profitability through cause relationships. For nonprofits, cause marketing is the new fundraising and marketing tool that helps raise revenue, create awareness and achieve important mission goals.

Passion: Making a Difference

A critical part of cause marketing is passion for bringing together both sides to combine assets and connect key company stakeholders, including employees, suppliers, retailers, and customers, to the mission and values of the nonprofit partner's cause. When organizations and people come together with passion, change can happen.

Unlike traditional philanthropic gifts, cause marketing focuses on publicly communicating a corporation's support using marketing tools. Cause marketing visibly demonstrates in the workplace and marketplace through advertising, corporate and product promotional material, and employee engagement what a company stands for, how it contributes, and how it is making a difference at a societal level.

The Passion Movement

In 2003, a Harris poll found 86% of those surveyed said that they wanted more fulfilling work.[1] The 2004 Cone Corporate Citizenship Study showed a company's commitment to a social issue was important when Americans decided where to work: 81% said this was important.

The surveys reflect a trend, started in the mid-1990s and dubbed the Passion Movement. This movement saw people no longer wanting their work to be a place to sacrifice or swap their hours for dollars disconnected from their values. Work is such a big part of most people's lives it had to have meaning and be a reflection of who they are and what they believe in. Corporations have taken note and started to connect to their employees and consumers through cause marketing. The growth of cause marketing is an outcome of the Passion Movement.

Profits: Creating Value, Communicating Values

Finally, cause marketing creates social and shareholder value and publicly communicates the values of those involved. Done right for nonprofits, it can be more productive and broader support than traditional corporate philanthropy. Cause-marketing relationships bring value beyond just dollars; they further validate nonprofit activities, help achieve mission, create brand awareness, disseminate information, change behavior and attitudes, bring valuable corporate expertise, and help leverage additional resources.

Corporations recognize more active cause-marketing relationships give the company a competitive advantage by creating tangible value and increasing their profitability. Cause marketing can help sell more goods and increase bottom lines; attract and appeal to employees, customers, and stakeholders; manage their reputations; and secure the license they need to operate in many markets. Most importantly, cause marketing publicly communicates a corporation's values and brings to life their commitment to the community. Cause marketing is the new marketing and corporate social responsibility tool.

Making the Pie Bigger

Corporate support still represents a small portion of overall philanthropic giving in North America. Less than 10% of overall giving comes from the corporate sector, even less from cause-marketing relationships. But the impact is greater than just financial support. The additional benefits of cause marketing come from the broader range of in-kind promotion, message dissemination, and employee and consumer engagement. Although some cause-marketing relationships receive money from the traditional corporate community investment pool of support, many involve a broader range of support from marketing budgets, human resources, and employee funds and even from corporate executive resources. What this means is that the corporate community pie has grown and will continue to grow as the benefits are proven and more companies turn to cause marketing to help them support both the community and their own bottom line.

A Growing Discipline

Only 25 years old, cause marketing is growing as the way the corporate and non-profit sectors are working together, and it is clearly here to stay. Cause marketing has come a long way since 1981 when the first programs were launched at the local level in California by American Express. The Cone Reports, through their 10-year-plus longitudinal research, track its development and define its evolution: from an initial one-off tactic meant to drive immediate sales while supporting non-profit organizations' efforts, to a more strategic approach geared to building customer loyalty and reputation, to deeper and longer term social commitments that brand a business with a cause, to the sophistication of many of today's leading programs that are the public face of a company's corporate social responsibility and that communicate a company's values and imbue its culture with support of a nonprofit cause.[2]

Cause marketing is defined through seven different types of relationships under the umbrella of: Products, Promotions, and Programs. Products-type relationships include product purchases, purchases plus, and licensed products; promotional cause-marketing initiatives focus on issues and messaging; and program initiatives are deeper forms of signature cobranded promotional events and programs and public social cause-marketing programming relationships established to impact and change attitudes and behavior.

THE WAY FORWARD

The number of cause-marketing initiatives and financial and other support being generated because of cause marketing is growing. Corporate experts predict a philanthropic component might, in the near future, be considered an integral part of any responsible marketing campaign. Nonprofit leaders predict cause marketing will grow as the way companies support the community. Either way, the impact is clear; nonprofits must learn how to present themselves to corporations in such a way that they are more marketing oriented and more supportable. Companies must understand the benefits of engaging in this form of community support for the company, products, brands, and internal culture.

The Wave of the Future—Don't Get Left Behind

If nonprofits aren't able to articulate their role and value to a company and participate in the conversation as a businessperson, they are going to get left behind on this trend. Nonprofit organizations are going to have to be more marketing oriented and strategic in the presentation of their cause and their relevance to the community and be prepared to find a way for their corporate partner to achieve their marketing and business objectives.

Don't Feel Daunted—Almost Any Nonprofit Can Do Cause Marketing

Almost any nonprofit organization, no matter size, scope, or geographic representation, can undertake cause-marketing relationships. Not all corporate support will be focused on cause-marketing initiatives with the nonprofit sector. There will always be dollars available for important causes that don't necessarily drive business and marketing objectives. But nonprofits that proactively develop their skills and position their organizations to be attractive causes stand to benefit from this growing trend.

Be Proactive and Disciplined—People, Thought, Action, Execution, Evaluation

Cause marketing requires a nonprofit organization to be marketing oriented and outwardly focused, looking at how best to present their organization and cause to an external audience. With the growth in the field and increasing sophistication, nonprofits must be businesslike and strategic in their approach.

Think, plan, and do. Follow the seven C's of "Getting it Right." Causes must be disciplined in their planning and internal organizing; be proactive in seeking collaborative partners, look to combine assets, and create value; and execute on what you promise, communicate what you're doing. Celebrate achievements, evaluate, and continually learn as the program moves forward.

Final Thoughts: Making a Great Society

I recently saw Charlie Rose interview Jim Collins to discuss his latest research and his two emblematic books: *Built to Last* and *Good to Great*. The interview focused on a number of issues, including what he felt the impact of these books had been. One of his key points was how these two books had inspired not only those working in the private sector but also those in the nonprofit sector. In the interview, he explained why this was important to him: "Successful business makes for a great economy, and successful social agencies and charities makes for great communities."[3] But what excited him more was what he saw as the new collaborative attitude between the two sectors. "When the two combine," he enthused, "they make for a great society."[4]

Cause marketing is about partnering for mutual benefit, working together to find solutions and advantages for all. Cause marketing is a new field for both the corporate and nonprofit sectors, and it is evolving and growing. It takes hard work, commitment, and an open, honest relationship built on trust and respect. Working in the nonprofit sector has never been more challenging. The need for corporate social responsibility has never been greater.

As nonprofit organizations and corporations continue to build mutually beneficial cause-marketing relationships and take advantage of this growing way to create shareholder and social value, I issue a challenge to both sectors.

Challenge to Corporate Partners

Accept the Challenge Cause Marketing Presents to Change Your Brand and Enhance Your Internal Culture

Cause marketing is a revolutionary concept. In less than 25 years it has taken hold as the growing way nonprofits and corporations are working together for positive social change and business impact. If a company accepts the enormous challenge of cause marketing and seeks the maximum benefit, it can't be done in half measures or without genuine dedication and a sincere presentation—both externally and internally.

Cause marketing has to be more than just a promotional gimmick; it must be part of the overall social responsibility and corporate citizenship efforts of a company. The brand and internal culture must reflect this commitment. Cause marketing has to be a commitment, not a campaign.

Help Create a Social Movement

Cause marketing can transform a cause from important, but little known, to front and center and can change the way people think and behave. Breast cancer's "For the Cure" is a great example of how cause marketing has raised this cause's profile, created awareness of the issue, and affected attitudes and behaviors. Today breast cancer is openly discussed, women have breast health as an important part of their regular health checks, and people understand the impact of this cruel disease. "Go Red for Women" is having the same impact for women and heart health. But there are many important causes. Can you help create a social movement?

No company is too big or too small to make a difference. Chose a cause, support it at every level, engage your employees, suppliers, and customers. Focus your support to help raise money, create awareness, and effect change. Then stand back and see the benefits for your business and your community.

Be a Kind and Generous Partner

Nonprofit organizations work with smaller budgets, fewer staff, and fewer resources than many of their corporate partners. But their level of professionalism and commitment is no less than that of their corporate partners. Be kind and generous, appreciate and respect the differences, celebrate the way you can work together for mutual gain.

Challenge to Nonprofit Partners

Embrace Change

Change can be hard for nonprofit organizations to accept. We can be masters of excuses: "We've been doing it this way forever," "Don't fix what isn't broken," "We don't have the resources to make changes." Will this drive to cause marketing mean some nonprofits will lose corporate support? If they remain in their traditional mode of expecting support because they are a worthy cause, without some kind of return, the chances are greater they will. The question will be, "Can nonprofits move from their traditional philanthropic route?" Don't wait to be pushed; embrace change.

Recognize the Potential Cause Marketing Offers for Greater Support

A key message of this book: cause marketing is so much more than just a way to generate additional revenue. In fact, many nonprofits put greater value on the publicity, in-store promotion, and the building of awareness with new audiences as the most important benefits of cause marketing. Look at the whole cause-marketing package and its value, not just the direct financial support.

Understand the Overall Benefits of Being More Marketing Oriented and Externally Focused for Your Organization

To be successful at cause marketing, nonprofits have to be entrepreneurial and marketing oriented. Any organization that becomes more outwardly focused and customer oriented will reap benefits beyond cause-marketing relationships. A tight "10-second" elevator message will help with other parts of a nonprofit's fundraising and marketing. Many nonprofits are recognizing the benefits of branding and positioning to help them raise their profile, be more relevant to the community, and in the end raise more money and support for their cause.

A Never-Ending Journey

As cause marketing continues to evolve, so too will the public's expectations about how companies address social issues and how nonprofits engage the corporate sector in their work. There is no turning back now. Employees, investors, communities, governments, and consumers will demand to know a company's values and their commitment to the community and the relevance of a nonprofit cause to society. With cause marketing falling at the intersection of marketing strategy and societal good, it is fast becoming a "must-do" business practice for the twenty-first century. This can be a great opportunity for nonprofit causes.

Cause marketing is a means, not an end. It will continue to develop and grow and be a force in society. Cause marketing was born out of necessity and innovation to meet the challenges of society and business. As each generation addresses the issues of the day, cause marketing will change and adapt to meet the new challenges. In the end, cause marketing is a process, one that will be never ending and ever evolving.

I am sure my own journey will include changes and lots more learning and adventure. I look forward to those challenges and the excitement of this ever-growing, ever-changing, ever-improving field. As Winston Churchill said, *"Every day you may make progress. Every step may be fruitful. Yet there will stretch out before you an ever-lengthening, ever-ascending, ever-improving path. You know you will never get to the end of the journey. But this, so far from discouraging, only adds to the joy and glory of the climb."*[5]

ENDNOTES

1. http://www.worthwhilemag.com/index.php.
2. Cone/Roper Cause Related Trends Report, 1999.
3. August 4, 2005, Charlie Rose interview on PBS.
4. Ibid.
5. www.quotationspage.com/quotes/Sir_Winston_Churchill.

Index